ETHICAL DECISION MAKING in SCHOOL ADMINISTRATION

Leadership as Moral Architecture

Paul A. Wagner
University of Houston–Clear Lake

Douglas J. Simpson
Texas Tech University

Los Angeles • London • New Delhi • Singapore • Washington DC

For information:

SAGE Publications, Inc.
2455 Teller Road
Thousand Oaks, California 91320
E-mail: order@sagepub.com

SAGE Publications Ltd.
1 Oliver's Yard
55 City Road
London EC1Y 1SP
United Kingdom

SAGE Publications India Pvt. Ltd.
B 1/I 1 Mohan Cooperative Industrial Area
Mathura Road, New Delhi 110 044
India

SAGE Publications Asia-Pacific Pte. Ltd.
33 Pekin Street #02-01
Far East Square
Singapore 048763

Printed in the United States of America

Library of Congress Cataloging-in-Publication Data

Wagner, Paul A.
Ethical decision making in school administration: leadership as moral architecture / Paul A. Wagner, Douglas J. Simpson.
    p. cm.
Includes bibliographical references and index.
ISBN 978-1-4129-5214-9 (cloth)
ISBN 978-1-4129-5215-6 (pbk.)

    1. School management and organization—Moral and ethical aspects. 2. Decision making—Moral and ethical aspects. 3. Educational leadership—Moral and ethical aspects. I. Simpson, Douglas J. II. Title.

LB2806.W24 2009
371.2—dc22   2008020273

This book is printed on acid-free paper.

08   09   10   11   12   10 9 8 7 6 5 4 3 2 1

Acquisitions Editor:	Diane McDaniel
Editorial Assistant:	Leah Mori
Production Editor:	Laureen A. Shea
Copy Editor:	Carol Anne Peschke
Typesetter:	C&M Digitals (P) Ltd.
Proofreader:	Victoria Reed-Castro
Indexer:	Jeanne Busemeyer
Cover Designer:	Candice Harman
Marketing Manager:	Christy Guilbault

ETHICAL
DECISION MAKING
in SCHOOL
ADMINISTRATION

To

My wife, Kerry, and my daughters, Emily and Nicole, and my sons, Eric and Jason

and

Judy and our daughters, Melanie and Letitia

Brief Contents

Preface   xi

1 Leaders, Ethics, and Schools: A Search for Clarity   1

2 Moral Theory   21

3 Leadership as Moral Architecture   47

4 Taking On the Big Challenge of School and District Administration   67

5 The Costs and Benefits of Inclusion   83

6 Factors to Consider When Making Judgments About Controversial Issues   103

7 The Pragmatic Value of Justice for All   119

8 The Role of Law in Moral Evaluation   135

Appendix A   Additional Case Studies in Educational Leadership   151

Appendix B   American Association of School Administrators
              Statement of Ethics for Educational Leaders   170

Appendix C   National Education Association Code
              of Ethics of the Education Profession   172

Appendix D   National School Boards Association Code
              of Ethics for School Board Members   175

Glossary   177

References   187

Index   197

About the Authors   207

About the Case Study Authors   208

Detailed Contents

Preface   xi

    Features of the Text xiii
    Acknowledgments xvi
    Case Matrix xvii

1 Leaders, Ethics, and Schools: A Search for Clarity   1

    The Inherently Moral Nature of Leadership 1
    Leader as Moral Architect 3
    Moral Architectures Stand Alone 6
    Distinguishing Between the Meta-Ethical and Prescriptive Morality 8
    It's Not Just Talk: Pointing Out the Do's and Don'ts of Communal Moral Life 8
    Taking Prescriptive Morality Seriously 9
    From the Great Conversation to Truth and Moral Commitment 10
    Leading the Great Conversation 12
    Professional Ethics 13
    Professional Ethics in Practice: An Example 15
    DISCUSSION QUESTIONS 18
    CASE STUDY 19
    ACTIVITY 20
    FURTHER READING 20

2 Moral Theory   21

    The Pragmatic Difference Between Scientific and Moral Theory 21
    A Spectrum of Moral Theory 22
        Virtue Theory 22
        Rationality and Moral Realists 24
        The Social Contract 27
        The Many Camps of Universalism 30
        Intuitionism and Social Sympathy 37
        Pragmatism 41

DISCUSSION QUESTIONS   44
CASE STUDY   45
ACTIVITY   45
FURTHER READING   45

3 Leadership as Moral Architecture 47

Sustainable Leadership   47
Morally Prescriptive Shared Vision in Education   49
The Four Corners of Educational Purpose   51
    Learning   51
    Developing Attitudes Appropriate for Participation in the Great Conversation   53
    Acquiring Important and Reliable Information   54
    Dispositions   55
The Challenge of Accommodating All Four Corners of Educational Purpose   56
The Educational Leader: Leading the Way to Accommodation While
Never Losing Sight of Principle   56
Beyond the Four Corners of Educational Purpose: Schooling
Dispositions and Attitudes   57
Political and Economic Challenges to Doing Good   60
Sustainable Leadership and Organizational Survival   62
DISCUSSION QUESTIONS   63
CASE STUDIES   64
ACTIVITIES   65
FURTHER READING   66

4 Taking On the Big Challenge of School and District Administration 67

Leadership, Management, and Policy   67
    Managers   68
    Bosses   69
Leadership: Moving Beyond Management   69
Start With Policy Review, Not People Review   71
Deming's Social and Managerial Idealism and Scheffler's Pragmatism   72
Getting One's Ducks in a Row   73
The Point of Policy: Getting Better All the Time   74
No Child Left Behind: A Source of Evaluation and Assessment Blunders   75
Pragmatic Idealism   76
Making Theory Responsive to Practice   79
DISCUSSION QUESTIONS   80
CASE STUDIES   81
ACTIVITY   82
FURTHER READING   82

5 The Costs and Benefits of Inclusion   83

Accounting: The Meta-Language of Costs and Benefits   83
Education for Inclusion   86
Respect for Persons and the Assault on Inclusion: Bullying,
Sexual Harassment, Sex Education, and Religious and Ethnic Tolerance   89
Conflicts of Duty   92
Education, Evaluation, and Funding: Putting Money Where It Belongs   94
What Does It Mean to Assess Education?   96
Boards, Unions, Politicians, Parents, and Colleagues   99
DISCUSSION QUESTIONS   101
CASE STUDIES   101
ACTIVITY   102
FURTHER READING   102

6 Factors to Consider When Making Judgments About Controversial Issues   103

Tolerance for Zero Tolerance   103
Racism and Hate Speech: Fragments of School and District Culture   111
Providing a Safe Environment: At What Cost?   113
Participation in the Great Conversation of Humankind   114
Summary Recommendations   115
DISCUSSION QUESTIONS   115
CASE STUDIES   116
ACTIVITY   117
FURTHER READING   118

7 The Pragmatic Value of Justice for All   119

The Pragmatics of Justice   119
Justice: A Linchpin Concept in Modern Theorizing   119
Justice, Promise, and the Relevant Origins of Enduring Morality   120
Bootstrapping Principles and Virtues and the Great Conversation   121
Properly Working Moral Architectures   122
Making Communities Better Through Better School and District Architectures   124
Sustaining Moral Architecture in the Face of Challenge   125
Elevating School and District Moral Architectures   128
Social Engineering, Schooling, and the Focus of Education   129
The Pragmatic Value of Justice   130
DISCUSSION QUESTIONS   132
CASE STUDIES   133
ACTIVITY   134
FURTHER READING   134

8 The Role of Law in Moral Evaluation 135

Law as Public Morality and Surface to Moral Architecture   135
Jurisprudence, Philosophy, and Practical Studies   135
The Nature of Law   138
Moral Courage, Prudence, and the Law   141
Law, Order, and the Feel of Justice   143
The Wisdom of the Law: Order and Social Justice   146
Summary   147
DISCUSSION QUESTIONS   148
CASE STUDIES   148
ACTIVITY   149
FURTHER READING   150

Appendix A   Additional Case Studies in Educational Leadership 151

Case A.1. Agonizing Over Ecstasy at Cedar Hill School   153
Daniel Vokey
DISCUSSION QUESTIONS   154

Case A.2. Justice and Zero Tolerance   154
Paul F. Bitting
DISCUSSION QUESTIONS   155

Case A.3. A Matter of Integrity   156
William Hare
DISCUSSION QUESTIONS   157

Case A.4. Possibilities at Lone Mountain   157
Ernestine K. Enomoto and Bruce H. Kramer
DISCUSSION QUESTIONS   158

Case A.5. Principal as Buffer at Man Dorr Primary   159
Kamla Mungal
DISCUSSION QUESTIONS   160

Case A.6. Professional Ethics and the Micropolitics of
Decentralization: The Dilemma of District Office Middle Managers   160
Lars G. Björk
DISCUSSION QUESTIONS   161

Case A.7. A Professional's Personal Challenge   161
JoAnn Franklin Klinker
DISCUSSION QUESTIONS   163

Case A.8. Rights of Students Versus Rights of Teachers 163
John Keedy
DISCUSSION QUESTIONS 164

Case A.9. When a Picket Fence Becomes an Offense in Standardized Testing 165
Elizabeth Campbell
DISCUSSION QUESTIONS 166

Case A.10. When the Saints Come Marching in 166
Sylvia Méndez-Morris
DISCUSSION QUESTIONS 168

Case A.11. Defending the Unempowered 168
Paul A. Wagner and Douglas J. Simpson
DISCUSSION QUESTIONS 169

**Appendix B   American Association of School Administrators
Statement of Ethics for Educational Leaders**   170

**Appendix C   National Education Association Code
of Ethics of the Education Profession**   172

**Appendix D   National School Boards Association
Code of Ethics for School Board Members**   175

Glossary   177

References   187

Index   197

About the Authors   207

About the Case Study Authors   208

Preface

We believe that what people make of their nation's schools will influence significantly how the country develops. No one plays a more important role in this development than senior-level school and district administrators. Senior-level educational administrators do far more than create flow charts, manage organizational structures, create and maintain budgets, design policy, and manage personnel. In addition to all this, they create a moral ambiance for the community, both within the schools and beyond.

The more we became aware of this impact of senior-level school administrators, the more two concepts pressed themselves upon our minds. The first idea is that of a Great Conversation of Humankind. This concept has been around in various forms since antiquity. Usually it takes the form of a shared search for knowledge (Wagner & Benavente, 2006). In 1959, Victor Frankl described a great conversation of humankind in Rousseau-like fashion as expressing the collective will of the human spirit. The most popular use of the term in recent history probably stems from the failed attempt of the *Encyclopedia Britannica* to establish a canon for the Western world through its Great Books series (Hutchins, 1952). Although many other writers have used the term in increasingly more generous terms regarding content (Adler, 1998; Born & Whitfield, 2004; Melchert, 2006), we use the term in a much more technical sense, embracing the idea of a shared search for knowledge and a quest for establishing an understanding of the general will of the human spirit. Moreover, in our technical use of the term *the Great Conversation,* we will identify both process and criteria for its content. Specifically, the process the authors identify as constitutive of the Great Conversation is the sincere and passionate search for truth as moderated by critical thinking and respect for both the shared purpose of all participants and the commitment to engage every potential truth seeker. Content is any and all generalizable inquiries perplexing the human mind, regardless of the artificial boundaries that exist in the world. This specialized technical notion refers not only to an expression of human willfulness but to the epistemic ambitions of human understanding in general (Wagner & Benavente, 2006). Because of the specificity of this technical notion, we will capitalize it throughout the text so the reader keeps in mind that we are not speaking of conversation in any ordinary sense, nor even in step with Rousseau, Frankl, or the editorial board of *Encyclopedia Britannica*. We will describe this concept in more detail in Chapter 1. Suffice for now to say that the Great Conversation designates the general purpose of education, understood grandly as a search for and the inclusive sharing of understanding in the search for truth of every sort.

The more we thought of schools, education, and senior-level administration, a second idea impressed itself on our minds: the idea of a moral architecture. The term *moral architecture* will be discussed at length and used throughout the book, but for now suffice it to say that the term *moral architecture* refers to the moral ambiance that is created in large part by how senior-level administrators go about their daily tasks. The need for such a specialized term became evident as we came to realize that sustainable leadership in general and educational leadership in particular depend critically on the moral ambiance surrounding its practice. Like an architect, the educational leader plans, designs, and constructs a framework that accomplishes a set of desirable goals. In the case of the architect these goals may be beauty, functionality, or a combination of both. For the educational leader these may be present, but even more imperative is that goals and processes are pursued in an ethically sound manner and result in a more credible, informed, and civil society. In this sense, competent leadership develops and sustains a moral ambiance that manifests the credibility of the goals pursued (Kouzes & Posner, 1993; Whitney, 1994).

This book is about management theory and practice. However, it is not the type of book on management theory and practice many readers typically expect. Whereas some books in management theory focus on strategic planning, operations research, school law, and logistics, and others may focus on organizational behavior, accounting methods, auditing procedures, personnel, and community relations, this book focuses distinctly on the moral aspects of leadership, administration, and school management. Thus, the reader will learn some necessary moral theory and even a bit of philosophy, biology, and psychology in addition to some leadership principles, law, and policy considerations.

Aristotle cautioned that theory without practice is empty, and practice without theory is blind. John Dewey and a host of American pragmatists hold similar views, as do we. In what follows there will be an account of the inherently moral in leadership and educational management. In Chapter 1 we will develop the complementary ideas of the Great Conversation and moral architecture. In Chapter 2 there are thumbnail sketches of foundational moral theories, followed by hints at how each might be pressed forward as pedagogical and administrative recommendations. The chapter ends by suggesting a strategy for minimizing moral error in practice. This very pragmatic strategy is not itself a moral theory but rather a way of bringing moral theory into practice with minimal risk of compromising the genuine and legitimate moral concerns of others.

The quest for applicable moral theory in human affairs is nothing new. Humans could have never survived as social beings without the cohesion provided by a generally shared moral conscience (Maxey, 2002). Indeed, leadership credibility itself is largely sustained by having and exhibiting commitment to a shared, public conscience. In Chapter 3, the idea of organizational conscience is further developed through elaboration of the concept of moral architecture. Chapters 4–7 focus on morality and leadership in practice and show that morality permeates so much that it is often taken for granted as standard administrative decision making.

In Chapter 8 we show how moral decision making brings together law, policy, emotive feel, and moral alertness into a very complex decision-making process. We show in detail that although public conscience is often exhibited in laws and codes of ethics particular to a community or profession, respectively, the credibility of the leader must always go beyond mere adherence to written dictates. To sustain a position of moral authority, the leader must be seen as one who understands the spirit of what is written and may even further articulate that spirit through word and action. Appendix A is designed to help us recognize that we often process ethical data too quickly and sometimes reach unsound conclusions as a result. Often, we need to reconsider our initial impressions in light of other information. This other information may include conversations with others, study of expert argument and analysis, and personal reflection. This two-step process does not assume that initial inclinations or tentative conclusions are incorrect. Rather, the two-step process is an intermediate heuristic meant to remind us that ethical decision making is more likely to be sound when moral agents are open to reconsidering initial instincts and early conclusions.

FEATURES OF THE TEXT

To underscore the focus on practice throughout, including the early theoretical chapters, we include pedagogical devices to stimulate immediate reflection on an important idea or issue as it appears in the text.

A Reflective Break: Sometimes it is important to pause from what one is reading and contemplate what is being said. It may even be time to go back and reread. In the Middle Ages this type of reading was called *lectio divina*. We don't think we are offering anything divine, but a contemplative pause may be in order.

A Group Discussion: This exercise is designed to prompt collaboration and shared understanding with others engaged in reading the same material. This exposes the text to greater variety of criticism, and we believe everyone can benefit from such moments of focused dialogue.

A Reality Check: This learning aid reminds the reader that in the end the goal is always to seek application to the realities of classroom, school, and district.

Questioning the Authors: We have nothing short of reverence for the idea of the Great Conversation, so these offerings are intended to prompt the discriminating reader to join in the Great Conversation and either take us to task for something we have said or offer greater support to make a loosely contrived idea more secure and reasonable.

A Practical Assignment: This is essentially a mini–case study that underscores the text's emphasis on putting theory into practice.

A Philosophical Question: This technique stimulates extended reflection about issues always and centrally close to the heart of philosophy, namely epistemic questions such as "What do you mean?" and "How do you know?"

Clarifying the Concept: For readers unfamiliar with philosophy, it may be something of a surprise to learn that before proceeding into further discussion it is essential periodically to stop and do a meta-analysis of the meanings of the terms central to the unfolding line of argument.

In addition, we intersperse tables and figures in the chapters to provide both summative information and heuristic frameworks for encouraging further deliberating in principle and in greater depth. Moreover, for further convenience to the reader, the first time technical terms appear they are in bold type to alert the reader to refer to the glossary for a precise definition. At the end of each discursive chapter there are case studies, discussion questions, and an activity. We also include suggestions for further reading.

Finally, we include examples of three professional codes of ethics. Appendix B is the American Association of School Administrators Statement of Ethics for Educational Leaders; Appendix C is the National Education Association Code of Ethics of the Education Profession; and Appendix D is the National School Boards Association Code of Ethics for School Board Members.

Probably the most noted intellectual historian of the 20th century was José Ortega y Gasset. In *The Revolt of the Masses,* Ortega y Gasset (1931) wrote that democracy's emphasis on egalitarianism was eroding general respect for legitimate expertise. Indeed, he noted, there are ideological movements today that object to nearly any claim of authority, truth, or knowledge. The trend he warned against at midcentury has only become more pronounced. For Ortega y Gasset, expertise didn't end at the portal leaving the sciences. He insisted that there was true expertise in art, artistic criticism, history, morality, and a host of other matters as well. By indicating his concern, he was not arguing for a blind acceptance of research or argument by authorities in certain fields. Instead, he was encouraging us to show critical receptiveness to ideas that are based on pertinent evidence and argument, an idea repeated in the work of some of the most rigorous theorists even today (Hare, 2000).

With regard to moral expertise, probably every reader can recall a time when he or she sought advice about some moral problem from someone presumably of greater wisdom and experience. This advisor may have been a mentor at work, an older sibling, parent, grandparent, aunt, uncle, or even professor. Mentors are sought and recognized, presumably because of some wisdom, experience, or expertise they manifest through personal word and deed. This suggests that at the level of real-world experience Ortega y Gasset may well be right in saying that there is real expertise in a whole host of matters, ranging from athletics to the arts and from moral and social affairs to the physical sciences.

In the text that follows, we try not to present a strong, personally favored foundational position. In some ways, this is a modest challenge because neither of us feels ready to place his chips behind one theory as yet. Along with the reader, we are refining our thinking and expect to continue doing so for the rest of our lives. At the very least, however, we think we offer several heuristics that will help readers partially avoid the most obvious pitfalls of moral reflection in the practice of leadership. Because we have both had a number of leadership roles, our writing is informed by practical insight and experience from a variety of contexts and is not limited to erudite scholarship. As a consequence, some may even criticize us at times for being too practical, but that is a criticism we gladly bear.

Although we do not delve greatly into religious ethics and leadership, we are aware that many followers of Buddhist, Jewish, Christian, Muslim, Confucian, Hindu, Taoist, and Native American beliefs are influenced by religious precepts and practices. These influences are of great importance to adherents of these traditions and to many contemporary scholars, but our work has a much more narrow scope. In the most modest manner possible, our goal is to help school administrators in the English-speaking world answer immediately practical questions, such as, "Whom do I owe in my role as an administrator?" "What do I owe each stakeholder?" and, finally, "How do I know when I have at least minimally paid my debt to those to whom I am morally obligated as an administrator?"

We go to special lengths to take note of the disempowered, the disadvantaged, different ethnicities, and class, racial, and other groups as school and district stakeholders. We do so because we believe that thinking and acting ethically involves considering the rights and interests of everyone. This interest in the unempowered, oppressed, and marginalized not only is apparent in our discussions but also is reflected in our choice of guest case writers in Appendix A. Their experiences and expertise contribute in invaluable ways to this project.

The great jurist Clarence Darrow, defender of Scopes and a host of unpopular and unempowered others, once observed in response to a question from reporters about his defense of Loeb and Leopold (two wealthy and notoriously privileged youngsters accused of murder), "This is America. In America even the rich deserve a fair trial." His point—and one of our major points throughout the book—is that respect for others is a moral principle for which we are sympathetic and which we think is indispensable for administrators. This is an admitted bias, one that we think undergirds both multicultural education and social justice emphases. Furthermore, and along these same lines, we think administrators owe as much to the gifted and talented as to the intellectually and behaviorally challenged, as much to girls as to boys, as much to one ethnic group or religiously affiliated group as to another. More specifically, we think that all students and professionals deserve every opportunity possible to reach their respective degrees of excellence. These are commitments necessitated by the concept of the Great Conversation, which we think helps define the profession.

To bring people together in the Conversation requires thoughtful and focused effort on the part of all constituents and a commitment to understanding diversity in all its forms, including the social and moral. Still, both of us know and appreciate the importance of keeping things simple whenever possible. We write with an eye to the simple acronym so fashionable today, K.I.S.S.: *Keep it simple, Socrates.*

ACKNOWLEDGMENTS

Many people have contributed to the development of this text, far too many to acknowledge individually, and so both the names omitted and those mentioned here undoubtedly contributed far more to our collective thinking than any acknowledgment can make clear. To begin, the following reviewers helped greatly in challenging us to make the text more accessible and keeping us to our promise to feature the practical: Penny S. Bryan, Chapman University, Orange; Loretta M. Delong, Minnesota State University, Mankato; Nirmala Erevelles, University of Alabama; Meta Harris, Georgia Southern University; Karen Hayes, University of Nebraska at Omaha; Marla Susman Israel, Loyola University Chicago; Steve Jenkins, University of Texas, Permian Basin; John W. Kalas, University at Albany–SUNY; Robert E. Kladifko, California State University, Northridge; Judith K. Mathers, Oklahoma State University; James O. McDowelle, East Carolina University; James C. Moses, Lewis University; Caroline Roettger, University of Toledo; James Sherrill, former Associate Dean of Graduate Studies and Research, University of British Columbia; Linda R. Vogel, University of Northern Colorado; and Elaine L. Wilmore, Dallas Baptist University.

We also wish to thank those who so generously contributed ancillary case studies in Appendix A. A special thanks therefore goes to Paul F. Bitting, North Carolina State University; Lars G. Björk, University of Kentucky; Elizabeth Campbell, University of Toronto; Ernestine K. Enomoto, University of Hawaii; William Hare, Mount Saint Vincent University; John Keedy, University of Louisville; JoAnn Franklin Klinker, Texas Tech University; Bruce H. Kramer, St. Thomas University; Sylvia Méndez-Morris, Texas Tech University; Kamla Mungal, University of West Indies; and Daniel Vokey, University of British Columbia.

We also need to thank a variety of people who have directly or indirectly contributed to the writing of this book. In addition to the just named, a special thanks goes to cohorts one and two in the educational administration doctoral program at the University of Houston–Clear Lake for assisting with and patiently working through earlier drafts of the text, commenting on reader friendliness, practitioner utility, and so on. I (Wagner) owe a further debt to my former teacher, Christopher J. Lucas, who taught me to avoid jargon and keep the intended audience in mind. In addition, I owe a more remote but no smaller debt to Professor Israel Scheffler, the dean of American philosophy of education, who through his writings and personal observations reminds those around him that education can be well served by serious philosophy, and so one should never take short cuts or apologize for taking the time and effort to make ideas clear. In addition, I (Simpson) would like to thank the students in my educational and multicultural ethics courses who have raised questions, identified issues, pinpointed assumptions, challenged conclusions, and advanced thinking about being ethical as a person and professional in a multitheoretical, multicultural, multiethnic, and multiracial society. Similarly, I would like to express my appreciation to the professors, teachers, and ethicists whom I have learned with and from. Almost needless to say, I am indebted to the thinking of John Dewey even when we diverge in our theorizing.

Finally, we both owe a great debt of gratitude in our editor at SAGE, Diane McDaniel, who was patient with us, as was necessary, and had a wonderful eye for reader accessibility. In addition, Dr. McDaniel solicited reviews from some first-rate reviewers who chose to remain anonymous. To all who helped with the preparation of this book we owe a debt of gratitude. The errors that remain are fully ours, and ours alone. Our arguments are more carefully crafted because of the reviewers, and any flaws that remain reflect our shortcomings in appreciation of the wisdom of others.

CASE MATRIX

Case Number	Case Title	Key Concerns	Key Issues	Page Number
1.1	A Case of Good Intentions?	Procedural fairness Good intentions Competing duties	How do you fulfill your duty to competing stakeholders?	19
2.1	When Policy, Personnel, and Prudence Collide	Following rules Threats Professionalism	When does following the rules become a violation of professionalism?	45
3.1	Should the Captain Go Down With the Ship?	Openness with staff Personal risk and staff needs	How much personal risk are you duty bound to take on behalf of faculty and staff?	64
3.2	A New Schooling Mission	Personal integrity and professional ambitions Hurt feelings and underserved students	Should you ever sacrifice integrity in your quest for professional advancement?	64
3.3	Stand by Your Man?	Protecting the innocent Fearing the influential Fighting a losing battle	To what extent are you obligated to protect an innocent from being victimized by the system?	65
4.1	Holding Teachers Accountable for Test Scores	Accommodating faulty policies Rejecting financial rewards Ought implies can	To what extent should you be willing to sacrifice the financial well-being of others on grounds of principle?	81
4.2	Great Conversation of Humankind Versus Unsatisfactory Test Scores	Test scores and educational goals Ethnocentric curricula Grading	To what extent should you be willing to subordinate schooling goals to fulfill less demonstrable educational goals?	81
5.1	Imposing Values on Children	Imposing values Promoting religion	What is the relationship between imposing values and promoting religion through schooling practices and protocols?	101
5.2	The Bully With a Coach's Cap	Administrative courage Staff timidity Professional bullying	How much should courage be valued as an administrative virtue?	101
6.1	The Teachers Gone Wild Blog	Insubordination Institutional integrity Electronic dangers	Are there any limits to protecting institutional integrity?	116

(Continued)

(Continued)

Case Number	Case Title	Key Concerns	Key Issues	Page Number
6.2	The Terrors of Bluegrass High School	Personal conscience Professional commitment Private lives Public pressure	To what extent are you obligated to follow your personal conscience and professional commitment?	117
7.1	Sex Education: Considering Conflicting Opinions and Promoting Educative Learning	Diverse moral opinions Cowardly strategies Doing the right thing	How can you show respect for diverse moral positions?	133
7.2	A Request for a Letter of Reference	Ethical priorities Stereotypes Duty and honesty versus compassion and paternalism	How can you evaluate a subordinate's professional competence without misleading those who depend on your good faith evaluation?	133
8.1	The King of Snide at Westside Middle School	Teacher professionalism Moral disrupters Hasty decisions Collegial advice	How can one balance monitoring instructor professionalism with securing one's own future? Do we have duties that extend beyond self, or should psychological egoism account for all moral behavior?	148
8.2	The Christian Biology Teacher	Professional competence Academic freedom Religious tolerance	How can you protect both academic freedom and religious tolerance?	149
A.1	Agonizing Over Ecstasy at Cedar Hill School	Compassion Consistency Fairness Proportionality	If a teacher intends to avoid immoral consequences of lawfully sanctioned, standardized tests, should these intentions be considered as mitigating factors in deciding how to deal with the acknowledged transgression?	153

Case Number	Case Title	Key Concerns	Key Issues	Page Number
A.2	Justice and Zero Tolerance	Equality of punishment Equality of wrongdoing Absolutist policy Reflective thinking	What constitutes fairness: ensuring equality of punishment or establishing equality of wrongdoing?	154
A.3	A Matter of Integrity	Competence and character Flaws and faultfinding Professional judgment and pride	How good is a "good enough" effort for identifying competent faculty?	156
A.4	Possibilities at Lone Mountain	Desires and duties Equity and equality Rightness and prudence	Duties subordinate wants, but should wanting fairness ever trump ensuring equality?	157
A.5	Principal as Buffer at Man Dorr Primary	Principles and directives Low-performing students and low-performing teachers Authoritarian leaders	Should nobility of principle ever trump institutional directive?	159
A.6	Professional Ethics and the Micropolitics of Decentralization: The Dilemma of District Office Middle Managers	Professional disloyalty Personal disregard Communication problems Policy and supervisors	Is disloyalty to policy or person ever justified?	160
A.7	A Professional's Personal Challenge	Rival goods Friendship and leadership Compassion and professionalism Students or colleagues	What's good for all may not be good for one, so how does one choose between goods?	161
A.8	Rights of Students Versus Rights of Teachers	Empathy and duty Motives and consequences Democratic decision making	How should our understanding of the mitigating circumstances of an individual be balanced with professional duty?	163
A.9	When a Picket Fence Becomes an Offense in Standardized Testing	Violating testing procedures Conscience and public law Advocating for children	How can we manage the personal conscience of others in the face of public morality as evidenced in law?	165

(Continued)

(Continued)

Case Number	Case Title	Key Concerns	Key Issues	Page Number
A.10	When the Saints Come Marching In	Religious tolerance Professional judgment Procedural problems	How can we balance religious tolerance and respect for professional judgment?	166
A.11	Defending the Unempowered	Disparate power holders Identifying the unempowered Cultural differences New immigrants	How can we find fair solutions to disputes between disparate holders of power when it is unclear who is unempowered in a situation?	168

CHAPTER 1

Leaders, Ethics, and Schools

A Search for Clarity

THE INHERENTLY MORAL NATURE OF LEADERSHIP

As Thomas Sergiovanni (1990, 1996) and Robert Starratt (2004) observed, educational leadership is productively conceived in terms of service to students, staff, and society. Although there are lots of ways to get into leadership, sustaining leadership over time requires moral sensitivity and sophistication, always with an eye to service on behalf of others. **Ethical issues** such as accommodating high-stakes testing, preserving free expression while limiting hate speech and religious solicitation, and discouraging cheating and **violence** of every sort are examples of common morally laden assignments for school administrators. In addition, service-oriented moral leadership confronts a host of **ethical dilemmas** (Price, 2008). The moral dilemmas they confront include such things as equitable distribution of resources among departments, alleged but unintended harassment among employees, the equitable implementation of various employee incentive protocols, and balancing of the contentious claims of adversaries, to name but a few.

The point of doing ethics both as individuals and collegially with others is to solve problems for the well-being of all involved (Howard & Korrer, 2008). There would probably be less stress in leadership positions if leaders pay attention to developing and maintaining an appropriate moral vision for their schools and districts (Strike, 1999). Such vision, when realized, is constitutive of the moral architecture of a school or **community.**

Until recently no distinction was made between ethics and **morals.** Indeed, a cursory review of college course catalogs in any decade or century shows that regardless of course title (*morals* or *ethics*), course substance is largely the same. *Ethics* and *morals* both equally referred to prescriptive rules or principles of **action,** rules presumably designed to make things better in some important sense by guiding appropriate action. Note the use of the word *action* where one might have reasonably anticipated the word *behavior.* The moral world is not about behavior per se but rather about action.

The term *action* is distinguished from the term *behavior* in that it implies intent. Behavior that is accidental is usually morally excusable unless one is accused of being unduly negligent. Moral praise and condemnation both are usually reserved for acts intended by the actor, and hence we have the fashionable use of the term *action theory* in philosophy and social psychology today (Thompson, 2008).

Morals and *ethics* both still refer to prescribed rules or principles of action in general parlance even today (Millgram, 2005). But in the wake of logical positivism in **law** schools, courses titled "legal ethics" began limiting their focus to descriptions of sanctions for specific violations of rules. The American Law School Association Committee on Ethics recently began an attempt to reverse this trend, reasoning that rules make sense only in light of shared commitment and general moral vision (Simmonds, 2007). Starting in the 1970s with a renewed interest in medical ethics, a similar distinction between **morality** and ethics was initiated by some social scientists studying the professional world of physicians. The word *ethics* came to be used for the rules, regulations, principles, and sometimes shared moral commitments common to a distinct group of professionals. In contrast, the word *morals* was shunted aside, said to refer only to personal moral commitments and principles. The distinction is heuristically useful in some contexts and probably will continue to be made in some professional literature. Nonetheless, the distinction does not yet establish a hard line of demarcation between the two terms in most parlances (Posner, 1998).

Several observations illustrate the difficulty if not undesirability of separating ethics from morals. To begin with, how can a profession agree on ethical **obligations** if there is not a shared and personal moral commitment to the aforesaid rules? And why would a school board employ a principal who said she was not personally committed to the profession's code of ethics but would merely act in the light of them? Moreover, it is not clear that a person could *be* truly professional if she behaved in accord with a wrongheaded institutional "ethic," that is to say, prescriptive rule. What counts as a wrongheaded institutional ethic (prescriptive rule) is something that the reader will figure out with greater experience, theoretical **understanding,** and reflective study. For the time being, consider the following real example as a prompt to understanding this caution.

In the late 20th century, a district school superintendent in Mississippi mandated that as a matter of district policy no interracial couples would be allowed at the high school prom. The superintendent insisted that the prohibition was necessary because of rising racial tensions in the area, and the presence of one or more interracial couples may have prompted a serious disruption at the event. As an administrator you have a **duty** to follow your superior's directives generally and formal district policy specifically. On the other hand, your moral commitment as a professional is to show equal respect to all people. Imagine you are assigned to chaperone the prom in this situation. An interracial couple appears at the door in defiance of district policy. You recognize the couple. Both are honor students and good citizens. Teachers working the front desk turn to you, wondering what should be done as the students approach. What do you think should be done?

The district policy is clear. Your personal and professional moral commitments are also clear. The two sets of commitments—one to the district policy and another to the principle of equal respect—seem diametrically opposed to one another in this case. What is your *professional* obligation? Do you follow the superintendent's directive, or do you act on your personal and professional conscience?

Before reaching your decision, reflect on another true incident. During the Vietnam War, a young lieutenant, presumably on orders from his company commander, had his troops destroy a village and begin killing the inhabitants until an American helicopter placed itself between the inhabitants and the lieutenant's troops. Upon formal review the lieutenant claimed he was only doing his duty by following orders. The military tribunal court-martialed him, saying he was always responsible for his own actions. He could never have a duty to act in a criminally offensive way, even if commanded to do so by a superior. More generally, from the mid-20th century and to the present, people brought to trial as war criminals have often pleaded they were acting under orders and so were not deserving of punishment. Is that a good defense? Is it a morally upstanding defense? Are such considerations relevant to the educational scenario described earlier?

To return to the hypothetical of the administrator on duty at the prom, what should you do? As you look about, all seems calm. There is no impending danger. However, as the night wears on it is quite possible that various prohibited intoxicants will begin to take their toll on some of the students. Some of the boys may become a bit edgier and quick to challenge another. Still, these are only possibilities at the moment. On the other hand, you are the district's representative. If you don't uphold and honor school policy, why should anyone else? And yet again, if you engage in an act of overt prejudice, don't you discredit not only yourself but the school, the district, the community, and the profession as well?

It may be premature to require you to risk a solution to this hypothetical, but as an administrator you can be sure that although you may not face this particular dilemma, you will face situations equally challenging to your wits, your sense of social sympathy, your honor, and your integrity. The closest you will come to a plausible answer at the moment may be to reflect on the notion of what it means to be a professional. Such reflection may lead you to conclude there is less of a gap between professional ethics and your personal moral convictions than you may have once suspected.

LEADER AS MORAL ARCHITECT

Leadership is a ubiquitous and practical exercise of human understanding and skill. Leadership shows up in all aspects of communal living and association. Leaders may do good or evil. They may lead through democratic processes, or they may lead through authoritarian demands. Their personalities, paths to **authority,** and sense of **responsibility** may vary greatly. In short, there is no generic template for all aspects of leadership in actual practice and in every context. There is no one-size-fits-all template for sustaining one's role as a leader in an educational community and under shifting schooling pressures. So much depends on context, and contexts are always in flux. Nonetheless, there is much that can be identified generally as relevant to sustainable leadership in an educational community.

When one looks more generally beyond **education,** any list of leaders belies the flaw in efforts to construct a one-size-fits-all template for leadership. For example,

St. Benedict, Joseph Stalin, Che Guevara, Seligman the Great, Lee Iaccoca, Mother Teresa, Mao Tse-tung, Martin Luther King Jr., Robert Oppenheimer, Joan of Arc, Golda Meir, George Washington, and Maria Montessori were all leaders of historic proportions. Yet think how different one is from the other. Think how different the contexts and challenges were that confronted each. One could easily argue that both St. Benedict and Joseph Stalin were authoritarian, and yet one must admit that each had strikingly different moral visions and led others from within very different contexts. Che Guevara and Mother Teresa were both said to be open to democratic processes in leadership, and yet again they were quite different from one another. Each had sharply different moral visions, and each led communities filled with strikingly different social dynamics. Of course, this does not mean that every kind of leadership is morally right minded. If just any moral vision were acceptable in education, then there would be no need for you to read this book, much less for you to attempt to think and act ethically. But the fact that we are dealing with educational leadership helps focus our considerations, especially our moral concerns, and that is fortunate because the productive study of leadership must limit itself in scope and sequence to be of any serviceable value to practitioners (Fasching, 1997).

Like all leaders, educational leaders work in specific contexts that limit the range of goals and probably social dynamics. In the case of educational leaders, these limitations emanate first and foremost from their professional commitments, but other factors such as time, place, and general social dynamics all play a limiting role on what is apt and appropriate as well. The leader may be an architect of a community's or **organization's** moral ambiance, but that does not mean he has a free hand at what materials he must work with or when a change in design may be necessary. For example, the profession's shared moral vision sets boundaries to what a leader can do or properly demand of fellow professionals. Like physicians following the Hippocratic code, educational leaders are constrained from the outset to do no harm to those they serve. And just as the Hippocratic oath isn't limited to doctors from Greece in antiquity but rather extends to physicians across millennia and many geographic borders, the shared professional vision of educators spreads across the globe in time and space. In addition to doing no harm, the professional vision of educators entails bringing people together in the sincere search for and sharing of truth. This bringing together of all peoples in the sincere and skillful search for truth and understanding is what we mean throughout this text by the term *Great Conversation of Humankind*. Professional vision may both limit what the leader can do and fulfill the leader in her attempt to get things right. Changing circumstances may both limit and advance the cause of professional leadership in education (Wagner, 1992).

A REFLECTIVE BREAK

To what extent are doing ethics and being ethical dependent upon context, personality, character, cooperation, and thinking with others? Explain your thinking.

American president John F. Kennedy famously implored his compatriots, "Ask not what your country can do for you but what you can do for your country." In asking citizens to engage in such reflection, Kennedy was acknowledging that leadership cannot succeed by focusing solely on the person at the top to make everything right. Successful leadership is a collaborative and community undertaking.

Leaders exist only in the context of community. Communities may be construed in light of geographic constructs or in light of shared professional interests (and, of course, in other ways). Communities make and sustain leaders in one way or another as much as do the individual talents and moral vision of the leaders themselves.

The apparatus sustaining a community is its moral architecture. Architecture typically is a dynamic interplay between the architect and her design and the engineers materializing the design. The same is true of moral architecture in the schools. The leaders bring important designs that they articulate and, more importantly, that they role model. All other stakeholders in the school and district are analogous to the engineers who through practice and willingness to commit to their own interpretation of the designs create a dynamic that brings the moral architecture to fruition.

Except in cases of sheer anarchy or absolute despotism, leaders are brought into the somewhat limiting constraints of a community's existing moral architecture. Over time leaders are bound to affect the moral architecture of the community, just as the architecture inevitably affects them. By respecting the most commendable aspects of existing moral architecture, stakeholders and leaders alike show respect for one another, the community, and its vision. Leaders committed to working with stakeholders further develop the moral architecture, creating and strengthening bonds between other leaders, staff, and students.

Leadership is inherently a dynamic between the **character** and **personality** of a leader and the further dynamic of the leader working in concert with followers of somewhat like mind in an action-focused context. Few understood this latter dynamic better than President Kennedy. In a recent conversation with Christopher Kennedy Lawford, one of the authors recalls Lawford telling the story, "When I was 5 the Democratic convention nominating Uncle Jack occurred in California, where I lived. My uncle came into my bedroom the night he became the party's nominee and asked me if I would help him win the presidency. I said I would tomorrow but I was tired now" (personal communication, April 17, 2007). The point in this amusing anecdote is that Kennedy recognized just how richly textured the dynamic between leader, followers, and context is. Here Uncle Jack was securing the commitment of all possible stakeholders. Such efforts are the very heart of leadership in democratic environments. Put another way, leadership demands both an awareness of and the ability to develop a robust moral architecture involving all stakeholders as fully as possible.

Beyond organizational structure and social hierarchies, every community also has a moral architecture. The moral architecture permeates both formal structure and social hierarchy. Moral architecture also illuminates the respect, moral imperatives, traditions of decency, and **courtesies** animating communal consciousness. (See Case Study A.6 in Appendix A.) Moral architecture is distinct from and does not replace decision-making protocols, nor does it replace law, policy, or organizational hierarchy. Moral architecture reflects in dynamic fashion stakeholder response to all these communal elements but goes further to reflect social graces and collaborative style. In summary, moral architecture is about how Munoz, Bernstein, Muhammad, and Jones treat each other collegially.

Moral architectures may range from so-called flat structures in which either anarchy or "might makes right" despotism results in dominance of the many by the capriciousness of a few, to lofty architectures with high-level commitments articulating honored principles and virtues generally accepted by all. Leaders either fit or fail to fit into an existing moral architecture. The best leaders, and those most likely to sustain a leadership position, affect the existing moral architecture in important ways, making it better in the eyes of nearly all.

This book argues that the heart of leadership begins in character and moral commitment. Individual character and shared commitment, as they are spread throughout a school or district, reflect qualities of moral architecture. Reflective, **strong character** on the part of individuals and shared moral commitments give the moral architecture an elevation necessary for adjudicating between the inevitable and transient diversity of claims that are bound to occur from time to time. In contrast, unreflective, **weak character** and fear of shared commitments deflate a moral architecture, limiting access to diverse perspectives and democratic resolution of disputes.

Although leaders play the most conspicuous roles in elevating and modeling participation in a moral architecture, their efforts alone cannot sustain its benefits. As the great contemporary philosopher of Chinese moral theory Antonio Cua (1979) insists, leaders must be paradigmatic of the best of ideals of a community if those ideals are to extend into the future. Nonetheless, the life of an institution's moral architecture depends on no one person.

MORAL ARCHITECTURES STAND ALONE

Group dynamics as studied by social scientists are descriptive of how people typically engage one another. In contrast, the study of ethics and morality draws attention to how people *ought to* engage one another. Moral architecture is a collection of principles, virtues, and courtesies that people in a given organization implicitly agree ought to guide their collaborations. Collaborations are most sustainable when underlying shared moral theory supports a given architecture. The point of this book is to focus attention on the nature of morally responsive leadership most likely to guide organizational success over the long haul.

Figure 1.1 depicts many of the elements of a moral architecture, namely, principles, virtues, courtesies and related values and manifestations, communication patterns, personal relationships, school policies, collective attitudes, educational aims, moral commitments, and reflective habits. At the center of the figure, imagine a theory of human betterment. When fully developed, this theory will relate an ideal of education, with experience lived well, generally. Moral architecture is a dynamic always in flux. Some elements of architecture are more noticeable at one time or another, only to recede from the foreground later as circumstances change. For example, school courtesies, communication patterns, and democratic processes may recede to the background when school personnel sacrifice these values as they rush to meet pressing state or federal mandated deadlines. School leaders need to ensure that temporary imbalances do not become permanent features and deflate their schools' moral architectures.

Figure 1.1   The Complexities of Moral Architecture: Ideals, Beliefs, and Behaviors That Permeate an Organization

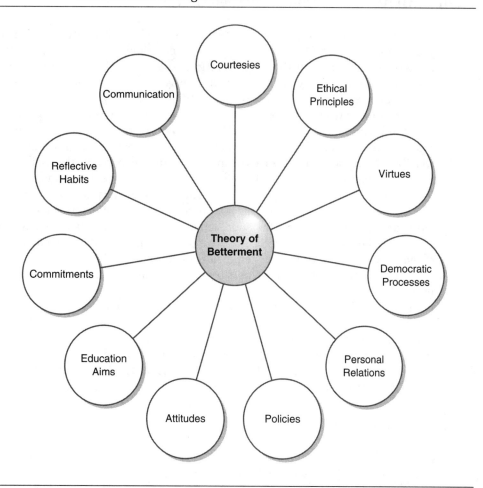

School leaders seeking a healthy, dynamic moral architecture center on sustained service to others and on a vision of human betterment. Commitment to such service requires strength of character, and strength of character has long been recognized as a straightforward moral virtue. Even more than service to others, commitment to human *betterment* is central to the notion of morality generally. Before a leader can model or agree to these recommendations meaningfully and direct her daily practice accordingly, she must have in mind clear and precise definitions of the key moral terms necessary for such reflection. For example, the educational leader must have explicitly in mind definitions for virtue, character, morality, human betterment, and, in the terms of this text, moral architecture.

DISTINGUISHING BETWEEN THE
META-ETHICAL AND PRESCRIPTIVE MORALITY

The ancient Greeks advised frequently that it was important to clarify one's terms. "Define your terms!" is often heard in history courses describing the ancient Greek search for **knowledge.** Since roughly the 1950s the effort to define terms precisely has been elevated to a technical subspecialty in philosophy known as meta-ethics (Blackburn, 1984; Darwall, 2006; Hare, 1954; Jackson, 2000; Korsgaard, 1996; Sober, 1975).

There is much work to be done in clarifying specific moral terms. Consequently, it should be no surprise to anyone that there are specialists at work on the project, and their work can be usefully explored by the practicing educational administrator (Price, 2008). This text will not explore meta-ethical issues in any depth other than to note the usefulness of such investigations from time to time. The glossary defines a number of relevant moral terms in light of the accumulated work product of meta-ethicists, and this should suffice for the practical investigations prompted in this text. In addition, we define at length two technical terms devised specifically for the approach of this text, namely *moral architecture* and a term yet to be defined more fully, *the Great Conversation of Humankind* (hereinafter also called the Great Conversation or simply the Conversation).

Clarity in moral language makes possible more exacting execution of considered and well-planned moral action (Adams, 2002; Crisp, 2006; Jackson, 2000; Millgram, 2005). For example, it doesn't do much good to tell either teachers or students that cheating is wrong if the teachers or students aren't exactly sure what counts as cheating or what it means to say that something is morally wrong in a specific context. Understanding what counts as cheating and what amounts to wrong, either morally or at least in some institutional context, makes violations and potential violations more evident to all. Such shared understanding should minimize the extent of unnecessary disagreement and conflict (Stevenson, 1944).

A GROUP DISCUSSION

If your district engaged in a discussion of democratically responsive leadership, how would you help clarify such a grand concept? Is there any reason to conclude that democratic leadership should have universal application in educational contexts or in the context of public schooling? When unpacking the term *democratic leadership,* what related concepts must be understood? Do you think you have identified all the *concepts* that must be grasped in order to understand the concept of democratic leadership? List the concepts you think must be understood in order to understand democratic leadership. Finally, what exactly are you saying when you modify the term *democratic leadership* with the further modifier *responsive?*

IT'S NOT JUST TALK: POINTING OUT THE
DO'S AND DON'TS OF COMMUNAL MORAL LIFE

When people think about ethics and morality, they have in mind something specialists call prescriptive moral theory. In prescriptive moral theory the theorist is genuinely trying to distinguish not the meaning of terms themselves but rather right from wrong action and character. The point of prescriptive morality is to construct rules, identify principles, or recommend virtues for living a morally upright and ethical life. At the level of practice, the principal or superintendent who is trying to decide whether a particular act is right or wrong (e.g., whether an alleged case of bullying or sexual harassment exists) is thinking prescriptively about possible moral choices. Moreover, he or she is living through and role modeling the virtues of a deliberative moral agent (Hursthouse, 1999). Such modeling is indispensable for adding elevation to institutional moral architecture.

Just as educational leaders must clarify the *meaning* of certain morally relevant terms, they must have warrant for anticipating the right-mindedness of action and policies in the contexts for which they are designed. In an educational context this right-mindedness is generally guided by an eye to human betterment (Darling-Hammond, 2006; Haidt & Joseph, 2004). Thus, conscientious educational leaders must not only take time to clarify the moral terms they use, they must also think through how people will be affected by given acts, the implementation of specific rules or policies, and the modeling of transparent virtues. The consequences that result from implementation will extend beyond any immediate challenge. Those consequences will further temper the evolving institutional moral architecture.

In short, the educational leader's lived moral experience affects more than just his or her situation in an organization or community. The leader's lived moral experience reverberates throughout the moral architecture, shifting architectural shape regardless of original and intentional design. As Cua (1979) notes, the more prominent a person's role in an organization, the more her ethics influence others. This role-modeling effect of Cua's "paradigmatic individual" can perhaps be more exactingly described (at least in mathematical terms) as an attractor effect (Skyrms, 2004). The attractor effect is the predictable effect that powerful figures have on the lives of others, depending in part on the *strength* of the exhibited virtue, **vice,** or disposition and the *proximity* of others to the role model. Suffice it to say that educational administrators play the major role in the dynamic that brings about an organization's sense of right-mindedness in matters large and small or, as we describe it, the organization's moral architecture.

TAKING PRESCRIPTIVE MORALITY SERIOUSLY

Whether in the case of individuals, professions, or communities of any kind, moral thinking aims at sentences that prescribe or prohibit virtues and vices, actions, and attitudes. Despite the recent flurry of opinion that there is no truth or point to "getting it right" in moral thinking, empirical evidence and studies from all over the world suggest much to the contrary (Adams, 2002; Audi, 2005). Three of the most prominent examples of mounting empirical evidence can be found in the American Psychological Association's endorsement of Peterson and Seligman's (2004) study of universal virtues and character strengths, Gert's (1996; 2004) studies of universal moral rules, and Sober and Wilson's (1998) extensive meta-analysis of the biological foundations for moral universals. Simply put, we have far more information about human morality generally than some relativists allow.

For readers who desire a better understanding of recent research in this realm, a wealth of multidisciplinary research is available (Axelrod, 1984; Blackburn, 2001, 2003; Coles, 2000;

Englehardt, 1986; Fehr & Fischbacher, 2003; Fletcher, 1993; Frank, 1988; Gaylin, 1979; Gazzaniga, 2006; Gibbard, 1990, 2003, 2008; Glimcher, 2004; Rapaport, 1991; Valliant, 1998; D. S. Wilson, 2002; J. Q. Wilson, 1997). Because every leader in an organization is a seminal architect of the organization's moral architecture, this literature is invaluable to responsible and reflective leaders. There is good reason to believe that human betterment can be achieved (Dugatkin, 1999). If there is any doubt that human betterment is achievable (Wright, 1955), consider the history of slavery. It took several thousand years for the last nation on Earth (an island nation off the west coast of Africa) to formally outlaw slavery in 1983. Now, when slavery does occur, it is at least formally condemned as contrary to both local and international law (Sowell, 1995). So there is evidence that people tend to agree cross-culturally on some moral prescriptions (Gordon, 2008; Koble & Garcia-Carpintero, 2008). Nonetheless, when researchers study ethics, they still need to consider grounds for moral agreement as well as moral diversity (Gibbard, 2008). For example, there is evidence of surface-level disagreement, or cultural endorsements of specific diverse ethics, however, there is compelling evidence that some universal moral structures run beneath local sources of agreement and disagreement (Scriven, 1976).

Surface-level variance in ethical rules and commitments increasingly appears analogous to what linguists have observed about human language (Hauser, 2006; Warneke, 2008). Just as languages differ on the surface (so Mandarin looks and sounds very different from Spanish, for example), there is compelling evidence that the species possesses a deep structure that makes human linguistic practice in general a possibility (Chomsky, 1988). Analogously, it might be noted that the cross-cultural transition away from opposing ethics involving issues such as slavery illustrates Dewey's (1938) notion that moral knowledge, like medical and other kinds of knowledge, converges as issues and principles are progressively studied and clarified (Alexander, 2007).

When students and staff from diverse backgrounds are brought together for the first time, they may sense little shared agreement on surface-level rules prescribing and prohibiting social behavior. At first glance institutional moral architecture may not be readily apparent. In addition, each person may bring along a mix of conflicting messages from both television and home about how to deal with "we–they challenges," "self-interest versus **altruism,**" and other apparent dichotomies of human social engagement. For example, compelling kinship affiliations (Hamilton, 1964) may draw them in one direction while principled instruction may draw them in another. Finding underlying moral structures alluring to all or otherwise creating grounds for convergence and creating a common sense of right-mindedness can be an Olympian task for educational administrators, their faculties, and their staffs. Yet regardless of how great the challenge, students and staff must learn that there is a source of respect in the human spirit (Strike, 1991) that makes bigotry, **racism,** and **sexism,** among other things, as universally unacceptable as slavery (Kohn, 2008).

FROM THE GREAT CONVERSATION TO TRUTH AND MORAL COMMITMENT

Albert Einstein once said that there would be no point to doing science if there were no reality about which scientific statements might be right or wrong (Isaacson, 2007). Analogously, moral theorists in education (Strike & Soltis, 2004) claim there is truth in morality, although it may look different from truth in other areas. In sympathy with both of these insights, we suggest that there is no point to morality or ethical theory if there is no such thing as getting it right or getting it wrong. As we alluded earlier, the history of slavery is in part at least a history of people and their leaders slowly moving away from error and coming to get things right.

Educational leaders must meet moral matters head on simply in order to do their respective jobs of principal, superintendent, educational policy maker, and so on. Educational leaders inherently make decisions about what *ought* to be done and (presumably) for what *good* ends. There is no way of pretending they can avoid moralistic decisions and commitments. However, in the best circumstances, highly principled moral architectures supporting virtues and eschewing vices advance the causes of productive planning and execution of collective purpose. They do this in part by developing communal attitudes and courtesies, accommodating a genuine concern for the well-being of others.

Fortunately, the educational leader is not left to construct a sense of organizational good out of whole cloth. Education has been around for millennia. More pointedly, the profession of teaching is one of the four oldest, along with doctoring, lawyering, and preaching. The professional traditions of education have accrued much in the way of hard-won and time-tested truths in the quest for morally respected practice. There have been high points and low for educational practice, from the Golden Age of Greece and the Age of Confucius to Nazi and Stalinist attempts to use education to propagandize. The former sought criticism in the pursuit of truth; the latter suppressed criticism in order to enforce oppressive socialization.

The term *Great Conversation* has been around seemingly forever. Although our use of the term is not fully identical with previous uses of the term (such as when the *Encyclopedia Britannica* used it to introduce their Great Book series back in the 1950s, a series disproportionately laden with Western male thinking), we share with previous definitions the idea that the Great Conversation is a process for seeking generalizable truth and understanding. Importantly, we extend the definition of the Conversation to make explicit the entailment of **multiculturalist** commitments to respect the voice of others, share understanding, and promote human well-being through the search for truth. In our more explicit definition, the commitment to pursue truth requires that participation in the Conversation be kept open to every source of potential truth and that everyone be heard and every idea exposed to earnest criticism aimed at moving all participants further away from error (Johnson, 2008). Presumably, as one moves further from error the only direction open is toward truth (Koble & Garcia-Carpintero, 2008). Moreover, the direction away from error also leads beyond matters of mere personal taste and idiosyncratic expression. As people move away from error they move toward others sincerely committed to truth, even when those others are not people we would often find ourselves agreeing with on other matters.

Truth claims should be held tentatively by those genuinely concerned with getting things right. Truth is difficult to ascertain, but that doesn't mean we cannot recognize personal and collective moves toward it. Our definition of the Great Conversation separates the concept of truth from definitions open to wildly disparate accounts associating truth with the simple expression of power, willfulness, or simple sympathy with the opinion of others. Perhaps most importantly, our definition of the Conversation entails commitment to the independent voice of every participant, with the goal of sharing as fully as possible all that is learned. In short, truth and the Great Conversation go together in matters of morality just as the two fit together in every other subject matter or cognitive discipline.

The Conversation seeks the possibility of generalizable insights of high utility for every aspect of human endeavor. Consequently, the Great Conversation depends on critical inquiry and fostering appropriate attitudes and virtues (Zagzebski, 2004). These derivative attitudes and virtues include respect for truth and for other truth seekers, open-mindedness to different ideas and evidence, humility in the quest for truth, tolerance for differentiation between levels of justification, and much more (Hare, 1992). In addition, the authentic search for truth is an inclusive practice as well as a practice with inclusion as its goal. Specifically this means that the Conversation must be an "every person" sort of affair, inherently global and multicultural in interest and actual engagement of others. To grasp the moralistic core of the Great Conversation, the reader must learn much more about moral theory itself. The goal of Chapter 2 is to familiarize you with most of the major branches of moral theory. Educational administrators are responsible for more than hosting this Conversation in their facilities.

LEADING THE GREAT CONVERSATION

Educational administrators are responsible for a number of training programs, socialization, and schooling practices. Each of these responsibilities must be accommodated in the organization's moral architecture in addition to the context necessary for fostering the Conversation. Because these further obligations are often imposed by civil authorities and other stakeholders outside the educational profession, cases of potential conflict of purpose may arise. Administrators must anticipate these conflicts and in some cases accommodate

A REALITY CHECK

Assume that you know condoms have been shown effective in protecting against pregnancy but that the Centers for Disease Control and Prevention (CDC) acknowledge that they do little to protect people from many sexually transmitted infections (STIs) or the depression that often accompanies becoming infected with one (Meeker, 2002). Some parents object to students being exposed to this information for a variety of reasons. Consider this: Do you consider the sharing of such knowledge an educational goal, or do you consider it a socialization goal mandated by society? Explain your thinking. Is it a good thing to share such knowledge with students? Explain. What considerations should determine whether it is good practice to share such knowledge with students? Before you answer, consider the possibility of conflicting parental concerns, the strength of the CDC's supporting research, society's interests, your professional commitment to truth, the students' and your own religious commitments, and other claims that may be a source of distress in arriving at a decision about sharing information about STIs with students. In sharing such knowledge, are educators at any legal risk? Are educators obligated to present such information while showing no moral concern? Explain your thinking.

conflicting interests under a single robust moral architecture with explicit commitment to the Great Conversation at every level.

The educational administrator is a moral agent who works with others to rearrange the present in order to do good, that is, to bring about human betterment. Doing good or bringing about human betterment through the Great Conversation is not something an educational administrator can do alone. Faculty, staff, and parents must share largely in the same vision of the good. A moral architecture must emerge that includes the shared sense of vision of all these stakeholders, ultimately including students as well. As Aristotle (1958) famously remarked in *The Politics*, "It makes no small difference what habits we develop, rather, it makes all the difference." The idea of human betterment can be realized in an educational organization only if all stakeholders' eyes are set firmly on the range of responsibilities assigned to the school or district, with special attention focused on the centrality of the Conversation.

PROFESSIONAL ETHICS

If the Great Conversation is the heart of education, then the moral architecture supporting the Conversation must be of a very special type. It must focus on inclusion as much as respect for the individual, passion for truth as well as tolerance for emerging opinion, and critical thinking as much as acquisition of facts, theories, and learning strategies and tactics. Clearly there is no way to get everyone to agree on every detail underpinning large concepts, policies, rules, protocols, and conventional courtesies of a school or district's moral architecture. Nonetheless, diversity of conscience or understanding need not eliminate the possibility of generally shared moral commitments within a community (Darling-Hammond, La Fors, & Snyder, 2001).

If a democratic, deliberatively derived moral architecture is not developed, an accidental, flat one will often evolve by default. And flat architectures, suffering as they do from an absence of lofty ideals and shared vision, are unsuitable to fostering the Great Conversation. Formal codes of professional ethics help articulate the lofty ideals and shared vision that sustain a moral architecture that fosters the Great Conversation.

Indeed, codes of ethics emerge as a result of efforts to bring into view a shared moral vision to which all members of a profession might aspire (Rich, 1984). A code of ethics should not be seen as a negatively motivated demand for **accountability** from wayward souls. Rather, the spirit of a code of ethics should be positive and proactive. Codes of ethics are meant to be both enduring in spirit and responsive to practical matters throughout changing times. Therefore, codes cannot be too specific in articulation. Human understanding of immediate circumstances is always tenuous at best. Moreover, social milieus are always in flux. Consequently, prescriptive details such as previously decided cases can only reveal trends upholding the lofty principles descriptive of the Great Conversation in circumstances that are not always wholly applicable in the immediate present.

The first written code of ethics for any profession was written by Hippocrates for physicians. Central to Hippocrates' original code is the imperative, "Do no harm!" The practice of medicine has changed greatly in the more than two millennia since Hippocrates wrote. Yet the general principle for physicians to "do no harm" remains as professionally prescriptive today as when the principle was first adopted by the local Greek profession of physicians. What counts as doing harm has changed many times and in many ways over the centuries and in different cultures, but the universal principle for physicians (even among many who never heard of Hippocrates) continues to be honored, namely, "First, do no harm." This bit of professionally prescriptive morality represents a generalized, shared moral vision of physicians past and present. Specifically, it directs practitioner attention to their shared obligation to seek the well-being of all they serve.

Codes of ethics prescribe in the most general terms a shared sense of moral vision for members of a profession. Codes of ethics may also be used to initiate the accumulation of a track record of decisions made on behalf of the profession to reprimand or sanction members who seem to be acting at odds with the evolving sense of right or wrong of the profession. A code of ethics itself provides only a general direction for shared specialist concern; specific decisions to reprimand or sanction a fellow practitioner add a bit more specificity to the profession's prescriptions to itself. But even the precedents establishing more precisely articulated prescriptions for members of the profession can never capture the full range of excellence in right-minded, professional action. Even a well-established record of precedent sometimes ignores or oversimplifies significant ethical considerations. Consequently, there is never enough direction in any formally articulated code or case-based derivative precedent to prescribe what the professional ought to do in every case. The proper moral considerations of professionals are bound to extend beyond such matters (Gaziel, 1997, 2003; Sergiovanni, 1996).

Being a professional is an understanding. In a profound sense it becomes for the practicing professional a state of mind that cannot be captured in a single written document. The range of unanticipated novelty is ever present and vast. Nonetheless, those on the inside of a profession, with code in hand, have a sense and familiarity with the moral vision they share with professional colleagues across geographic borders and over historic epochs. However much the details change, there is something about the moral vision of the four oldest professions (doctors, lawyers, preachers, and teachers) that makes it possible for fellow practitioners to recognize one another over the centuries and across cultural and geographic borders. In the case of educators, that something is perhaps best summed up in the concept of the Great Conversation. If this is so, and we believe it is, then the concept of the Great Conversation can serve educators well as the moral compass of a school or district. In short, the Great Conversation focuses professional vision on the necessities of an appropriate moral architecture for classroom, school, and district.

PROFESSIONAL ETHICS IN PRACTICE: AN EXAMPLE

As noted earlier, the shared commitment of professional educators may serve as a base from which an administrator can navigate between the competing claims of stakeholders with regard to a potentially tumultuous topic such as the balance between self-expression and constraints of religious tolerance in the schools.

Under the rubric of religious tolerance and First Amendment **rights** to self-expression, the courts are addressing criteria for student dress codes, how and when students might assemble for religious purposes, and public expressions of personal religious testimony. What is ahead in law in each of these areas is far from clear. And the enthusiasms and irritations of many groups of stakeholders in the schools seem bound to conflict. Consider now how an organizational moral architecture committed to the Great Conversation might help the administrator manage such a source of stakeholder conflict.

As a consequence of their commitment to the Great Conversation (and as specified in a variety of codes of ethics for educators in specific states), educators must promote sincere inquiry but never by making others feel intimidated or in any way silenced by the ongoing inquiry of others. The Conversation is committed to inclusion, not exclusion. The directive here seems clear enough, at least on the surface. But in practical situations the underlying spirit of surface-level prescriptions must be relied on to elucidate what is needed to sustain a moral architecture supportive of the Conversation. Moreover, the educational leader will find that there is much that is never anticipated by the straightforward language of law, policy, ethical codes, or other surface-level directives. Is a Tibetan child who spins a prayer wheel in school during free time expressing his cultural identity, or is he creating an environment hostile to learning by imposing his religion into the world of all others? Is a Native American student (Nighardt, 1961) who refuses to cut up an animal in biology just to learn techniques of dissection and see the internal operations of an animal excluding himself from the Great Conversation on religious or cultural grounds? Should devout Christian teachers be allowed to wear a small cross around their neck (and what about gang members for whom the cross may be an article of gang membership, a cultural artifact, or just an item of idiosyncratic self-expression)? Theories of creationism may not be permitted in biology courses, but what about in a course on the history of science or, more particularly, the history of biology? Does it make any difference which department might teach such a course? How can the educational administrator exhibit tolerance in such a way that all stakeholders are likely to understand the administrator's position as both tolerant and respectful of each stakeholder? Because much of this is not yet fully resolved by the courts or by anything written in local policy or codes of ethics (or even the derivative literature), what should the morally conscientious administrator do?

Earlier we mentioned the principle doctors fall back on when no other guidance seems evident: "Do no harm." We advised at the time that this principle might serve well the interests of educational administrators, and here is an apt example. Several of the questions in this section seem to suggest zero-sum games as options. In other words, what is done to favor the quest for truth, sharing of an alleged truth, or self-expression by one person seems to be at an equal cost to another's search for truth, sharing of that truth, or self-expression. So what is an administrator to do, and how does he or she create a moral architecture that does no harm in all these cases and yet fosters the best ideals of the Conversation?

There are no easy answers to any of these questions nor any specific directives that can be looked up somewhere in a text. On the contrary, day in and day out the administrator will be called on to get things right when addressing such dilemmas. Without specific guidance from the law, district policy, or professional codes of ethics, the administrator is largely on her own, yet she cannot just throw her hands in the air and act on **intuition** or personal conscience. The moral theories developed over the centuries and surveyed in the next chapter provide grounds for resolving such dilemmas. For example, in the absence of any other guidelines the utilitarian will try to figure out what course of action will bring about the greatest net pleasure (Hare, 1992). An advocate of an ethic of caring (Noddings, 1988) will focus on maintaining bonds of shared commitment between stakeholders even if it doesn't promote the greatest net pleasure. So in the case of wearing a cross, a utilitarian administrator in the absence of any other guidance may allow the widest possible interpretation of self-expression in order to produce the most overall pleasure. In contrast, the advocate of caring may bring stakeholders together and attempt to persuade others that they need to come to a collective solution without intimidating anyone into acquiescence (Hekman, 1995). The point here is that even in the absence of formal guidance, familiarity with moral theory gives the practicing administrator more to go on than her own subjective suspicions. By reaching beyond the impulse of her subjective conscience alone, she shows that she is truly committed to a moral architecture fostering respect for all stakeholders and the inclusiveness of the Conversation. This proactive respect for all trumps any individual's idiosyncratic preferences of the moment (Phillips & Freeman, 2003) and shows that she senses her **professionalism** demands respect for a vision beyond mere personal conscience.

Obviously, we have not given the reader specific prescriptions for what to do in each imaginable case of religious tolerance. But that was never the intent. No one can get the right answers every time to all such cases in advance and in the abstract. However, there are principles, virtues, and other understandings generally that may help the practitioner avoid moral error a bit more often than not by knowing more about the directionality of moral focus appropriate to the task of educational administration. The primary task of the rest of this book is to show how conflicts between personal moral conscience and professional duty can be avoided through deep moral reflection. Part of this will involve recommended heuristics aimed at doing the generally right thing in context-specific situations. For example, consider Table 1.1. This template is a heuristic tool for beginning responsible moral analysis in cases of applied situational complexity.

Keep in mind that the table is a heuristic tool, not an algorithm for calculating moral truth. The table is designed to prompt more exacting thought about applicable practice and its effects on the organization's developing moral architecture. There are many dimensions to moral architecture, too many to get a fix on without extended and deliberative attention before each immediate challenge is encountered. For example, schools and districts are becoming increasingly diverse, and as a consequence they are expected to accommodate often incompatible surface-level moral prescriptions or differing notions of educational or schooling purpose. For this reason, the model illustrates that especially at the surface level there may be several ethically plausible solutions to a controversial issue among a community of stakeholders. Because it is so important to secure the integrity of the community under the broad umbrella of one moral architecture, when differential support for alternative surface-level ethics appears evident, grounds for ultimately favoring one over another must become transparent and open to critique to all stakeholders (Zakhem, 2007).

Table 1.1   A Model for Analyzing and Addressing Ethical Issues Supportive of a Resilient Moral Architecture: A Multitheoretical and Multicultural Approach

Reflections	Responsibilities	Interests	Considerations
Problem Identification	Talking with relevant parties about their views and concerns	Ensuring that you and others understand the precise problems and issues of the parties involved	Listening carefully to the parties involved so that their personal and cultural perspectives are understood
Problem Clarification	Interacting again with relevant parties when there are ambiguities and uncertainties	Ensuring that key concepts and preliminary questions are clearly and fully answered	Raising questions to make sure that all nuances, haziness, and conceptual confusions are understood or clarified
Moral Commitments	Determining which moral principles or virtues (e.g., fairness, equity, freedom, caring) are linked to the situation	Ensuring that different people express their exact ethical concerns, (e.g., harassment, dishonesty, offensiveness)	Discussing details to encourage involved parties to explicitly state the causes of their anger, hurt, or moral indignation
Data Collection	Gathering cultural and empirical information, facts, and data that have a bearing on the issue	Ensuring that the facts and interpretations of them are as stated and have a relationship to the problem	Pursuing all relevant facts and information from as many sources as needed
Theoretical Scan	Scanning ethical theories and their subtypes for the insight they offer	Ensuring that relevant ethical considerations are used in reflection and practice	Thinking broadly about the problem from diverse legal, policy, and theoretical perspectives
Solution Construction	Working with others to construct the best possible hypothetical solutions in the multicultural context	Ensuring that the best solutions are discussed with relevant people	Seeing whether the collective wisdom leads to more than one practical solution to the challenge
Consequences Considered	Imagining with others what the probable consequences of proposed solutions may be	Ensuring that the consequences of possible solutions on all parties are considered	Examining both the potential positive and negative outcomes of perceived solutions

(Continued)

Table 1.1   (Continued)

Reflections	Responsibilities	Interests	Considerations
Solution Reconsideration	Reconsidering previously proposed solutions in the light of probable outcomes and new information	Ensuring that the forthcoming plan of action is based on all relevant ethical considerations	Rethinking plans in view of different perspectives, diverse peoples, and probable outcomes
Action Plan	Deciding on a plan of action that will be guided by the ethical decision	Ensuring that a decision is acted on in an ethical and holistic manner with clear communication of the decision to all parties	Making certain that the plan is understood as part of a broader moral architecture or school culture
Evaluation Plan	Determining what went well in the process and outcome and what was learned for future similar situations	Ensuring that ethical decision making is seen as a community learning process that informs better decision making in the future	Contributing to the ongoing thinking of staff about building a classroom, school, or district environment that is ethically informed and growing

Users of the model should avoid several temptations. We have already noted the temptation to use the model as a lockstep process. The model is intended only as a checklist of all that should be considered before arriving at some decision. Another temptation to be avoided is to use the model as a substitute for psychological or sociological theories of personal or group dynamics, stressful interactions, or group information processing. This temptation would lead to an inexcusable omission of much relevant theory and empirical data needed to construct a comprehensive picture of relevant context. The model is about the moral context in which all other adult social dynamics take place. Although that sounds quite grand (and it is), it is deliberately limited to the morally relevant elements needing deliberative attention. With these considerations in mind, the model in Table 1.1 should prove useful to readers throughout this book.

DISCUSSION QUESTIONS

1. What is the difference between a good person and a good school? In what sense, if any, does the word *good* successfully modify nouns such as *person* and *school*? What might be the grounds for counting Shannon Wright, Marva Collins, and Jamie Escalante as paradigmatically good teachers?

2. What makes a person virtuous? Does it matter to you that staff and students see you as exhibiting certain virtues and avoiding certain vices? Explain why such perceptions should or should not matter.

3. What do you think about when you reflect on the sentence, "Educational leadership is moral architecture"? What images come to mind? What questions do you have?

CASE STUDY

Case Study 1.1. A Case of Good Intentions?

Imagine the following scenario. Finances for education have become a problem at the state or provincial level and, more oppressing, in your district. You are the district superintendent. The school board has great confidence in you and is likely to endorse your recommendations for how to cut costs in order to give the school professional staff a raise and increase the number of teachers in order to reduce class size. Specifically, the board has asked you for a plan to downsize entitlements to pay for these additional costs.

Because you value the opinions of your colleagues and think their voices should be heard, you create a committee of long-term school personnel who understand the district and represent all district human resource categories. At the end of deliberations and several surveys, you and your committee present a plan to the school board. Your plan (which saves the district money) goes as follows: Employees will no longer be served by a single comprehensive health plan. Instead, employees will be offered a choice between a costly preferred provider organization (PPO) and several inexpensive health maintenance organizations (HMOs). The PPO has high deductibles and an across-the-board 60/40 split for out-of-network medical services. The HMOs are much less expensive, but access to medical care is limited. In addition, the wait time to see specialists is long. The board adopts your plan. Unexpectedly, organized protests emerge from groups throughout the system. Those with the lowest incomes are the most implacable, accusing you and your "gang of eight" of being self-serving and unfair. What should you do? Explain where and how you will start analyzing the matter and then address it.

Some questions may help you tease out issues in this situation: Are there some key words you need to consider? Will agreement on key words help focus attention on the right-mindedness of your proposal? Moreover, in the face of so much agitation by the lowest-paid employees, just how right-minded is the social justice of your proposal? Was it right to create a committee of only long-term employees (even though every occupational category was represented)? What are your moral obligations at this point? Did potentially dissatisfied school employees have a duty to voice their concerns about the "gang of eight" early in the very open and public process before controversy developed? Did you have a duty to ask for widespread input about the *process* of developing the proposal before the plan was developed? Some employees accuse you of self-interest. Is the nature of intentions ever relevant to figuring out the nature of another's actions?

ACTIVITY

Activity 1.1

List five moral terms or phrases frequently used in educational discourse that often seem to lead to inflammatory disagreements. Go to the *Encyclopedia of Philosophy,* the *Encyclopedia of Ethics,* the *Encyclopedia of Educational Philosophy, Black's Law Dictionary,* and a textbook in education that specifically defines each of the five terms.

Look also in the glossary of this book to see whether it contains the word or phrase. Write down the definitions you find in each of these authoritative sources. (Do not rely on ordinary dictionaries for this activity.) For each of the five sets of definitions, note whether the definitions agree closely with one another. Construe a detailed and explicit definition for each of the terms and describe the extent to which this carefully honed definition reflecting expert usage is captured in the inflammatory disagreements that you first had in mind. How pragmatically useful do you believe it is to insist that whenever possible stakeholders should define or clarify critical moral terms before launching into what could lead to contentious debate?

FURTHER READING

Gordon, L. (2008). *An introduction to African philosophy.* Cambridge, MA: Harvard University Press.

Hare, R. M. (1954). *The language of morals.* New York: Oxford University Press.

Johnson, B. (2008). *Radical hope: Ethics in the face of cultural devastation.* Cambridge, MA: Harvard University Press.

Koble, M., & Garcia-Carpintero, M. (2008). *Relative truth.* New York: Oxford University Press.

Peterson, P., & Seligman, M. (2003). *Character strengths and virtues.* New York: Oxford.

Rest, J. R. (1979). *Development in judging moral issues.* Minneapolis: University of Minnesota Press.

Sternberg, R. J. (2003). *Wisdom, intelligence, and creativity synthesized.* New York: Cambridge University Press.

Thorndike, E. L. (1940). *Human nature and the social order.* New York: Macmillan.

CHAPTER 2

Moral Theory

THE PRAGMATIC DIFFERENCE BETWEEN
SCIENTIFIC AND MORAL THEORY

Aristotle was wise in so very many ways. He is known today as the father of many subjects, including democracy and virtue theory, and Aristotle's skills and propensity for theoretical reasoning may be unparalleled. In any case, what may be the most astonishing thing about Aristotle was his simultaneous penchant for the practical, requiring the execution of great skill in common-sense thinking. Perhaps better than anyone else in history he brought together theoretical excellence and worldly savvy (Smith, 2009). Presumably as a consequence of these intellectual traits, he was able to recognize that all investigations are limited by the nature of the subject matter (Aristotle, 1958). For example, he noticed that moral theory cannot be as exacting as physics. Although Aristotle could know nothing of quantum physics, he wisely recognized that in general, different subject matters afford different degrees of certainty. As Aristotle says, moral truth may be more difficult to attain than, say, truth in physics.

Although certainty may be a bit much to ask for, it is possible to move away from error and accomplish much in the process, according to Aristotle and even modern pragmatists (Dewey, 1929; Putnam, 2002; Quine, 2004; Scheffler, 1974).

To validate theorizing about the foundation of law, codes of ethics and morality generally begin by looking at the basic assumptions and animating motivations of morality itself. According to an ever-increasing number of researchers, there must be an animating moral faculty prompting humans to become the kind of social animal empirical observation shows us to be (de Waal, 2006). If correct, this means that there must be some self-correcting feedback mechanism limiting brutish self-interest (Hellman, 2008). For example, consider the abandonment of brutish self-interest in the now-universal legal prohibitions against slavery. (The last nation to outlaw slavery did so in 1983; Sowell, 1995, 2005.) Slavery may still exist in places, but now it is formally condemned as a wrong, much in the manner of murder or some other universally recognized wrong. Such convergence on universal or nearly universal prohibitions and prescriptions suggests a feedback mechanism, awareness or whatever, beyond enculturation of surface-level rules or attitudes (Dugatkin, 2006; Hauser, 2006). Surface-level rules are localized or cultural phenomena, but that does not mean they are not driven by deeper cross-cultural intuitions about human well-being generally (Rothschaeffer, 2008).

A REALITY CHECK

List three characteristics that you think make a moral theory useful. Explain your reasoning.

A SPECTRUM OF MORAL THEORY

What follows is a survey of some very sophisticated moral theories fashionable today. We have admittedly risked oversimplification in what follows, but we also provide the reader with substantial additional resources to dig into matters as personal and professional needs and interests require. Because moral theorizing is designed to lead to practical advice, we complete each theoretical synopsis with an indication of the sorts of things some major moral theorists might say to present-day school leaders.

Our discussion of moral theories falls under the following headings: "Virtue Theory," "Rationality and Moral Realists," "The Social Contract," "The Many Camps of Universalism," "Intuitionism and Social Sympathy," and "Pragmatism." To be objective and fair we have attempted in each case to note widely circulating criticisms of some of the theories as well.

Virtue Theory

Aristotle

Virtue theory is a popular approach to moral theory (MacIntyre, 1981; Peterson & Seligman, 2004; Taylor, 2005). It began long ago with Aristotle, who believed that human reason is too unreliable for determining rightful action in every case. Instead, Aristotle advised, attention should be focused principally on virtues that equip people for living communal life and developing personal excellencies (e.g., cooperation, tolerance, sympathy).

A PRACTICAL ASSIGNMENT

Which virtues do you think are most necessary for educational leadership? What reasons or observations support your selection of these virtues?

Aristotle constructed a heuristic for identifying right-minded virtues. He said that people should look for the mean between opposing, natural instincts (e.g., the virtue of courage is found between the instinct of fear and the instinct to be reckless). Fearfulness inhibits life's pleasures. Recklessness is likely to shorten life altogether. Where there is no fear, there is no courage. Nor is there courage in the absence of self-conscious risk taking. Courage is a *reasoned* willingness to risk stepping toward a source of fear. It is the mean between two extremes of natural human instinct. Consider what people are most likely to admire about an administrator's moral sensibility. Robotic-like adherence to rules rarely earns the admiration of subordinates. Similarly, reckless endorsement of every cause seldom wins lasting approval by subordinates. Instead, an administrator's reasoned support of a subordinate even in the face of personal risk to self is likely to be favorably remembered by all. Such an administrator seems to exhibit courage, loyalty, and integrity under such circumstances. To act in moderation and exhibit worthy virtues makes the administrator a person subordinates will more willingly support in good times and bad.

Aristotle's Advice for Educators

Teachers:	Develop in students skills of both practical and theoretical reasoning. Especially develop in them an understanding of virtues appropriate for democratic participation and personal excellence.
Principals:	Model appropriate virtues for students and staff. Remember that the mean between opposite instinctual extremes can be a guide to finding appropriate character traits to model.
Superintendents:	Interpret the needs of society and develop students into citizens that can support democracy and the flourishing of fellow citizens.

Linda Zagzebski (1996, 2004), a prominent contemporary virtue theorist, lays out a theory of moral motivation that weaves together character and personality traits along with desires, instincts, reason, and purpose. No one can know what to do in every case, she observes, but someone of virtue—that is, a person of courage, patience, honor, and loyalty, respectful of self and others, disciplined, honest, and compassionate—is more likely to do right by self and others than is someone who is unreflective, is overly confident in a prescribed set of rules, or believes she is simply free to do as she pleases. In the absence of certainty, morally conscientious people are best served by embracing generally honored virtues (Adams, 2002; Zagzebski, 2004).

Zagzebski's Advice for Educators

Teachers:	Show students the difference between their motivations and desires and the consequences of each for establishing appropriate moral commitments.
Principals:	Reassure teachers that student character can be developed despite turbulent **personality traits.** Change is both possible and probable if teachers and

students work together, and it is the teacher's professional duty to help students develop character.

Superintendents: District policy is a community's best predictor of the common good in the future. Ensure that the district is developing people with the right set of virtues, not mere adherence to district rules and regulations.

Summary

Virtue theory may be an especially potent guide for educational administrators (Sergiovanni, 1984; Starratt, 2004). As Aristotle and Zagzebski advise, people are most likely to follow educational leaders who exhibit integrity and are recognized for their embodiment of virtues generally (Smith, 2009). (See Table 2.1.)

Table 2.1   Virtue Theory: Emphases and Questions

Theorists	Emphases	Questions
Aristotle	Personal virtues and not reason alone make for better communal living.	Are we developing in ourselves and students virtues that fall between opposing natural instincts (e.g., between fear and foolhardiness)?
Zagzebski	Character, personality traits, desires, and reason are more important than external rules.	Are we nurturing the development of virtues or settling for mere obedience to school rules and regulations?

Rationality and Moral Realists

Plato

For some, an emphasis on virtue may sound Pollyannaish. Popular books such as *All I Really Need to Know I Learned in Kindergarten* (Fulghum, 2004) and *Chicken Soup for the Soul* (Canfield & Hansen, 2001) give the impression that morality is a simple matter of virtue and reduces to the ambiguous disposition of "being nice" to others. But surely, others argue, there is more to the moral world than merely trying to be nice (Levine, 2008). There must be reliable rules and other dictates as well. There must be lines drawn in the sand at times. Where would we all be today if Martin Luther King Jr. hadn't insisted that the time had come to draw a line in the sand and declare prejudicial policies, practices, and behavior morally unacceptable?

The need to draw definitive lines in the sand is particularly apparent to anyone with onsite management responsibilities in the schools. But the lines to be drawn are not always, clear and local circumstances make knowing the right thing to do difficult. For example, deciding whether a first grader should be expelled for bringing a toy pistol to school may not be a simple matter. The issue cannot be decided simply on grounds of "being nice." A line of demarcation between acceptable and unacceptable behavior must be drawn. But exactly where should that line be drawn in each case? What is the surrounding environment like? How real looking is the toy gun? What appears to be the student's intent? Were other students threatened or in any way made fearful by the presence of the gun? Is the presence of the toy gun likely to prompt student cynicism toward the rules if something isn't done to punish the transgression?

Aristotle's mentor, Plato, understood this administrative lament and recommended that educated and experienced leaders reflect seriously about the truth involved in such matters and then courageously rule accordingly (Boyes-Stones & Brittain, 2008). Plato (1992) believed that true leaders can see clearly into the light of truth and make local rulings that capture the spirit of true moral absolutes.

Plato's thinking may seem very provincial and indefensible. Yet how often does literature from around the world tout the hero who does not compromise principle and stands firmly his or her ground (Gordon, 2008; Lai, 2008)? Consider the lives of Gandhi, Martin Luther King Jr., Bishop Tutu, and the American women suffragists.

In sympathy with Plato, Ortega y Gasset (1931) warns that in the postmodern world we increasingly fail to appreciate the value of expertise and the courage to follow through on well-reasoned convictions. Plato and Ortega y Gasset would be quick to note that ideas of social justice, extending rights to indigenous peoples, peoples of color, adherents of different faiths, women, and children, usually originate with wise and thoughtful leaders and rarely among the masses. Popular consensus usually fails to lead to human betterment, whereas the recommendations of experts often are fruitful.

A HISTORICAL GLIMPSE

Think of an ethical issue regarding school operations that once seemed fuzzy but now seems clear and well grounded. What wisdom derived from others helped you better understand the previously fuzzy issue? Were previous errant ways just a consequence of popular ignorance, as Plato might predict?

Surely, the vision of learned and experienced mentors is too valuable to ignore, as Ortega y Gasset reminds us. Even if moral prescriptions cannot be derived from eternal forms, as Plato supposed, some people nevertheless seem to exhibit an uncommon knack for doing right. It would be foolish to ignore their advice.

Plato's Advice for Educators

Teachers: People act wrongly only out of ignorance. Teach students **discipline** in rigorous thinking, and they won't act wrongly except when confronted with inadequate or incorrect **information.** Show them the wisdom of seeking insight from experienced moral thinkers.

Principals:	Teachers must learn to lead students away from ignorance by asking them the right sequence of questions. Moreover, teachers must know where they intend to lead students with their carefully crafted questions. Teacher workshops should develop such skills. Applied mathematicians, computer scientists, professional philosophers, attorneys, or logicians should be the workshop instructors because of their formal skills and specialized training.
Superintendents:	Like that of the philosopher king, the superintendent's extensive study and practical experience place him in a position to make the best possible decisions for others. His decisions should be based on the well-being of others, not the administrator's own well-being. He should think of himself as a servant, carrying the burden of responsibility for those he leads.

More on Realism

Plato is known as a moral realist (Rice, 1997). He believed there is truth to be gleaned from expert, moral reflection (Denyer, 2008). Halfway around the world in significantly different cultures, Confucius (Al-Ghazali, 1963; Dawson, 2001) and Lao Tzu (Laozi, 2001) similarly aligned themselves with moral realist thinking (Lai, 2008). Like Plato (Denyer, 2008), Confucius and Lao Tzu believed that by serious and rational thinking one can come to see previously obscured truth in moral matters. However, these Chinese thinkers would distance themselves from the abstractness of Plato's moral ruminations. Confucius and Lao Tzu (Chen & Lee, 2008; Lai, 2008) saw moral expertise as grounded in practical day-to-day challenges of right living. Whereas Plato's moral expert was an intellectual giant with insight into grand absolutes, Confucius and Lao Tzu's moral expert was probably intended to be a paradigm of moral living, presumably someone like Calcutta's Mother Teresa.

Critics charge that with moral realism it is not always clear who possesses the wisdom needed to address a case at hand (Haidt, 2003). And all becomes a matter of "your guess is no better than mine." Lao Tzu confronts this challenge in a parable wherein a youth asks a respected sage what should be done if one's sister falls into a raging stream. If nothing is done, she will die. On the other hand, if a male touches her in public, she becomes violated and dishonored. Lao Tzu's response is to have the sage observe simply, "You don't understand the point of morality."

Lao Tzu's point here is that the youth is confusing a social convention *encouraging* respect with an actual moral principle itself (i.e., "respect and treasure the well-being of others"). The youth's alleged confusion is allowing a mere social convention to dominate the point of moral principle itself.

Morality is about the well-being of all. Lao Tzu's admonition to the youth is that social conventions are important to the extent that they advance moral concern for others. But one should never confuse a transient social convention (what we are calling surface-level moral rules) with the point of morality, which in the end is always about right action toward self and others.

Confucius's Advice for Educators

Teachers: Initiate children into proper behavior. Train them in attitudes of honor, respect, and dignity.

Principals: Education should never be given freely. If students are to value their education, they must be required to give something of value in return for what they receive.

Superintendents: The betterment of society depends on proper behavior being instilled in students by expert moral teachers and not by the whimsy and capriciousness of the transitory fashions of society.

Traditions and conventions can blind us to both harmful and healthy moral principles. Morality should free us from provincial thinking at the surface level and take us beyond to more penetrating levels of reflection.

A GROUP DISCUSSION

As a district superintendent in a rural, conservative part of the country, what local traditions do you suppose might distract you from your moral commitment as the area's senior educational leader?

Consider the same problem anew, this time from the perspective of a superintendent in what is often called a very politically correct, urban school. Why do you suppose it is so easy, as Lao Tzu believes, to confuse moral principles with transient local conventions?

Summary

One can take a softer spin on moral realism than that favored by Plato, Socrates, or even Confucius and Lao Tzu (Augustine, 1998; Fischel, 1967; Long, 2002). Moral realism is not restricted to antiquity. Major philosophers today (Adams, 2005; Audi, 2002) continue to develop arguments regarding moral truth. They believe that the moral world is as real as rocks, wetness, and stormy weather. The idea that we can be definitively and profoundly wrong about moral matters is a key factor in defining one's position as a form of moral realism. Table 2.2 is a prompt to thinking as a moral realist.

The Social Contract

Aristotle and Hobbes

It's difficult to get far from Aristotle. In one way or another he seemed to write something about almost everything. Although he is definitely a virtue theorist (Aristotle, 1958), he also

Table 2.2   Rationality and Moral Realists: Emphases and Questions

Theorists	Emphases	Questions
Plato	Study and experience are essential to moral maturation.	Do we study ethics and design experiences to help ourselves and our students grow in their thinking and behaving?
Ortega y Gasset	Expert knowledge should always be valued.	Who are the experts to whom we should turn for advice in matters of morality and application of ethics?
Confucius and Lao Tzu	Moral practice and moral knowledge are one and the same.	How do we integrate moral practice into classrooms and model what we understand?

initiated what later came to be called social contract theory. Aristotle says we are social animals by nature (Smith, 2009). For him and others, social organization is instinctual (Aquinas, 2001; Sigmund, 1987). This instinctual urge makes a social contract inevitable as an expression of public morality. The purpose of public morality is to figure out how best to distribute and shoulder responsibility for a well-run state or, in the case of education, well-run schools.

Hobbes, another social contract theorist, sees things very different from Aristotle. Hobbes (1651/1996) sees people pushed together by self-interest. People selfishly have many overlapping desires, and so they always are in fear that other humans will take from them what they most desire and possess. Hobbes calls this the most natural state of nature, and he laments that it is a horrible situation to be avoided at all costs. The only plausible option is to organize in groups sufficiently strong to protect members from the predatory behavior of others (Martinich, 1999).

> ## A PHILOSOPHICAL QUESTION
>
> Does adolescent behavior seem driven by self-interest or fear? Describe what a Hobbesian social contract would look like in a school community; remember to include all stakeholder groups.

To secure some degree of security, Hobbes proposes that people seek contractual alliances with one another. Each contracting party agrees to give his or her personal power to a central authority. The central authority then enforces rules and regulations. This enforcement of rules and regulations protects a limited range of liberties for participants by imposing order and social structure. Moreover, the order that is imposed creates a force sufficiently strong to repel intrusion from predators outside the social contract

(Zimmerman, 1996). In today's schools, from classroom management to school and district security protocols to arrangements between groups, cliques, and gangs of students, Hobbes's recommendations seem manifest as common-sense **protocols.**

[handwritten note: → social Order]

Hobbes's Advice for Educators

Teachers:	Because fear is the most powerful and disquieting emotion, root it out of the classroom so students can fulfill their other desires.
Principals:	The first order of business in a school is security for students and staff.
Superintendents:	Maintain a balance between the competing interests of the schools and protect the school system from intrusion by outside interests.

Summary

Are things really as simple as Hobbes's insistence on social order would lead us to believe? Something must be said about the notion of moral obligation in Hobbes's contract theory. Moral obligation and not some force of nature is central to the theory. Moreover, whatever evolutionary function may have led to the human sense of moral obligation, it is clear that obligation in large part represents a reciprocal exchange of implicit promises.

Promises are probably the greatest of all human inventions. It is the exchange of promises that makes cooperation between large groups of people across time and place possible. Promises make possible the cooperation necessary for commerce, extended families, banking, large-scale science, and so on. Participants in the social contract implicitly promise one another to cooperate. Promising *obligates* people to one another (Austin, 1962). So in addition to fear and self-interest, the moral force of promising makes possible the very institution of social contract, Hobbesian or Aristotelian.

A REFLECTIVE BREAK

Explain how an implicit exchange of promises is necessary between students and staff (and within the community more generally) to create and sustain social order. How would an Aristotelian approach to a school or district-based social contract differ from a Hobbesian approach?

Promising may have developed hand in hand with the acquisition and unexplained richness of human language generally. But however promising and obligation came about, it is clear that they constitute moral facts and are as much a part of human reality as self-interest and aversion to fear.

District or school cohesiveness, whether explicit in written contract and policy or sustained by implied convention, depends in the last analysis on promising and the moral fact of obligation. Promising is so central to human social fabric that contract law itself is generally summed up as the law of promise keeping (Black, 1951). See Table 2.3 for highlights of social contract thinking.

Table 2.3   Social Contract: Emphases and Questions

Theorists	Emphases	Questions
Aristotle	Ethical responsibility is best shared between community members.	How should we distribute moral responsibility through the district, school, and greater community? What promises should we make to one another?
Hobbes	Organizational power is meant to serve as a safe harbor from fear and the self-interest of others.	How should power be used to make a school or district a safe harbor? What promises must we make to one another?

The Many Camps of Universalism

The term *universalism* has a common technical meaning in philosophy. It is generally associated with philosopher Immanuel Kant's criteria for legitimating surface-level moral rules as unbiased and equally applicable to all. However, we will use the term *universalism* more generally and colloquially to mean merely any moral system that musters a criterion for determining in advance how everyone ought or, is inherently compelled, to use criteria for assessing surface-level moral prescriptions. Thus in this more colloquial terminology, utilitarianism—a moral theory usually set against Kantian and neo-Kantianism along with game theory and developmental psychology, cognitive psychology, and neuropsychology— will be included here as one taxonomic entry. This taxonomic convenience should secure further utility for practitioners who have limited time for choosing only one or two moral theories for more advanced study beyond this book.

The most prominent universalist theorist is Immanuel Kant. Kant began looking for the only good that is good in itself. The one good thing that he determined is good in itself is a good will, that is, a will that stands in awe of moral law itself. Moral law is open to understanding by everyone able and willing to reason while keeping in mind that there is nothing more valuable in the moral world than the well-being of other autonomous agents. Kant (1998) named the governing principle that resulted from his extended reflection the *categorical imperative* (CI). The CI was said to determine the admissibility of all lower-order moral principles. To be admissible under the CI, a surface-level moral rule must be universally applicable and never favor or disfavor any individual or group. In practice this means that no person should ever treat another person as a mere means to his or her own ends.

A PHILOSOPHICAL QUESTION

How, if at all, are ethical statements embedded in national constitutions and charters and professional codes useful to the administrator?

The CI is commensurable with the moral intuition that in spirit led to the first five amendments to the U.S. Constitution (and later to the 13th, 14th, 15th, and 19th amendments and later civil rights legislation). These amendments are legal and hence moral constraints on what the majority (any other citizen or any leader) may do to another individual or group. Kantian educators such as Paulo Freire (2000) believe that true professionals enlightened by the universalism of the CI may be called on courageously to stand against popular and powerful forces in order to protect an individual from disenfranchisement or some other mistreatment, even in an ostensibly democratic environment.

Kant's Advice for Educators

Teachers:	Develop students' personal **autonomy** by nurturing excellence in reasoning.
Principals:	Take corrective action of student misbehavior in light of student capacity for autonomy. Withdrawing privileges may be necessary for 5-year-olds, whereas sound explanation may be sufficient for 16-year-olds.
Superintendents:	Moral rules must be universally applied throughout the district in order to ensure fairness for all.

Not All Universalists Are Kantian

Jeremy Bentham is the founder of utilitarianism, but its best-known advocate and the one whose texts we rely on here is John Stuart Mill (2007). Utilitarians, such as Mill and Bentham, think that the purpose of moral activity is to maximize pleasure (because that is something we all want) and to minimize displeasure (again, something we all want). For utilitarians, what we want is the only empirically based guide to what is good in itself. And what is good for one (pleasure vs. displeasure) is equally and universally good for all. Utilitarians argue that sometimes there is no choice but to treat one or even a few as a means to the vastly greater good available to others when an inevitable imbalance of interests becomes apparent.

Utilitarians devised a hedonic calculus as an exacting tool for avoiding apparent conflicts of duty: Evaluate how to maximize pleasure while minimizing displeasure and then act accordingly. Utilitarians acknowledge that sometimes a few must suffer for the benefit of the many, but such trade-offs are just in the nature of the way the world is. Utilitarians also acknowledge that the many may suffer *minor* inconvenience if there is *overwhelming* benefit to a few. The goal is always and everywhere the same: Maximize pleasure and minimize displeasure.

The inclusion of some students in the least restrictive environment may pose a minor distraction, inconvenience, or even discomfort to most other students; nonetheless, if the benefits of inclusion for the few are vastly significant, then pleasure is maximized and displeasure minimized, and so this is sensible utilitarian practice. But, as critics charge, there is no precise way of weighting pleasure and displeasure, and so utilitarian thinking is bound to be forever a hit-or-miss thing.

Imagine **punishment** administered to a whole class for the misdeeds of one student. On a grander scale, imagine a district-wide discontinuation of a football season because three star players from one school are arrested for severely beating a star player from the team of another school the night before the game. Order in each case is secured by harsh punishment of guilty and innocent alike. Presumably happiness is maximized in both communities generally, but only at the cost of making the innocent suffer along with the guilty. Such possible **consequences** reveal a deeply counterintuitive flaw in utilitarian thinking. Utilitarians think punishment and **penalties** are largely indistinguishable from one another and are justified simply on grounds of their ability to extinguish or deter behavior leading to disproportionate displeasure. By contrast, Kantians think punishment should be retributive and limited only to wrongdoers. Utilitarians retort that the only good of punishment is how it might lead to more happiness in the future. (Of course, it is legitimate to ask—even on utilitarian grounds—what is the long-term cost in accrued happiness of role modeling behavior that punishes the innocent for some short-term gain in pleasure.) It is no wonder that Kantian and utilitarian instincts continue to be expressed frequently in faculty and school board meetings around the world today. Each has some appeal, and the truth of such principles and instincts is not easily settled.

Mill's Advice for Educators

Teachers:	Get to know the range of each child's abilities. Push students toward personal excellence and fulfillment. In the end, they will thank you for it.
Principals:	Be sure the school is kept open as a marketplace of novel but well-supported ideas. The net increase of pleasure depends significantly on access to ideas promising of a better future.
Superintendents:	Insist that all policies, acts, rules, and regulations create the greatest amount of pleasure while reducing displeasure.

A Striking Angle on Universalism

A variety of philosophers have attempted to pull together both utilitarianism and Kant's **principle of universality** (CI). The effort is usually called rule utilitarianism (Hare, 2000). Rule utilitarianism seeks the optimization of pleasure and the minimization of displeasure but—and here is the nexus of their recommended improvement—*never* by treating any person as a mere means to the ends of others. Kenneth Strike (1991, 1999) adds something more to the rule utilitarian framework. He recognizes that even with an improved and exacting hedonic calculus and the unwavering Kantian prohibition against using others as means, there are still bound to be times when conflicts of duties arise. Such conflicts are most evident when unimpeachable opposing arguments lead to conclusions that seem deeply counterintuitive (e.g., the cheerleading squad should consist of only the best candidates, or the cheerleading squad should focus first and foremost on representing school diversity). Something more must be brought to bear on the problem-solving process in such situations. In their moral theory *reflective equilibrium,* Strike and Jonas Soltis (2004) recommend that every agent should take notice of his or her own personal intuitions in such matters.

CLARIFYING THE CONCEPT

Illustrate how principals or teachers might use each other or even students as mere means. How might students use each other as means? Are teacher and administrator bonuses for student success on state-mandated standardized tests likely to encourage or discourage treating students as means rather than ends? Explain your thinking.

must have some degree of relativism

Strike doesn't pretend intuition should rule the day. Instead, what Strike and Soltis recommend is that intuitions are signals that alert the agent to the fact that at some level all may not be right. In such situations, administrators, as moral agents, should think through once again anything that seems deeply counterintuitive (Strike, 2006; Strike & Soltis, 2004). Minds may not change, but surely such intuition is an appropriate alarm signaling the need for further review and reflection.

Strike's Advice for Educators

Teachers: Develop student reasoning but don't dismiss their intuitions about matters of morality.

Principals: Always try to make the best of a difficult situation but never victimize one person in order to secure the well-being of others.

Superintendents: Keep in mind that laws and codes of ethics and school policies are surface-level contrivances. They effectively guide administrator thinking in most cases, but commitment to net success, freedom from victimization, and respect for intuition must always be a part of the administrator's conceptual apparatus.

Universalist Psychology: A Sense of Justice

Another attempted synthesis of the Kantian and utilitarian ethic was hinted at by psychologists Jean Piaget (1995) and later Lawrence Kohlberg (1981; Clark, Higgens, & Kohlberg, 1991). Each attempted to bring empirical data to bear on adoption of a neo-Kantian ethic. Both psychologists claimed to see evidence that as people got better at moral decision making they moved toward a universalist position, moving through utilitarianism and settling finally on a more neo-Kantian outlook on morality. Kohlberg himself was especially fond of identifying the final stage of moral fulfillment with the moral philosophy of John Rawls, perhaps the most famous of all neo-Kantians.

John Rawls (2001) brought together social contract theory with rule utilitarianism to construct a foundation for moral theory that was responsive to irreducible psychological conditions of human nature. He even portrayed his own theory as beholden at times to a universalist reading of Karl Marx (Rawls & Hermann, 2002).

QUESTIONING
THE AUTHORS

?

If there are universal tendencies toward self-interest and altruism, how can administrators, teachers, and students know when to support which tendency when they conflict?

Rawls recognized that people exhibit tendencies toward both self-interest and altruism. He described the altruistic tendency in an essay he wrote titled "The Sense of Justice." For Rawls (1969) a sense of justice is a capacity humans have for recognizing that ventures ought not to be undertaken that assign anyone a *disadvantage* (as opposed to a mere difference) before the commencement of some practice or distribution of goods. In addition to a universally distributed sense of justice, Rawls saw social contract theory as integral to moral theory as well. Rawls sees the exchange of reciprocal promises taken from behind a veil of ignorance, preventing any contracting party from anticipating personal benefit as crucial when creating social contracts animating moral communities (Skyrms, 2004). Moral communities such as schools reflect local conventions (surface-level moral rules) but no more than they reflect awareness of social justice universally and an implicit contract on the part of each to protect every community member from avoidable harm.

Rawls's Advice for Educators

Teachers: Because students seldom have an opportunity to assent to the community arrangements that surround them, teachers are under a special duty to act on their behalf to secure each student's greatest welfare.

Principals: No good can be so good that the minimal welfare of any staff or student can be ignored, even temporarily.

Superintendents: When making policy or advising a board on policy, imagine that all participants begin behind a veil of ignorance. That is, no one should know what role they will actually have when the policy or rule is implemented. Consequently, each should want a situation that meets the minimal welfare of even the so-called lowliest while accommodating divergence in talent, merit, and reward distributed by principle beyond that minimum.

Universal Gaming

The Rawlsian synthesis is probably the most popularly known neo-Kantian position today. Even so, there continue to be other ventures into what we are calling universalism. Most notably, these ventures exploit mathematical modeling and game theory to make moral thinking more exacting. For example, mathematical psychologists (Barash, 2003; Rapaport, 1991) and logicians (Skyrms, 2004), economists (Axelrod, 1997; Frank, 1988), and mathematical biologists

(Nowack, 2006) are but a few of the more famous theorists working in this domain. It is clearly informative to see how a simple universal rule such as "cooperate unless others refuse to do so," as exhibited in Rapaport's Tit for Tat computer program, can exhibit so precisely the survival cost of failing to act cooperatively with others. In Tit for Tat, if a competitor competes rather than cooperates, Tit for Tat retaliates the next time around. The competitor quickly finds his winning edge disappearing in such circumstances as both parties' scores (there is a stipulated scoring system) spirals downward. In the round after the retaliation, Tit for Tat returns to a cooperative strategy and continues in that strategy unless the other side violates the implicit offer to cooperate. Tit for Tat continues in this fashion until the other side learns it is better to cooperate rather than suffer the consequences of retaliation. Tit for Tat shows that in encounters where there is no limit to the number of rounds of play, it is generally better to cooperate with others than to compete with them. (In the case of a limited number of rounds, self-interest may entice one or both players to violate previous accommodations and make one last big score when the possibility of retaliation no longer exists.) The value of Tit for Tat and other game modeling is that it shows cooperation is generally a better life strategy than competition. As every educator knows, and as Rapaport (1991) acknowledges, on the last day of school or the last day or so before graduation all bets are off as some students realize that retaliation costs are at a minimum, and so they may act in self-interest to score big one last time. In short, when the rounds of play are specified, self-interest may trump cooperation during the last round of play. At all other times game theory makes cooperation appear a more attractive strategy for survival, and moral appraisals are distributed predictably in that light.

QUESTIONING THE AUTHORS

?

Are there occasions at school when competition might be more advisable than cooperation? What reasons do you have for your selections?

Competition can't be inherently bad... but especially w/ children, there is a need to teach how to ~~cope~~ handle the outcome

---

Rapaport and Axelrod's Advice for Educators

Teachers, principals, and superintendents:	Promote the idea that it is nearly always to everyone's advantage to cooperate with others and never to sabotage their efforts toward self-improvement. This is especially true among stakeholders in schools, where continued contact between parties seems inevitable.

but what if others forgo self-improvement for the sake of winning?

The Biological Grounds of Universalism

The challenge to create a natural and causal account of moral universalism has been undertaken in recent years by economists, anthropologists, psychologists, applied mathematicians, and, as always, philosophers (Ridley, 2003). These researchers try to account for human moral experience by looking more generally at the evolution of humans as social animals bonded by a rich linguistic repertoire (Dugatkin, 1999; Joyce, 2006; Sober & Wilson, 1998). By wading through streams of empirical research, they identify universal distributions of different forms of cooperation and, most importantly, altruism. Where game theorists begin with the fact of cooperation in their modeling efforts, these theorists begin with kinship affiliations as ground zero for moral theorizing, reflecting an underlying assumption of evolution as grounds for moral theorizing.

Clearly kinship governs relations between lower-order animals that lack the resources to plan cooperative efforts as humans do. Interestingly, cooperation and even altruism have been demonstrated with enormous precision to be predictive of behavior in a wide variety of species according to the well-known **Hamilton equation** (Hamilton, 1964, 1975)—from bacteria (Skyrms, 2004) through ants and bees to guppies, wolves, deer, and humans (Dugatkin, 1999; Wilson, 2002) just to name a few. However, as creatures evolve and become more complex, kinship relations become less predictive of moral phenomena such as altruism and some forms of cooperation. For instance, humans often *act* altruistically on behalf of other humans and even members of other species in the absence of any evident kinship bonds (Schmidtz, 1996).

No educator should ever forget the name of Shannon Wright from Jonesboro, Arkansas. Despite having children of her own to care for, she kept rushing into the line of rifle fire to save the lives of children unrelated to her. This same sort of educator altruism was observed at Columbine High School and often even in the ordinary day-to-day decisions of educators in schools throughout the world. Humans act contrary to self-interest on behalf of others, even those unrelated to them.

A GROUP DISCUSSION

How do linguistic tools and the capacity for self-reflection increase the administrator's ability to build a moral architecture? How should these tools be developed for use by the entire school community?

Biological universalism is increasingly detecting complex social tools humans use to ensure the survival of succeeding generations. These tools include forward-looking cooperative planning and binding formal and informal agreements ensuring the cooperation of future generations (Windekind & Milinski, 2000). The source of many of these tools is a function of the evolved richness and texture of human language extending human capacity for self-reflection, negotiated arrangements, and organizational proficiency (Dugatkin, 2006).

Many of these universalists describe their approach as evolutionary psychology (Tooby & Cosmides, 1998; Turiel, 2005) to underscore that origin as much as function is needed to understand human moral and social life. They claim that natural selection eliminates infirm species, not just infirm individuals. So what is good for the species (in the case of humans, a rich linguistic repertoire and resulting moral capacities) is what gets transmitted across a succession of generations, sustaining species' competitive fitness. Natural selection in addition to current circumstances accounts for human morality and social integration.

Sober, Wilson, and Dugatkin's Advice for Educators

Teachers: Discourage students from thinking exclusively in terms of self-interest when considering consequences of their actions. Do not encourage students to think that every social situation can be fully analyzed from the perspective of each participant thinking, "What's in it for me?"

Principals: Implement various forms of cooperation in the broadest possible realm of applicable situations. Make sure faculty explain to students the evolutionary value of altruism to organizations, communities, and the species as a whole. In short, make more apparent the nature of democratic responsibility and the attendant rewards for all.

Superintendents: Contrary to Thomas Huxley's evolutionary dictum—that "nature is red in tooth and claw"—individual species often thrive through cooperation. Slogans such as "might makes right" do not appear to represent much current understanding of social organization. An open door, a good heart, and commitment to democratic processes exhibit how schools and school leadership can best model how humans were naturally meant to organize with one another.

Summary

The experienced educational administrator should see that nurturing cooperation and altruism is a natural tendency that can be harnessed for organizational and instructional success. Organizations fostering cooperative rather than competitive associations tend to be favored by selective forces. Admittedly, a self-interested scoundrel may flourish at times in a community of other-regarding individuals. However, if self-interest comes to dominate a social species, its fitness landscape will change. Selective forces are always present. Widespread and manifest self-interest is counterproductive to the survival of inherently social species. From Rawls to Sober, universalists are likely to echo Abraham Lincoln's warning to all: "Together we stand, divided we fall." Table 2.4 shows how universalist thinking might apply in the schools.

Intuitionism and Social Sympathy

Intuitionists and social sympathy advocates are critical of universalists. For instance, G. E. Moore (1903/1993, 1936) warns against committing what he calls the naturalistic fallacy, and David Hume cautions against is–ought violations. The naturalistic fallacy occurs when thinkers conclude that our belief habits confirm the right-mindedness of how we ought to think about morality. That is, if we habitually consider the well-being of our own children before we think of others, then we ought to think of our own children before considering others. This may be true, but Moore cautions, "How do we *know* it is true?" Similarly, Hume notes that how the world is in fact can never tell us how it ought to be.

Table 2.4   Universalism: Emphasis and Questions

Theorists	Emphases	Questions
Kant	Legitimate moral rules are those that everyone would be willing for herself and others to live by.	Are we willing for everyone to live by the rules we are creating?
Mill	Actions are right or wrong in proportion to the degree of happiness or unhappiness they produce.	Is our school culture designed to nurture the greatest degree of proportional happiness for all stakeholders?
Rawls	A sense of fairness enables people to be interested in the well-being of others.	Do we truly listen and empathize with others when reflecting on the social justice of a certain policy, rule, or practice?
Rapaport and Axelrod	Cooperation rather than competition is generally in the best interest of everyone.	Does our school's moral architecture feature the value of cooperation?
Sober, Wilson, and Dugatkin	Cooperation and altruism appear to be species-wide tendencies promoting evolutionary fitness.	In what ways can schools nurture altruism and cooperation? In what ways can the moral architecture of schools and districts benefit the fitness landscape of the surrounding communities?

A REFLECTIVE BREAK

If people have a sixth sense (as Moore believes) that informs them that it is morally wrong to handcuff a student to a desk or bicycle rack, how are we to understand the behavior of a teacher or principal who does such an act? Does such behavior refute the idea of a sixth sense? Why or why not?

Moore proposes that humans have a sixth sense enabling them simply to see rightness and wrongness in proposed rules, policies, and acts. Some things such as moral goodness and evil are just too obvious to need further account, according to Moore.

Moore's Advice to Educators

Teachers: Some moral rights and wrongs can simply be shown to students as examples of right and wrong, without further explanation, because their character is self-evident.

Principals: Psychology, economics, biology, and philosophy have little to offer when it comes to engaging the moral world appropriately. Explain to teachers that they

	can best develop students' moral sense by calibrating their observations with the observations of mature observers such as the teacher.
Superintendents:	Your leadership position is so far away from where the action is that you may be most vulnerable to committing the naturalistic fallacy. This realization should underscore your recognition of the need for democratic management of the school by those who hold professional status.

Providential Intuition

Søren Kierkegaard (Mullen, 1981) is an intuitionist with both a religious and an **existentialist** bent. He faults foundational moral theories that do not recognize the hand of Providence. For Kierkegaard (2000) the divine will alone is the ultimate source of all morality. For Kierkegaard moral diversity exists because God may speak to each person differently. The Native American Black Elk makes a very similar point, as reported in *Black Elk Speaks* (Nighardt, 1961). For such spiritually derived moral theories, moral rightness is something of a secret existing in the soul of one in communion with the divine.

Kierkegaard's Advice for Educators

Teachers, principals, and superintendents:	In general, behave according to the rules, laws, and traditions of your community, but always be alert to a higher calling requiring you to risk safety, convenience, and credibility to do what's right from the very highest perspective.

No Principle Can Replace the Need for Social Sympathy

The father of a social sympathy approach is David Hume (1748/1966, 1739/2000). In addition to criticizing universalists for violating the **is–ought gap** (i.e., for assuming that how the world is can be a reliable indicator of how the world ought to be) Hume and Yale law professor Stephen Carter (1997) believe humans are drawn to sympathize with the fortunes and misfortunes of others. So we simply sense that our actions, rules, and policies are right when they lead to increasing concern for the well-being of others.

Hume's Advice for Educators

Teachers:	Students are inspired by exemplars. Present them with clear examples of noble action likely to inspire their sense of social sympathy.
Principals:	Explain to faculty the importance of permeating all that goes on in a school with a shared sense of compassion and delight in the well-being of others.
Superintendents:	Don't let the ease of policy administration lead you to overlook legitimate grounds for sympathizing with others.

A Sense of Bondedness

Like Hume, feminist educators and moral theorists (Benhabib, 2004; Foot, 2002; Jagger, 2006; Nussbaum, 2006) are sympathy theorists. They predicate the nature of human moral life on a shared proclivity toward bondedness. Nel Noddings (1992) describes this sympathetic bondedness as an ethic of caring. Sympathetic bond sustains moral alertness among people. It is not a principle of any kind but rather an emerging feeling to watch out for others, perhaps, as Carol Gilligan (1982) would add, as a consequence of evolving relationships.

A REALITY CHECK

Proponents of an ethic of care sometimes encourage educators to ask particular kinds of questions, such as how can schools put an end to intimidation among students, faculty, and staff? How do we make boys less rule governed in their moral thinking and more open to the value of association that seems to come so much more naturally to girls? Can gender differences create an insurmountable divide between colleagues? How should an administrator circumvent such a potential divide?

A paradigm in feminist thinking might be found in the life of someone such as Mother Teresa, a person driven by a sense of social sympathy who lived by an ethic of caring. Certainly not all feminists would agree. Other feminist writers as diverse as Catharine MacKinnon (2006) and Christina Hoff Sommers (1994) fear that such an approach would open proponents to easy victimization. Nonetheless, nearly all feminists accommodate in some way Noddings's ruminations on caring as a directing sense of social sympathy.

Noddings's Advice for Educators

Teachers: Morality is about showing care for others. Some children may have a bit more trouble learning this than others, and so special attention should be given to help them come to terms with this idea.

Principals: Most faculty do not need to labor under the explicit moral direction of administrators. Create opportunities for bonding between staff and students, and there will be little risk of drifting far from the community's moral compass.

Superintendents: Elaborate policies and regulations may blur the focus on a common vision that should be shared naturally by all. Shared sense of community, not rules and regulations, is key to establishing an appropriate moral foundation in the schools.

Table 2.5   Social Sympathy and Intuitionism: Emphases and Questions

Theorists	Emphases	Questions
Moore	Moral intuition is a sixth sense.	Do some administrators, teachers, and students intuit the rightness and wrongness of certain policies better than others?
Hume	The natural impulse to help others indicates what is right.	Does our school culture stymie or cultivate the impulse to relieve the suffering of others?
Kierkegaard	Community ideals are generally right, but God sometimes speaks to the individual about what is right and wrong.	Should genuinely held religious beliefs ever trump school or district policy?
Noddings	Teaching and role modeling can advance human bonding.	How does a school's moral architecture facilitate human bonding?

Summary

Moral theories based on intuition or social sympathy begin with poignant criticism aimed at universalists, and they conclude by drawing attention to the morally intuitive. Moral development, whether in an individual or organization, hangs not so much on surface-level rules or policies and not even deep principles and **virtues** but rather on a developing sense of ever-broadening horizons of relatedness. Think further about Moore, Hume, Kierkegaard, and Noddings and applications of their thoughts for the practice of school leadership. (See Table 2.5 for further prompts.)

Pragmatism

Although pragmatism prides itself in being about the here and now, this may be what makes it a widely misunderstood moral theory. Everyone has heard the exhortation, "We must be pragmatic about this or that immediate challenge." The expression is often used by laypersons—not philosophers—who want to emphasize the importance of so-called common sense. However, the expression is also often used by a **boss,** perhaps to excuse cold-hearted or ruthless behavior. The declaration comes perilously close to Machiavelli's "The ends justify the means."

Pragmatism is not a simple-minded invitation to settle every matter through trade-offs or cost–benefit analysis. Although pragmatists insist that the good is established by reference to a problem set in the here and now, they do not discount the value of moral reflection, nor do they endorse a cavalier or simplistic moral relativism. In fact, pragmatism began as a search for truth (Peirce, 1992).

C. S. Peirce marveled at a human inferential ability that seemed uncannily apt at moving away from error and toward truth. He called this inferential ability *abduction.*

Presumably, this ability is as apt in moral deliberation as it is in other disciplines. Neither Peirce, John Dewey (1938), nor any other pragmatist then or now thought truth was knowingly within reach. On the other hand, all recognize progress in moving away from error. Dewey (1938) went so far as to conclude that some statements are so well supported that they can be treated as if they are true. Dewey certainly acknowledged human fallibility, yet he added that moral principles can be prima facie true and derived not from logical reasoning but from an expanding conversation with the peoples of the world.

Dewey's Advice for Educators

Teachers: Develop a democratic classroom so students learn that morality begins with open communication and learning to work with others at each given moment.

Principals: Morality is about individual fulfillment through communal life. Democratic practices should be encouraged as much as possible at every level of school life.

Superintendents: Celebrating differences is one thing. In contrast, separating peoples one from another is quite another. Schools are meant to prepare all people for *sharing* community in a democratic fashion. Consider extolling the virtues of Martin Luther King Jr.'s "I Have a Dream" speech.

Today's Pragmatists

The unifying purpose that pervades moral thinking for all pragmatists is perhaps best captured in Hilary Putnam's choice of the French *fraternité*. For Putnam (2002, 2004) the omnipresent purpose of morality is collegiality and the betterment of all. Putnam's colleague Israel Scheffler (1973, 1974, 1985) similarly notes that pragmatically based moral commitments aim at making the best of individual potential generally and indiscriminately. Explicit in Scheffler (1985) and Putnam is a commitment to **freedom** and universal respect regardless of the context of an immediate problem. Such unwavering commitment hardly settles well with stalwart relativism.

Putnam and Scheffler's Advice for Educators

Teachers: Create tasks for students requiring cooperative action, but do not specify the direction on how to create such cooperation. Cooperative tactics are something they must discover for themselves in the process of creating cooperation.

Principals: Empower teachers to be experimental, creating as many democratic arrangements as possible.

Superintendents: Avoid "zero tolerance" policies and other schemes that thwart the effort to think through moral challenges arising at the moment.

Table 2.6   The Principle of Minimizing Substantive Moral Error: Planning for Actions That Are Least Likely to Offend People

Key Ideas	Assumptions	Questions
Reactions to moral decisions	Everyone faces moral dilemmas.	What decisions are least likely to prompt deep-set counterintuitive negative reactions? How and when should intuitions about right and wrong be examined?
Interest in moral accuracy	Moral appropriateness matters in widely diverse populations.	How can school leaders learn about the moral interests and concerns of stakeholders? What kind of professional and parent consultation expedite the sharing of competing moral concerns among all stakeholders?
Common moral interests	Diverse people often have common moral beliefs because of their ethical utility.	Some moral differences are semantic in nature. Others are embedded in the prescriptive traditions of diverse populations. How can these differences be resolved fairly? (We do not advise using a formal system here, such as Hare, Borda, Condercet, or plurality voting. This is intended to be a conceptual ideal only.)
Moral utility	Utility in a moral sense means we need to focus on applications that disadvantage no one.	Differential treatment may have moral utility as long as it leads to no a priori disadvantage to another. What utility is there to ensuring consideration of stakeholder inclusion at every level?
Human error	People are aware that they are prone to make mistakes at times.	How important is it that some intuitions and assumptions have been wrong and others have been right?
Minimizing moral error	Moral differences exist in schools and districts, but their potentially divisive effects can be accommodated if not eliminated through this pragmatic principle.	How can school administrators and staff work together with others to identify moral intuitions and beliefs that are least likely to offend if acted on? How does this approach help protect the sincere moral commitments of those who disagree with the majority?

A Pragmatic Assessment of Moral Theory

Implicit in the very act of recognizing community is acknowledgment of some moral architecture. Communal development is in part a process of gathering support for an evolving moral architecture and, ideally, a commitment to further enriching that

Table 2.7 Pragmatism: Emphases and Questions

Theorists	Emphases	Questions
Dewey	Democratic school cultures are critical means for teaching and learning democratic values.	How much attention should we give to nurturing the democratic values of equal respect, freedom of inquiry, and fair treatment of everyone?
Putnam and Scheffler	Maximization of human potential and human moral intuition is crucial.	Do we develop equitably the potential of all students? What grounds do you have for your beliefs?

architecture. This architectural challenge rests on five presumably uncontentious assumptions (Wagner, 1982): People confront dilemmas of unfolding consequence for self and others, most people naturally care about moral rightness, research shows evidence of moral convergence, moral utility is reflected in such convergence, and although convergence is evident, the possibility of moral error is ever present. These assumptions, represented in Table 2.6, ground the effort to move away from moral error and toward moral truth.

This initiative presumes that in practice the best people can and should hope for is a general moral ambiance, an ecology (Goodlad, 2004), that is least likely to offend the diversity of all stakeholders. Clearly this procedure will not guarantee moral right-mindedness. But it does help capture the intuitions most have that no stakeholders should be ignored or minimized as the community struggles to distance itself from the likelihood of moral error.

Summary

Pragmatists claim that human nature exhibits great plasticity and potential, so robust flourishing of every individual should always be the aim of every moral consideration. Admittedly, becoming all we can become and the moral requirements necessary for such individual fulfillment remain somewhat elusive, as the prompts in Table 2.7 suggest (also see Case Studies A.8 and A.9 in Appendix A).

DISCUSSION QUESTIONS

1. The great logician Alfred Tarski (1981) defined truth as a sentence mapping onto the world without error. As an example he wrote, "The sentence 'Snow is white.' is true if and only if snow is white." How do you define truth? How would you define the term *moral truth*?

2. Briefly describe the moral position you think most likely to meet the criterion proposed by the principle of minimizing substantive moral error. What factors led to your selection?

3. In what ways can an administrator be wrong when making moral decisions?
4. If there is no such thing as a moral foundation, in what sense can schools productively contribute to student social and moral development?

CASE STUDY

Case Study 2.1. When Policy, Personnel, and Prudence Collide

Your district has a board-sanctioned policy against weapons. Ms. Igetem teaches family relations. Her husband is a very vocal member of the school board. This is your second year on the job. Ms. Igetem brings to your office a student of color who is a senior and who has recently been awarded an appointment to West Point. This student is wearing his Eagle Scout shirt and a pair of pressed jeans. His name is Ausifer Cannydit, and he is third in his senior class ranking. Ms. Igetem explains she noticed a bulge in Ausifer's pants and had him empty his pockets, and out came his Eagle Scout pocketknife. Ausifer explains he forgot the knife was still in his pocket after last night's scout meeting. You believe him.

The district's zero tolerance policy requires that Ausifer be expelled. His expulsion will cost him his congressional appointment to West Point. Ms. Igetem threatens to tell the school board if you make an exception in this case. What should you do? What moral theory helped you decide?

ACTIVITY

Activity 2.1

Identify five of the most generally accepted moral principles you can imagine. Create a Likert scale and survey a dozen or so people asking them which principle they find the least likely to offend their moral sensibilities. This is a modified Weber Voting Approval strategy (Poundstone, 2008). Use the same five principles and a Likert scale and ask people to indicate which principles they most strongly approve. Write a summary statement indicating whether people tend to agree generally on the principle least likely to offend their moral sensibility more than they are likely to agree on which statement secures their collective approbation. Do your informal findings suggest any further lines of inquiry?

FURTHER READING

Axelrod, R. (1997). *The complexity of cooperation*. Princeton, NJ: Princeton University Press.

Dewey, J. (1938). *Experience and education*. Indianapolis: Kappa Delta Pi.

Lao Tzu. (1979). *The complete works of Lao Tzu* (H. C. Ni, Ed. and Trans.). San Francisco: Seven Stars Communication.

MacIntyre, A. (1998). *A short history of ethics* (2nd ed.). South Bend, IN: University of Notre Dame.

Noddings, N. (1992). *The challenge to care in schools.* New York: Teacher's College.

Scheffler, I., & Howard, V. (1995). *Work, education and leadership.* New York: Peter Lang.

Sober, E., & Sloan Wilson, D. (1998). *Unto others.* Cambridge, MA: Harvard University Press.

Zagzebski, L. (2004). *Divine motivation theory.* Oxford: Oxford University Press.

C H A P T E R   3

Leadership as Moral Architecture

SUSTAINABLE LEADERSHIP

After the theoretical exploration of ethics in the last chapter, you are probably eager to return to discussions centered on practical problems in schools. Still, the serious work of Chapter 2 was necessary. Understanding ethical theory is important in figuring out in full and subtle detail how to treat others right-mindedly and not settle for the expedient, or what a sportscaster might call "a near miss." Therefore, we shouldn't rely on ethical one-liners, slogans, or clichés because they seem to make our job easier. Sound bites cannot create a responsible and mindful understanding of moral consequence. In the educational world, it is imperative that moral matters are thought through from a responsible *and* theoretical foundation. Moral theory is only briefly sketched in the previous chapter. Consequently, you should consider reading some of the references listed that flesh out more thoroughly notions that seem provocative or prompt in you a desire for fuller understanding. However, you should have sufficient basis to consider further the idea of educational leadership as moral architecture or, as Goodlad (2004) might say, moral ecology.

A library computer or Internet search will show that many people have written about leadership in nearly every walk of life. Much of the literature is about leadership techniques, often actions and devices aimed at influencing others to do one's bidding. Tricks and gimmicks may get people elected, hired, or appointed to positions of power in the short run, but what matters more is how to sustain one's leadership credibility over time (Dryfoos, 1996). This is what being a leader is all about ultimately.

Keeping things simple, Dwight Eisenhower made clear what it takes to be a leader. He said bluntly, "A leader is someone others will follow." Eisenhower truly hit the mark here. No jargon, no pontification, no razzle-dazzle, just plain common sense, direct and to the point. A leader is someone others will follow. This idea has much that is built into it. Consequently, much unpacking is needed to really grasp the implicit profoundness of Eisenhower's observation. For example, take the word *follow*. It is one thing to follow a young Teddy Roosevelt up a hill charging into enemy fire, as occurred at the battle of San Juan Hill, and it is quite another to follow the neighborhood schemer in his latest get-rich-quick scheme. In fact, in the latter case, if a person chooses to go along with the schemer she may choose the words "follow along with" rather than "follow" to make clear a guarded willingness to cooperate with the schemer rather than commit to his leadership. In following a leader up a hill in the face of enemy fire or continuing with a medical team into the heart of a deadly epidemic requires both faith in the leader and commitment to the merit of the enterprise. The same distinction between *following along with* and *following* applies equally to the willingness of teachers and parents to align themselves with a school administrator's leadership.

CLARIFYING THE CONCEPT

Can an administrator lead others for long without sharing her vision of some morally responsible end to be achieved? Do people want school administrators who avoid making waves at all costs or do they want leaders who are progressive and courageous? Are teachers likely to follow enthusiastically administrators who always try to fly a school or a district "under the radar"? Can an administrator's ethical commitments as expressed in both word and deed be powerfully motivating to staff and consensually bonding? What characteristics, beyond integrity, are most likely to cause teachers to follow a leader rather than merely "following along"?

Many enterprising people in search of a few dollars are willing to join forces with a schemer in an alleged "slam dunk" venture. Usually, these "followers" are alert to any problem and are quick to bolt in view of any threat or danger. These so-called followers are not really following; rather, they are merely coasting until the going gets tough. And when the going does get tough, as it nearly always does, those merely "following along" will get going—far away from the schemer. The same kind of coasting or following along may occur in a school or district when administrators direct attention toward a goal of dubious schooling value, such as raising test scores to the neglect of all other educational efforts.

For an educational institution to succeed, followers cannot coast; they cannot merely follow along. Rather, they must believe in both the cause and the leader. There must be evident a clear reason for going above and beyond in the quest for institutional success. Followers are willing to risk personal inconvenience when they believe in the cause and believe in the leader. Those merely following along will not take personal risk because they have found neither cause nor leader (Deal & Peterson, 1999). The moral architecture of a school or district determines whether its human capital is built on a foundation of committed followers or a mere ghostly apparition of support by employees just following along.

In traditional management theory much is often made of the importance of leaders creating shared vision in order to create a resilient organization. Certainly shared vision is important, but more important in terms of organizational resiliency is moral architecture. People following along with a scam artist may well have a shared vision to make a bundle of money from selling widgets. But should things go awry, perhaps some legal violation arises, then those following along may disappear, demonstrating that their previously shared vision provided little organizational unity. In contrast, those who follow a leader they trust within a transparent and elevated moral architecture may go quite a distance to hold together in tough times and in good times. Moreover, in a resilient moral architecture, external forces may impose a change in shared vision (such as No Child Left Behind did in many schools), but even in the face of a transiently, fragmented shared vision organizations with a resilient moral architecture and reciprocal trust among leaders and followers may well stay together to weather the storm.

[handwritten margin note: Strong moral architecture can weather a storm]

In certain respects, education is somewhat like a battle against an epidemic: In both, the stakes are high and the enemy is elusive. The enemy in the case of education is the host of insidious elements that compromise student educational growth. The presence of such elements seems ubiquitous and yet never clearly defined to the untutored eye. Consequently, the leader needs to be capable and committed, her vision clear and focused, and followers must be confident in her integrity, competence, courage, and zeal to persist in the face of the most awesome challenges. Clearly, shared vision is important, but moral architecture contains elements that collectively weigh much more heavily in the organization's sustainability over the long run and over stretches of rough terrain.

If a person is serious about being an educational leader, it is crucial that she understand the nature of both education and leadership. She must also understand the surrounding communities that support or constrain district and school development. In this book we focus on the moral nature of leadership, especially its role as an animating force in education development. As will become increasingly clear, a host of virtues are needed for leadership: courage, honesty, compassion, trustfulness and trustworthiness, an evident sense of just and fair play, loyalty, self-discipline, and more (Hoyle, English, & Steffy, 1998). Ironically, the likelihood that a school administrator will exhibit such virtues depends greatly on the use of such virtues in her own previous schooling and educational experience and as role modeled by her own previous mentors. In helping to craft the moral architecture of schools, educational administrators through role modeling, policy, and other discursive directives serve as co-architects of the local community's future and, more generally, as co-architects of the nation's future.

MORALLY PRESCRIPTIVE SHARED VISION IN EDUCATION

[handwritten margin note: get rich quick vs commitment]

As we alluded to earlier, a scheme to get rich quick is not the sort of thing that typically secures unwavering commitment from those who follow along. In contrast, the challenge to do good creates conditions of consensual bonding. These conditions must be met in order to secure a truly shared vision. This point is more subtle than it may first appear. But persevering with a leader pursuing the well-being of children and society is significantly different from trailing a leader who is wholly self-serving and keeping the school and district "under the radar."

In his recent book *A Secular Age,* Charles Taylor (2007) speaks of an animating motive for adopting an ethic (what we are calling a foundational moral theory) across a historical epoch. His concern is that to make sense of such an ethic a common motivation must be identified. In the more narrow case of a historic profession such as education, he is almost certainly right. The motivation, or, as he calls it, the moral source, becomes the defining

what it means to educate

characteristic of the profession itself. This motivation or moral source is a unifying factor enabling leaders to lead and others to follow enthusiastically.

Educators should be people who want to educate. To want to educate is about more than wanting to cause others to behave in predictable fashion or to learn a select body of information. To want to educate is an expressed desire to expand the horizons of others' vision by increasing their knowledge and their capacity and disposition to follow a line of questions establishing how something might be truly known or at least what is meant by specific concepts, terms, algorithms, and heuristics. Educating others is about seeking universal human betterment and not simply about seeking the betterment of one's own place in the world. Education is about the genuine pursuit of truth. It is also about the desire to share with others a lifestyle in which both truth and other truth seekers flourish on equal terms and where social justice is a lived experience and sought on behalf of all.

If faculty and staff settle for less noble reasons for wanting to educate, it might be that they have in mind a disparate vision that focuses on mere social engineering or perhaps personal reward for a certain type of job performance. These less noble reasons for wanting to educate denigrate both practitioner and profession alike. Education is meant to enlighten everyone about the nature of reality and about what makes humans most noble (Drucker, 1967). When and where noble reasons for educating are absent among faculty and staff, the administrator is challenged to reconstruct an institutional architecture that fosters the merits of education for all. This begins with instilling in all faculty and staff the sense that education begins with their shared commitment to the service of others through education. This may be the most difficult challenge of educational leadership. Arguably it is perhaps the noblest challenge, and certainly it is at the heart of professionalism in educational administration.

Better than what?

A Philosophical Question

Do school leaders really need to be as service- and other-oriented as the authors suggest? Isn't it okay to enter the profession with an eye toward personal advancement, higher salaries, greater benefits, and a well-funded retirement plan? Why might or might not such a career plan be praised by teachers, parents, and the community?

Professionalism is about much more than holding a certain degree or union card, passing a licensure examination, or completing an apprenticeship. Being a professional traditionally has been considered far more comprehensive and demanding than mere technical proficiency. Indeed, professionals must be technically proficient, but they must also demonstrate a shared sense of moral obligation to those they serve.

Historically, there have been four professions. The four historic professions ranging across cultures are serving as clerics, doctors, lawyers, and teachers. Technical **training,** group membership, exhibited expertise, social esteem, and all the other sociological traits usually summoned to portray the character of a profession (Rich, 1984) may serve well enough to define a profession in most cases, but beyond these there is something that sets true historic professions apart from all the rest (Kultgen, 1988).

A GROUP DISCUSSION

As an educational leader, you are a member of a service-oriented profession. What does that mean to you? Whom does a superintendent serve? A principal? A teacher? If a professional educator fails to serve, has he or she failed in his or her professional duties? What arguments could be made for the claim that educational leaders fulfill their professional obligations based solely on motivations of self-interest? What arguments might be made for saying there must be more (i.e., administrators must be other-regarding to be truly professional)?

Each of the four historic professions is a service-oriented undertaking. Each aims ostensibly at the overall betterment of human well-being. Psychologically speaking, there are clearly less noble reasons that at times may motivate an individual to become a member of a profession, but we should not confuse such disparate motivations with the summative calling of the respective professions themselves. For example, an individual may become a doctor solely for self-serving reasons. Nonetheless, the purpose of doctoring *as a profession* is to contribute to human betterment through the skillful exercise of the healing arts. Similarly, regardless of an individual's reason for becoming an educator (Coulter, 2006; Gross, 1997, 2000; Koerner, 1963), the profession is about bringing people together in the Great Conversation.

The truly professional school administrator of the future probably will have to be more courageous, creative, and imaginative than at any time past in order to keep her school or district focused on its educational purposes in addition to its schooling and training purposes. These educational purposes include learning distinct cognitive skills, developing attitudes commensurate with shared participation in the Great Conversation, acquiring important and reliable information, and finally developing dispositions accommodating the communal quest for truth. These educational purposes are also relevant to many of the schooling goals of schools and districts in open and democratic societies. Consider now essential ways for addressing each of these four purposes. Figure 3.1 summarizes key concepts in these four domains.

THE FOUR CORNERS OF EDUCATIONAL PURPOSE

Learning

People can learn all sorts of things. Psychologists use nonsense syllables to study certain memorization patterns and capacities in people. Young children learn to make all sorts of peculiar sounds with their bodies. But none of this learning represents a set of skills ordinarily conceived as indispensable to becoming educated. When deciding what skills students should learn, educators since antiquity have had to make value judgments about the skills society ought to value generally. Moreover, at times they have had to distinguish these skills from skills with limited training application (Baron, 2000).

Figure 3.1   Four Corners of Educational Purpose

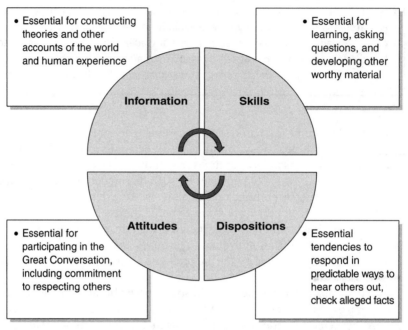

- Essential for constructing theories and other accounts of the world and human experience

Information

- Essential for learning, asking questions, and developing other worthy material

Skills

- Essential for participating in the Great Conversation, including commitment to respecting others

Attitudes

Dispositions

- Essential tendencies to respond in predictable ways to hear others out, check alleged facts

A REFLECTIVE BREAK

In schools run by the Taliban, reportedly teachers socially engineered children solely for a life governed by the Taliban state. How would people drawn to that sort of challenge be different from teachers drawn toward the profession as we describe it in this chapter? In what sense, if any, can administrators and faculty with the first sort of motivations be said to be less professional than educators with motivations more closely aligned with the historic profession as we describe it?

Learning to burp on command is a skill, and it may be great fun for a 9-year-old or a fraternity member. Nonetheless, burping on command is not a skill educators across culture and historical epoch are likely to consider central to educationally relevant learning. In contrast, deductive rigor and semantic precision are readily applauded by most teachers as worthy skills.

Clearly, variance between cultures about the priority of distinguishable skill sets exists. But it is not always clear whether such variance typically represents lack of agreement about education among local educators or a superposition from outside the teaching profession dictating the priority of certain schooling practices to the exclusion of education. This is a matter we leave for educational historians to resolve. For our purposes it is enough to simply acknowledge that in some dictatorial states training and socialization strategies are emphasized to the exclusion of educational skills such as reflectiveness and exacting thought. Fortunately, most readers for whom this book is intended are unlikely to be residents of such authoritarian regimes, and so attention will be focused on other causes of variance.

Variance of purpose and, less so, practice often is due more to influences from outside the local community of professional educators than to that likely to be found between one community of professional educators and another. For example, although the ancient Jews, Ethiopians, Chinese, and Greeks differed in many ways, they shared much in common with what we refer to throughout this book as the Great Conversation (Wagner & Benavente, 2006). Regardless of the strikingly variant social structures of these great ancient civilizations, each generally held in high regard the individual achievement of becoming educated.

Learning skills of distinctly educational import should not be placed in opposition to schooling objectives. Not only are both properly included in school and district planning, but more often than not they can usually be managed as mutually accommodating. For example, through special education courses and vocational education, school administrators create training opportunities for students to successfully enter society's economic world. In addition, such courses socialize students to engage others as friends, neighbors, and colleagues, skills (and information) essential to future communal harmony. Some of the former skills may be distinctly different from more strictly educational skills, but that by itself makes them no less important. In a democratic society, schools have a broader mission than education alone. This means that although the educational function should never be wholly subordinated to other schooling concerns, training and socializing do indeed have legitimate roles in schools and districts. Schools are intended to accommodate a wide range of responsibilities extending well beyond their educational mission. One of the ethical challenges of the educational administrator is to help stakeholder groups understand why schools have such responsibilities and to further explain how schools can responsibly manage all the additional tasks assigned to them.

Developing Attitudes Appropriate for Participation in the Great Conversation

People learn not only educationally appropriate skills but also educationally appropriate attitudes. For instance, at first blush one might suggest that students should learn to respect learning itself, without regard for what is learned. However, people can learn to be mean and disrespectful to others. There is an apt children's tale of a young frog and a snake who play together until their parents find out and teach each of them that snakes and frogs are destined to be enemies. Puppies and kittens raised together often live harmoniously as adults and do not, as is often said, "fight like cats and dogs." Learning an attitude of hostility toward others for no reason other than their differences is not an appropriate educational attitude for children to learn. Rather, a very different learning task, openness toward others, better captures the idea of educationally appropriate attitudes. The point is that of the many attitudes that are learned, some create distance and hostility between people.

learned attitudes

Such learned attitudes are not educationally appropriate and stymie the development of the Great Conversation. Furthermore, such learned attitudes may lead to a host of other vices as the young grow into their adulthood as bigots and enemies of one another.

In contrast to the learned attitudes that become vices, other learned attitudes are most appropriate to education because they represent virtues and character strengths (Peterson & Seligman, 2004). These latter learned attitudes include respect for other people as fellow participants in the Great Conversation and a learned attitude of passion for truth, not just acceptance of settled opinion or some personally favored idea.

Acquiring Important and Reliable Information

There is a bootstrapping process in education. Just as newly acquired skills and attitudes lead to the acquisition of more information, so too through the acquisition of additional information people can develop further educationally appropriate skills and attitudes. This is as true for teachers and administrators as it is for students. For instance, the more stakeholders learn about foundational moral theory, organizational theory, and social interaction, the more they may be able to develop or modify social skills and attitudes for the betterment of all. If such betterment takes place, everyone experiences an ennobling lift in the moral architecture they share. In short, skills and attitudes bootstrap the advance and productive use of additional information. At very nearly the same time, advances in skill and acquisition of productive attitudes bootstrap and thereby often lead to new insights, new information, and knowledge of new avenues for beneficial change. The bootstrapping process is a never-ending cycle of reciprocity in the individual and collective mental life of human beings.

Learning some information is a straightforward task. For example, students must learn the alphabet before they can write. Requiring students to sing the "Alphabet Song" is often effective for instructing them in this task. Direct instruction may be suitable for this learning task, but **indoctrination** protocols can be quite dangerous and usually are best avoided in more advanced curricular and instructional planning (Wagner, 1981).

Most learning tasks tend to be more complex than learning the alphabet. In more advanced learning tasks the optimal bootstrapping balance may not be as self-evident in terms of a controlled and predictable process. Nonetheless, the outcome of successful bootstrapping becomes evident when students demonstrate a critical understanding of the learned complex.

Students may be enticed to learn more information by prompting and developing their skills and their disposition to entertain epistemically searching questions. Serious questioning can create doubt as much as it can reinforce conviction, but in either case, serious questions are an indispensable part of the bootstrapping process.

The resulting cognitive dissonance created within a community entertaining Socratic questioning depends on stakeholders' sharing at least some background knowledge (Vygotsky, 1962) and some commitment to shared truth and understanding. Sorting out the right balance between conveying information and prompting skills commensurate with the disposition to doubt on one hand and encouraging initial commitment to a hypothesis without unduly prejudicing students in its direction on the other can be difficult. Bootstrapping success can never be more than opaquely evident, and even then it appears after the fact, hence the challenge to educators. Bootstrapping is indispensable to educational advance, but it brings an element of uncontrolled progression and uncertainty into the educational process. Certainly it doesn't lend itself well to the periodic intrusion of high-stakes testing aimed at students moving predictably up a series of well-defined steps.

Dispositions

A disposition is a tendency to act in the presence of an appropriate cue. The tendency may or may not be conscionable. In contrast, attitudes, skills, and information are usually relevant to the successful application of a precipitating disposition, but they do not constitute the disposition itself.

Some dispositions seem to be learned, whereas others seem hardwired, an inherent product of nature. For example, a *learned* disposition for an infant is to utter certain sounds when he needs his diaper changed. In contrast, infants are born with the disposition to jerk in the presence of a loud, sharp sound. From the entire range of imaginable dispositions, developmental, cognitive, and neurological scientists are still only beginning to unpack all that might be best described as educational dispositions. For example, from behaviorism to constructivism the credibility of each approach to learning theory depends in large part on the assortment of dispositions scientists believe are arranged under the discriminating categories of inherent and learned disposition, respectively.

Probably the most important *educational* disposition that comes to mind is the proclivity to ask two specific questions when trying to determine the **epistemic** soundness of any truth claim. To wit, the two questions are "How do you know?" and "What do you mean by this or that term?" Both questions can be asked skillfully or unskillfully. Both can be asked with appropriate or inappropriate attitudes. Both can be asked in light of any possible range of background information. In other words, the *disposition* to ask such questions is set apart from the skills, the attitudes, and the background information that constitute elements of the same *action* when that action is fully understood. Nonetheless, the disposition to ask such questions is critical to the overall purpose of education regardless of one's learning theory or any considerations about the other three corners of educational purpose taken in isolation.

There are other educational (as opposed to learning dispositions, more generally speaking) dispositions as well, but the disposition to secure epistemic soundness is surely the most agreed-to *educational* disposition of all. Without this disposition it makes no sense to foster the Conversation at all. Without this disposition commitment to inclusion and respect for all must be based on political grounds or other grounds external to education. Learning to ask these two penetrating questions is becoming disposed to a life of participation in the Great Conversation. Moreover, the authentic disposition to ask such questions entails welcoming the participation of others to check on and share the accumulating product of the Conversation. This element of the dispositional cornerstone of educational purpose is always a legitimate educational focus. From 5-year-olds to 55-year-olds, from students to educators, a sincerely asked question deserves always to be honored. For example, we can never know that we know anything or even have plausible grounds for our beliefs until we at least confront the question, asking, "How do we know?" (See Case Study A.8 in Appendix A.)

THE CHALLENGE OF ACCOMMODATING
ALL FOUR CORNERS OF EDUCATIONAL PURPOSE

The four corners of educational purpose—skill, attitude, information, and disposition—tend to pull against one another. Talented educators are challenged to blend synchronistically each of the corners to ensure the general educational development of each student. Sometimes, because of external pressures such as high-stakes testing (emphasizing the information corner over all else) the challenge to develop well-balanced and fully educated students becomes increasingly intensified.

If the focus is on one corner alone, say on the information corner, odd consequences may follow. For example, students may be taught to memorize the definition of different cell types. But how and at what point should students be invited to consider what may be the greatest mystery of evolution: the appearance of the eukaryotic cell? If a precocious student challenges textbook or curricular material with mysteries evolution hasn't yet been able to solve, how should teachers respond? The answers to such questions will never appear on any test, in part because the answers are being sought by the world's best scientists at this moment. How much time can students be given to explore such questions in class? It seems apparent that the answer will be very different if one is focused on only one corner of educational purpose—in this example, the acquisition of information—as opposed to a focus on all four corners. There is no time to consider the mystery of the eukaryotic cell's appearance if sharing of uncontroversial information is the exclusive focus of the school, especially because there is no way a test item about it could appear now or in the foreseeable future. On the other hand, if all four corners of educational purpose are to be honored, then clearly the question should be honored, its author should be respected, and the speculation and effort aimed at solving the dilemma should be celebrated.

Developing in students educationally appropriate skills and attitudes can unleash a passion-driven search for truth that does not settle well with the institutional mission to prepare students for the next high-stakes test. The bootstrapping effect between information and educationally appropriate skills, attitudes, and dispositions may lead to a Pandora's box of pedagogical and administrative nightmares. For instance, should students be invited to think creatively, on grounds external to classroom information, about somewhat exotic ideas such as Niles Eldridge and Stephen Gould's theory of punctuated equilibrium in evolution or DNA discoverer Francis Crick's hypothesis about celestial seeding (Crick, 1995; Eldridge, 1985; Gould, 2002)? In mathematics and social studies, is there time to think about the consequences of Godel's incompleteness theorems (Goldstein, 2006) and the consequences for mathematical knowledge or theories of human nature? Think of all the time such discussion might take. Then again, should students' drive for truth be subordinated to the institution's need to equip them with certain information?

THE EDUCATIONAL LEADER: LEADING THE WAY TO
ACCOMMODATION WHILE NEVER LOSING SIGHT OF PRINCIPLE

Educational leaders serve as society's custodians in many ways. They *preserve* cultural traditions while broadening participation in an ever more inclusive Conversation. But they also serve as society's *change agents*. Educational administrators are also leaders of a historic and noble profession. As such they are committed to extending human understanding, wherever that may lead.

These three roles—community leader, change agent, and leader of a profession—may place a school administrator in a political hotbed. Responsibility for the curriculum makes administrators responsible for the flow of information into the schools. But as noted earlier, there is more to education than managing the flow of information into developing minds. The Conversation must be preserved and all four corners of educational purpose realized in practice and not in mere rhetoric or theory. Important challenges are unavoidable if all four corners of educational purpose are to be addressed adequately. For example, how can administrators balance societal demands for limits and selection of information against the openness the profession aims toward when fostering in students educational dispositions and attitudes commensurate with the other two more neatly defined corners of educational purpose? How can the openness the profession embraces protect against exclusion of individuals and exotic opinions? How can critical inquiry be kept from evolving into derogatory attitudes or dispositions to assault authority at every level? (Epistemic anarchy dissolves the Conversation every bit as much as ruthless authoritarianism.)

And, as every experienced administrator knows, it is not just about education. Stakeholders want control over the information schools deliver. They may also want control over the attitudes and skills developed in students. Also, stakeholders other than professional educators may not distinguish well between educational purpose and schooling purpose. And finally, every stakeholder knows full well that there are legitimate schooling demands that must be addressed in addition to any purist educational concerns of the academic specialists. To stabilize what can appear to be an otherwise unstable situation, administrators must be able to articulate the rationale behind each corner of educational purpose to the minimal satisfaction of each stakeholder group (Campbell & Overman, 1991).

BEYOND THE FOUR CORNERS OF EDUCATIONAL PURPOSE: SCHOOLING DISPOSITIONS AND ATTITUDES

Identifying the limited range of learning, along with the entire range of educationally relevant skills, attitudes, information, and dispositions that ought to be featured in a district or a school, is an enormous and ongoing task. The challenge is not only to identify a set of curricula that meet the needs and interests of all students (i.e., an explicitly defined menu) but to set appropriate priorities as well. Prioritizing such a menu inevitably raises questions of paternalism and social engineering. For better or worse, it cannot be denied that the curricular menu reflects unavoidably and disproportionately what groups of stakeholders believe leads to human betterment. Administrators alone stand to resist inappropriate imbalance between stakeholder groups. In addition, administrators must ensure that due consideration is always given to educational purpose and that the Great Conversation is never silenced.

Beyond educational purpose, a host of schooling objectives need administrative attention as well. Schools just happen to be places where society can most efficiently address many recognized social needs, from vaccinating the young and the elderly, to serving as voting stations or safe harbor during natural disasters, and feeding children of the socially and economically challenged. Other schooling functions necessary for supporting the educational mission of the school may include collecting milk money, cafeteria services, emergency health support, and safe and reliable transportation for students. And there is more. Schooling objectives also legitimately include vocational and other training and various types of socializing and enculturation. So, from courses in woodworking and metalworking to saying the Pledge of Allegiance, there is much that administrators must accommodate side by side with all else the schools hope to accomplish educationally.

For example, teaching about the nature of **compassion** is surely a worthy educational objective. Compassion is about more than respect for persons and inclusion (matters essential to the Great Conversation itself). Compassion is also an expression of empathy, mercy, and perhaps heroic action on behalf of others. Compassion is a wonderful hybrid of attitude and disposition. But however meritorious it is as a virtue, it is not an attitude or disposition essential to participation in the Great Conversation. Learning about compassion is integral to the Conversation, certainly, but being compassionate is altogether another thing. Presumably, most would like to think, the more people learn about compassion the more it is likely to bootstrap into meritorious changes in learner attitudes and dispositions. Nonetheless, it must be remembered that not all attitudes and dispositions, any more than all skills and information, are matters of educational purpose, no matter how worthy such attributes are. The word *education* is no mere synonym for all that is worthy. It cannot be a conceptual dumping ground for all that people think is good. In addition, with any attempt to make education refer to every imaginable good, the term *education* becomes increasingly unwieldy and subject to bitter and unproductive debate. People do best advancing the cause of education when they agree to focus on a defensible shared meaning of the term.

To return to the example of compassion, it should be noted that socializing or enculturating students into becoming compassionate may indeed be a very worthy and legitimate schooling purpose. In fact, its very worthiness underscores the fact that schools legitimately do more than educate; they can do other things through socialization and enculturation for the betterment of all. Here's the rub: It is easy to imagine how specific stakeholders may disagree on the importance and operational practices suitable to compassionate action (Clark, 1984). For example, should students be taught to advocate for softening penalties for first-time drug offenders and to give money to homeless people on city streets? Certainly these are good and compassionate things to do. Certainly education should address such matters *in principle* as the unfolding Conversation lays bare the elements and central nature of human capacities and inclinations. But should students be explicitly schooled in standards of change for criminal punishment or for when and to whom they should give money?

If the role of compassion in the schooling and educational agenda can rise to the status of an administrative conundrum, try to imagine a really difficult challenge such as the appropriate accommodation of so-called sex education (Meeker, 2002). Are moral considerations of sexual behavior an educational matter or a schooling matter?

Creating dispositions to abstain from reckless sexual behavior will save lives and the unnecessary trauma brought on students and their families by serious illness. Enculturating in students a disposition to abstain from risky sexual behavior is arguably a social good. But the social engineering involved is not a legitimate part of something called education, and such social engineering may even run counter to educational purpose. At the same time, pondering the morality of sexual behavior, like all momentous questions, is legitimately a part of the Great Conversation and hence of legitimate educational merit. Oddly enough, however, stakeholders may be more eager to school certain dispositions in students and at the same time offended by open discussion of the morality of such behavior. Moreover, sex education that artificially restricts itself to descriptions of copulating machinery and rates of disease but disallows legitimate moral reflection sacrifices educational purpose altogether, save the one corner we describe as informational. In summary, bringing together an instructional menu of educational and schooling responsibilities is no easy task. Conflicts of duty abound.

preferences to teach certain behaviors who chooses?

How one balances competing claims between educational and schooling purposes shapes and reshapes school and district moral architecture. There may be truth in matters of morality, but human intellectual fragility combined with diverse forces of cultural and social conditioning make apprehension of moral truth an insurmountable challenge at times. **Surface-level moral** disagreements between stakeholders are inevitable. In the best of all well-managed worlds, disagreement should simply stimulate the intellectual climate of school and district alike. The enriched intellectual climate should lead stakeholders to common ground at a deeper level of moral reflection (Freire, 2000; Habermas, 1979). For most administrators these challenges will exist in something less than the best of all well-managed worlds.

Figure 3.2 illustrates how comprehensive institutional purposes may be distributed without formal demarcation between schooling and education as mutually exclusive categories.

Figure 3.2   Comprehensive Instructional Purposes: Education and Schooling

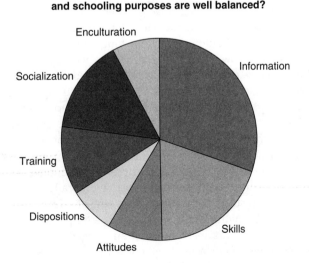

How does an administrator know when education and schooling purposes are well balanced?

The proportions here are only illustrative and are not meant to be prescriptive for any particular educational institution or organization.

Administrators cannot be the sort of people who are quick to settle for what most readily seems good enough for the passing moment. Educational leadership by its very nature seeks excellence, and "good enough" is never an apt substitute for excellence. Again, to recall Charles Taylor (2007), moral focus extends beyond the transient and the merely apparent. Moral focus is about setting school destinies in light of educational and schooling purpose (*schooling* will subsequently be used to refer also to training, socialization, and enculturation unless otherwise indicated).

POLITICAL AND ECONOMIC CHALLENGES TO DOING GOOD

Education has always reflected people's ideas of human betterment. This is also true of schooling, but ideas of human betterment evolving within education have been distilled over centuries and across cultural borders. In contrast, many schooling notions of human betterment are often limited to local environments and to moments in history. For example, in the 1950s a schooling objective aimed at community betterment was to teach students what to do in the case of nuclear attack. In contrast, an educational objective might be to help students understand the nature of nuclear fission or to understand human aggression or the rationality of annihilating whole populations.

Schooling concerns typically reflect a more surface level of moral discussion and a more immediate demand for predictable consequence. For instance, a schooling concern might be whether drug sniffing dogs should be used in school to deter drug use. The educational analog of such a concern might deal with such things as "What is the good life?" or "To what extent does one person have a right to advise or constrain the actions of another?"

Education has also always been about someone's idea of the truth (including, perhaps paradoxically, whether truth exists). Nonetheless, no champion in the educational literature from any culture or at any time in history has espoused the idea that education (again as opposed to schooling) should focus on teaching known falsehoods. As a practical matter, it is evident that we know much more about the world than we did some time ago. For example, we can now cure diseases that a century ago we didn't even know existed. It is also evident that we make mistakes and that our truths are always subject to further modification in light of new evidence or the need to make what is known a piece of one coherent fabric.

Schooling has never had such lofty ambitions as the quest for truth. Rather, schooling focuses on what those in power see as beneficial local conventions for the present and foreseeable future (Fiske, 1992). Schooling for the most part is intended to make students more engaged in the community in which they live; education seeks a broader horizon. From the viewpoint of schooling, it is often reasonable and morally inoffensive to consider contexts in which the ends justify the means (a fancy way of referring to cost–benefit analysis), so generally speaking, anything that works in a cost-efficient fashion ought to be embraced. Educational administrators are responsible and even held accountable by outside forces for attending to many formally articulated goals and objectives. These may not be neglected.

In the United States, teachers following a schooling modified curriculum have long (usually unknowingly) told students falsehoods, such as that drinking a single beer will kill five brain cells or that condoms will protect them from sexually transmitted infections. Because there is no evidence that drinking a single beer will kill five brain cells and little evidence that condoms protect people from any but a few select sexually transmitted infections, these are clearly not the sorts of things that represent good educational practice. That is, they do not represent our best understanding of the truth. On the other hand, if such tales lead to a decrease in reckless drinking and promiscuous sex, then such falsehoods ably serve a noble schooling cause and are thereby considered by many to be justified.

It is undoubtedly a good thing for society to do all it can to school young people away from behaviors such as imprudent drinking and sexual promiscuity. On the other hand, there is a prima facie *educational* objection to educators perpetuating false claims simply to secure a favored behavior. How should the responsible educational leader balance educational and schooling purposes in such cases?

School administrators must protect the soul of education and yet still initiate practices that modify student behavior and accommodate it to the surrounding community. Administrators are expected by all stakeholders to do the right thing, but the stakeholders themselves often have very different ideas about what the right thing to do might be. When all is said and done, the administrator's best shot at preserving his or her integrity and the moral architecture it supports is to have a clear-headed moral theory in mind. That moral theory should be so fully thought out that it suits all the uniqueness of modern educational administration, aligning schooling and educational purposes alike, with unimpeachable ideals always clearly in sight.

A PRACTICAL ASSIGNMENT

Ideally, schooling and education go hand in hand. But when there is conflict, how should it be managed? What deep moral principle or virtue might best prepare administrators for maintaining the proper balance when educational and schooling purposes seem to conflict? Give an example to illustrate your point.

Schooling is a matter of managing behavior, creating habits, arranging the flow of information, instituting and maintaining procedures for social cooperation, and expediting the effective and relevant exchange of information. Schooling is also about establishing and maintaining institutional robustness. Education is about establishing and maintaining intellectual robustness.

Without effective and appropriate schooling practices in place, education could never find a home for the Conversation in schools. Policy makers like to talk about the centrality of education in what schools do. Perhaps they do so earnestly. Even so, it is always tempting for them to subjugate the educational to the controlling demands of external schooling interests.

Managers carry out policy in line with the interpretations of superiors. Leaders play an active role in both creating and interpreting policy. Educational administrators must both manage and lead.

Administrators act as the profession's public conscience and make as clear as possible to policy makers the need for schools to stay focused first and foremost on matters of educational purpose. They use policy, faculty, and staff to capture the grandest of all multicultural

Figure 3.3 Dichotomous View of Institutional Purposes

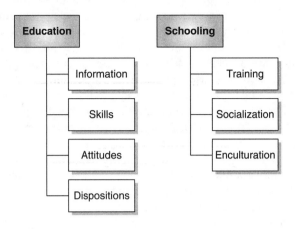

prizes: bringing all students into the Great Conversation. Administrators must never neglect schooling, largely because of what it contributes in the end to educational purpose and institutional function (Figure 3.3).

SUSTAINABLE LEADERSHIP AND ORGANIZATIONAL SURVIVAL

Obviously, there is more to sustaining managerial leadership than is involved in acquiring a formal position initially. More importantly, it is the ability to sustain one's leadership over the long haul that separates the ill-suited from the talented, well-prepared, and growing professionals who survive to make leadership a noble calling.

On one occasion, we asked a leader of one of the world's largest corporations what would make him follow another leader. After some thought, he summed things up in one word: *integrity.* Upon hearing this, an excited, enterprising, and ambitious young executive asked, "So how do you convince people you have integrity?" The room fell silent.

Integrity

A REALITY CHECK

If a candidate has great credentials and a winning personality but evidently lacks integrity, would you hire the person? All people have weaknesses of one sort or another. Is lack of integrity a weakness that can be overcome? Or is an evident lack of integrity a deal breaker from the very beginning? Explain.

Integrity is no gimmick. It is the embodiment of good character. Integrity cannot long be faked. There may be a few tips to help advance the career of the young executive, but the purely gimmicky will wear off. People sense when a person of integrity is in charge. As

Aristotle (1958) noted long ago, when discussing the leadership virtue of justice as an example, "To become just, one must do just acts. But, to *be* just one must do just acts *as a just person.*" Aristotle's point is that acts alone wear thin. True character is more permanent and evident. With integrity, as with all virtues, contributing to a leader's manifest destiny, the virtues must be lived. They cannot long be faked.

The educational administrator most likely to survive combines personal integrity with a clear-headed understanding of educational purpose. In good faith she accommodates all her responsibilities. Her accounting ledgers, like everything else about her, reflect what she values, and what she values is an unwavering commitment to education, respect for people, and the sustainable inclusiveness of the Conversation. Personal fulfillment through service, responsibility, and integrity are the perks that fulfill her. Salaries, parking spaces, and titles are certainly nice, but they are only incidental to the motivations of the truest of professionals.

A REFLECTIVE BREAK

How will a leader of integrity be reflected in the institution's moral architecture? How will a leader lacking integrity compromise the institution's moral architecture?

Those who choose educational leadership as a career for less than noble reasons expose our schools to unwarranted intrusion from outside interests who see schooling as the premiere purpose of schools. The most professional educational leaders must defend their schools from those both outside and inside the schools who would inequitably disturb the proper balance between schooling and education. Sustainable leaders in the educational context do not just hold on to formal authority. They do more. They use their authority to nurture the Great Conversation through effective planning and daily commitment to its purposes. They serve local communities and beyond through reasonable schooling practices and accommodations, always with an eye to ministering the Great Conversation.

DISCUSSION QUESTIONS

1. What is the leader's responsibility for creating cohesiveness in a situation where faculty, staff, and students all come from strikingly different cultures?

2. Some people, such as Linda Zagzebski, seem to think that virtue and strength of character are all there is to establishing a flourishing moral environment. What do you think? Can the moral architecture you hope to build in your organization be made out of a shared sense of virtue, or are principles and perhaps other elements needed as well?

3. What do you think is the noblest aspiration for an educational leader?

4. Create a working definition of sustainable leadership. List the three character traits you think most necessary for sustaining leadership. Explain the rationale for your choices and your priorities.

5. What makes a gang leader a leader? What do you think limits the tenure of a gang leader? In what ways is gang leadership like and unlike school leadership?

6. How will you control and, ideally, diminish the negative influence of gangs? Your leadership must be more influential than theirs. How will you diminish the influence of gangs and keep institutional attention on the purpose of education at the same time?

7. What is the best way for an administrator to make his moral commitment to the four corners of educational purpose explicit?

CASE STUDIES

Case Study 3.1. Should the Captain Go Down With the Ship?

Imagine you are principal at an elementary school in an inner-city area that is being revitalized. Tiny old homes are being bulldozed every day, and huge townhomes are being built in their place. These new homes are so expensive and with such small yards that they do not appeal to families. These are homes for wealthy seniors or young people who have no desire for families. This is happening all around your school service area and that of two adjacent elementary school service areas. Enrollments at all three schools are plummeting. Rumors abound. There will be school closings. Two of the schools will be closing if the rumors are correct. In addition, the district in general is not growing, and teachers especially feel that they will not be reassigned if their school closes but will instead be released from employment. You are the principal. What should you say or do to prepare all legitimate stakeholders for the possibility of the school closing? Do you bargain and strategize with central administration to save your school? Do you figure the handwriting is on the wall and look for ways to use your contacts at central administration to get reassigned yourself before the current house of cards falls in?

Case Study 3.2. A New Schooling Mission

Envision another scenario. Your school has been a magnet school for talented students in the sciences. Because of changing demographics, the district is changing your school back into a standard high school and is creating a new facility 9 miles away. That school is taking away 15% of your most talented and highly trained faculty. Central administration tells you that the reason for leaving you behind is that you are such a good leader, you will be critical to keeping the remaining faculty from becoming despondent and leaving. Moreover, they tell you that you alone can rally those remaining behind to continue doing their best. You don't know whether the administration is attempting to placate you or is being truthful. You are a good administrator and have often been complimented on your skills by your superiors. On the other hand, won't the new school need a talented administrator experienced with handling a science-heavy curriculum? Why not you? It feels as if you are being passed over for promotion, but then you learn that the principal of the new school will make only as much money as you now make. The faculty you have left is less talented, and many of your best students will be leaving. What do you owe the remaining faculty and students? What do you owe the district? How do you know when you have paid off your duty to those you owe in this case? Specifically, in the next year what will you implement to make the existing school whole and productive in its new role? How does the idea of integrity play a role in your decisions and discussions?

Case Study 3.3. Stand by Your Man?

A 30-year-old teacher that you know well and have respected for 6 years has been accused of making inappropriate remarks and touching a 15-year-old freshman girl. The girl is part of an intimidating gang. Two other members of the gang say they witnessed it. All three girls were failing the accused teacher's class before the alleged incident occurred. The girls—but neither you nor the teacher—are of the same ethnic background. In your heart of hearts you find it impossible to believe the accusations. Of course, the teacher denies the accusations. The girls will undoubtedly go to their parents and to the press if this teacher is not fired or at least suspended immediately. What do you do? Whom do you owe? What do you owe to each party? How do you know when you have fulfilled your obligation to all relevant parties? As you ponder these questions, the superintendent calls you. One of the girls' parents has called her and is threatening to go to the press if the teacher isn't relieved of duties immediately. What do you say to the superintendent, especially because she is new to the district? Now imagine you are the superintendent in the same case. The district has just recently been dragged through the muckraking media for some missing school travel funds. It turned out to be a nonissue, but for 4 days it was all over the press. Now this sexual harassment issue comes up. You don't know the principal very well and know even less about the accused teacher. Should these considerations matter to you? The principal is resolute regarding the teacher's likely innocence. Should that matter to you? You believe these parents will go to the press and fear the press will make ethnicity an issue. What do you do? How do you ensure that student safety and rights are honored, staff rights are protected, public perceptions are considered, ethnic concerns are honored, and district integrity is maintained? Explain the reasoning behind your proposed course of action. What plan do you wish the district had in place so that accusations of this sort can be addressed objectively by a diverse group or committee? When would you consider contacting local police to assist you?

ACTIVITIES

Activity 3.1

Identify a volunteer organization that is of interest to you. Get involved as soon as possible. Agree to serve on a committee or in another capacity, ideally in a group that does not have a leader at the moment. If a leadership opportunity arises, take advantage of it. As you serve, take notes on how the committee functions. If you were elected or appointed to a leadership position, explain the process and how you did or did not influence it. Specifically, why do you suppose others wanted either you or another person to lead? What did you learn about leadership? How is this position similar to and different from leadership in a school or district? Would this group elect you again to chair again? What message should you get from your answer to the previous question?

Activity 3.2

Ask someone to help you do some small job (such as moving a couch) as a favor. Ask someone different to help you move the couch for, say, $5.00. Finally, ask a third party to help you move the couch for, say, $20. Who worked the hardest to help you? Has this exercise helped you learn anything about social relationships and their accompanying reward structure, especially the sorts of reward structures that are most productive (Ariely, 2008)?

FURTHER READING

Beckner, W. (2004). *Ethics for educational leaders.* Boston: Pearson Education.

Fullan, M. (2003). *The moral imperative of school leadership.* Thousand Oaks, CA: Corwin.

Haynes, F. (1998). *The ethical school.* London: Routledge.

Sergiovanni, T. (2005). *Strengthening the heartbeat: Leading and learning in schools.* San Francisco: Jossey-Bass.

CHAPTER 4

Taking On the Big Challenge of School and District Administration

LEADERSHIP, MANAGEMENT, AND POLICY

The previous chapter addressed the challenge of sustaining leadership in education. It began by focusing attention on a common vision of education as identified through what we described as four foundational corners of educational purpose. This brief sketch of educational purpose is aligned with schooling functions that similarly must be addressed through institutional education. The authors denigrate neither education nor schooling but try to illuminate differences between the two institutionalized functions of public schooling. No reasonable balance between the two is possible if the difference between them goes unrecognized. Besides the technical task of maintaining balance between the two, the chapter concluded that the success of educational leadership depends largely on leaders' possessing certain moral qualities, most importantly integrity, moral focus, and a general awareness of how a working moral compass is integral to the moral architecture of the organization as a whole.

In this chapter we shift perspective a bit to discuss the educational administrator not only as a leader but as a manager as well. As alluded to at the end of the previous chapter, the skill sets and talents of leadership and management are not the same. However, both skill sets are needed to be a successful, senior-level educational administrator (Hoyle, English, & Steffy, 1998).

Leadership and management are not exclusive functions in education. Each depends on the successful operation of the other. In the realities of everyday institutional operation, the skill sets critical to these respective functions are commingled throughout the day. There are also some commonalities in the two respective skill sets. Nonetheless, there is little symmetry between the two functions and their respective skill sets. For example, education depends on effective management of schooling operations. In sharply definitive contrast, schooling and management do not depend on the fulfillment of educational operations in the same way. Capability in fulfilling one function is no guarantee of skill in fulfilling the other. For example, one could reasonably expect that a talented MBA could competently manage the schooling operations of a district.

Table 4.1   The Person in Charge: An Ethical Perspective

Administrative Leader	Manager	Boss
A paradigm of the organization's moral architecture, a true exemplar of the community's ethics and sense of decorum. Sets ideals and shared professional vision above personal convenience.	Works with others to organize systems of data collection, evaluation, and accountability aimed at organizational efficiency. Uses appeals to accountability to reinforce clearly articulated public objectives and goals.	First and foremost, relies on formal authority to get subordinates in line. May use techniques of intimidation, both subtle and overt. Insists on personal loyalty and getting the job done right away, with no complaint. If the assigned person cannot get the job done right the first time, the boss will find someone who can.
Elevates school and district moral architecture through example, policy, and protocol.	Sustains the level of moral architecture necessary to sustain current operational efficiency in the organization.	Tends to bring organizational architecture to its lowest level by creating a "might makes right" ambiance.

However, there is every reason to doubt that a person without specific training and experience in education could either lead or manage the educational function of a district, much less maintain the sometimes precarious balance between educational functions and schooling functions.

Because schools are about education, those trained in education are presumably far more likely than even a highly competent operational manager to recognize that educational purpose should nearly always have some prioritized edge over any set of schooling purposes. In a nutshell, a properly trained educational administrator knows what education is about, whereas a person whose training is limited to efficient managerial skills will inevitably fall short in genuinely educational contexts. See Table 4.1, which highlights the difference in sense of mission between administrative leaders, managers, and bosses. The ideas captured in the table are discussed in more detail here.

Managers

A good manager may keep a district or school afloat indefinitely but there may be little of educational value produced in a school or district that is merely operationally efficient. A competent and experienced MBA may run a cost-effective organization, and a competent attorney should help navigate districts through the risks of costly litigation. But what does an MBA or attorney know about education, faculty development, the theory and practice of teaching, student learning and development, and, most importantly, the idea of education as a Great Conversation?

MBAs have been trained as professional managers, not as educational leaders. School administrators who try to establish their personal competency on grounds of operational efficiency alone are helping to set the stage for their own replacement by cost-conscious and number-focused MBAs and attorneys who are well trained in such matters.

Educational institutions are unique institutions. Their closest analogs are perhaps local churches and the quickly disappearing institution of the community hospital. Each instance of such institutions is one that is in large part by the people and for the people. Educational institutions exist in part to bring about an educational ideal, not a financial, management, or political ideal. Of course, schools and districts, like churches and community hospitals, must be efficiently managed and responsive to community patrons, but they must be efficiently managed and responsive to community patrons in light of their unique ideals. In these unique institutions, the ideals are largely and essentially moral. More specifically, in the case of education the ideals are such things as inclusion, respect for the individual and diversity of culture, a passion for the pursuit and sharing of truth, open dialogue, and on and on (Dupre, 2009; Frank, 2009; Scanlon, 1998). Typical MBA or legal training does not focus on such ideals or on any articulated responsibility for promoting such ideals (Strike, Haller, & Soltis, 1998).

Bosses

As alluded to earlier, competent educational administrators bring together into a seamless whole management discipline, educational and professional vision, and leadership skills and talents. Any fragmentation of this triad fractures administrative proficiency. A striking example of fractured administrative proficiency is evident when an administrator gets a bit too comfortable and falls, however innocently, into the role of "boss."

Mere managers can and often do run things by falling back on the role of boss. They use power to push people. By contrast, leaders are usually most effective when they are seen as drawing people forward through personal example, vision, and courteous interactions. Some rather romantically slanted literature on leadership would have us believe that it is *always* better to act like a leader rather than a boss. However, given the diverse nature of human motivation this is probably an unrealistic expectation. Sometimes there are people who, for a time at least, need a more directive approach—they do need a boss at the helm. That is, they need someone who directs them toward a specific course of action in order to become properly animated. Institutions need to stay in motion, and at times that may entail a variety of initiatives and operational style.

Professional responsibility demands that duties are fulfilled, not that style should trump outcome. This dictum should not be taken as a recommendation that the ends justify the means. Rather, the point is that the ends are the rationale for the existence of the organization, and therefore whatever means are consistent with the organization's moral architecture are resources to be used in fulfilling professional responsibilities. The ends of an educational organization are so inclusive and democratic that bossiness as an administrative style should be only an exception to the rule.

LEADERSHIP: MOVING BEYOND MANAGEMENT

A leader with worthy educational aspirations, compelling personality, and noble commitments may fail as an administrator if he or she lacks managerial proficiency. In short, it is the entire range of professional skill and commitment that makes leaders and managers into successful administrators.

The successful administrator must blend command style with an eye for appropriate detail. That is, she generally fosters a democratic environment but also knows when she must shoulder the responsibility of being boss. She also knows that not all detail is worthy of her immediate attention. Obsession with detail makes it impossible to focus, to see the forest for the trees. With a balanced approach between variant leadership styles, detail, and the "big picture" and appreciation for sustaining the moral architecture of school and district, the truest administrators secure stakeholder loyalty and enthusiastic commitment to the Great Conversation.

In the Middle Ages, great tapestries were created as a record of a lord's achievements. Today the analog of such tapestries in the case of educational administrators is written policy. Just as with the tapestries, there are many fingerprints on every well-conceived policy, but in the end the aggregate of policy is a snapshot of the administrator's longest-standing institutional success. Consequently, it is to every administrator's advantage to know proactively how to *create* policy rather than always react to each crisis and apparent need with targeted rules and regulations. Professional managers know that effective policy stabilizes organizations. Leaders understand how policy controls and develops the growth of organizations (Lyubomirsky et al., 2005). Successful administrators know how to bring it all together for the benefit of stakeholders and institution alike (Gneezy & Rustichini, 2000).

In creating policy, the administrator must always begin by thinking through what the policy is meant to *do*. Noble intentions are not enough. The competent administrator must bring together policy purpose, practical constraints, and likely consequences in the context of shared vision and existing moral architecture. This aggregation of considerations must be as nearly complete as possible before one can throw open the door to stakeholders with the query, "What do you all want to do about this?" Premature open inquiry can lead to conceptual anarchy and disenfranchisement of more reticent or complacent personnel. Such consequences diminish the likelihood of inclusive, task-oriented participation. Premature open inquiry does not promote conditions for democratic leadership (Townsend, 1995).

Stakeholders want their fingerprints on policy (Byrne-Jiminez & Orr, 2007). They tend to resent authoritarian downloading of sets of directives. Even so, people are generally appreciative of being presented with fairly complete policies and protocols for review as long as they are able to review every aspect of the document, make recommendations as appropriate, and have their recommendations seriously considered. Openness to suggestions—even the suggestion to discard work done and start afresh—is the key to democratic leadership (Gardara & Contreras, 2009). It is always difficult to see one's work suffer criticism and modification. Nonetheless, the administrator must not be too proprietary about the destiny of the submitted document (Fasching, 1997). She should take heart in the folk wisdom that says committees tend to accept about 85% of the content of a formally submitted document. The other 15% is the price paid for stakeholder buy-in, evidence that stakeholder contribution genuinely matters.

In an environment of democratic openness, changes will be made to any proposal, no matter how well prepared. Even if the change lessens the policy's potency, this loss is usually more than made up for by the increase in stakeholder sense of buy-in and readiness to support the policy more heartily. Finally, savvy administrators usually learn through experience that there is little danger that a well-thought-out policy will be recklessly discarded in its entirety. When stakeholders trust in the integrity and openness of the administrator who is bringing the policy to the table, there is seldom any sustainable impulse to discard well-intentioned work.

In the end, the administrator must decide whether a policy is to be implemented. And in the end, it is the administrator who is held accountable for failure and praised for success (American Association of School Administrators, 1981). Nonetheless, she seldom has reason to fear that what might be lost in the deletion or modification of this or that detail is of greater cost than the loss of stakeholder buy-in if she proves unwilling to consider all well-intended recommendations for improvement. Administrative secrecy, obstinacy, authoritarianism, and prickliness in the face of criticism are each far more likely to cause problems for an administrator in the long run than is implementation of a less-than-optimal policy. As explained in Chapter 1, follower support is key to sustainable leadership (Hoyle et al., 1998; Kaiser, 1996).

START WITH POLICY REVIEW, NOT PEOPLE REVIEW

In the years of total quality management's heyday, W. E. Deming, Joseph Juran, Phillip Crosby (Crosby, 1985; Deming, 1982, 2000; Juran & Blanton, 1998), and other writers in business management theory touted the idea that it is process and policy that make or break an organization. If an institution is in trouble, assessment and subsequent evaluation should lead to identification of an inoperable process or policy for modification. The purpose of assessment and evaluation should never be to lay blame or subject a subordinate to retribution (Griffin, 1986). In the latter case such practices nearly always prompt suspicion of the administrator's integrity and commitment to work openly with others.

After assessment and evaluation, defective processes or policy should be fixed. Further review of the repaired policy should be scheduled in order to detect the next bottleneck, which will inevitably appear in any cooperative and complex organizational effort (Deming, 2000).

Change in process and policy is the source of institutional improvement. Denigrating fellow team members is never a productive substitute. The former enhances the administrator's credibility as a focused leader of integrity, whereas the latter threatens his credibility and compromises the willingness of subordinates to follow rather than just follow along.

> ### A GROUP DISCUSSION
>
> A good administrator never settles into the role of "boss" to lead an organization forward. How can you lead directly and forcefully at times without abusing the formal role of authority? What might happen if you lack the strength or courage to make difficult or unpopular decisions when called upon to do so?

Among all the early quality theorists, Deming alone addressed the human elements of administration in addition to the formalities of process and policy. Deming (2000) also pressed forward specifically to address quality control issues in education. Educational theorist Thomas Sergiovanni (1984) quickly picked up on Deming's insights and led the effort to apply them to public education. Deming and Sergiovanni both argue that with robust **plans** encompassing comprehensive policy, protocols, and procedures and with specific moral commitments, an organization can survive the inevitable turnover of personnel and change of contextual conditions while continuing to fulfill its institutional mission. This was a great insight into management theory, which in the past too often insisted blindly that the key to a great organization is a great manager rather than great management and great leadership.

Keep in mind that planning and its constituent policy must be fleshed out in detail and subject to review and revision again and again. It is through both review and revision that the cycle of continuous improvement and optimal institutional performance is secured (Sergiovanni, 2005). Educational administrators are responsible for ensuring assessment, evaluation, and further data-driven planning are used routinely in an unbroken cycle of continuous improvement. In the context of fostering a moral architecture, such striving for continuous improvement can be embraced by all and feared by none.

DEMING'S SOCIAL AND MANAGERIAL IDEALISM AND SCHEFFLER'S PRAGMATISM

Deming's work as the leading voice of a school of management theory called total quality management led him beyond quality control and into becoming something of a moralist. He espoused a program of 14 points. Five of his 14 points are highly moralistic (Walton, 1986): drive out fear; break down barriers that thwart congenial cooperation; eliminate slogans, exhortations, and other conspicuous behavioral prods to mass motivate personnel; develop pride of workmanship (professional accomplishment); and *lead* people to become more proficient (rather than bully, boss, and otherwise threaten them with consequences for substandard performance). Table 4.2 encapsulates Deming's thoughts in this area. What examples would you add to those listed in the table?

Deming decries management that relies on boss-like behavior for getting things done. Generally speaking, people work harder when they are led rather than pushed (Myers, 1999). Because people follow best those they admire, respect, and honor, Deming surmised, leaders must develop a full and appropriate repertoire of virtues (Walton, 1986).

A REALITY CHECK

How would you set about reducing fear among your faculty and staff? How does fear compromise an organization's moral architecture? How does a moral architecture compromised by fear suffer in terms of organizational proficiency, if at all?

Deming's moralism is resolute but not absolute. Actually, his moral position is similar to that of contemporary pragmatist Israel Scheffler (Wagner, 1997). Like Deming, Scheffler focuses attention on individual human potential and the drive for human betterment generally. Deming and Scheffler both believe universal human betterment can be achieved through appropriate education and organizational structures and the accompanying processes.

Table 4.2   Deming's Moralism

Advice	Explanation	Example
Eliminate fear	Fears that stymie trust, openness, caring, and discussion	Tell an employee how to further develop without criticizing his efforts to date.
Eliminate barriers	Practices and policies that inhibit cooperative staff reflection, planning, re-envisioning, and sharing	Create teacher discussion groups to meet on a regular basis.
Eliminate quotas (prods)	Behavior prods that push or pull staff toward performance markers	Making job continuance and any reward dependent on a single number lessens the likelihood of creative problem solving.
Develop pride	Commitment to high-quality performance	Show through your own example that you never settle for "good enough" but instead always strive for genuine excellence.
Maximize leadership	Leadership that respects staff and prompts them to follow (and not merely follow along with) together in a shared vision	Have an end-of-semester brainstorming session chaired by a teacher and attended by all administrators.

GETTING ONE'S DUCKS IN A ROW

"Getting one's ducks in a row" is an expression coined for the process of getting ready to solve a problem or meet a challenge. Problem solving does not begin in a vacuum. For a problem to be recognized, it must be framed in some context. Once the problem is appropriately framed, relevant background data on which a plausible solution might be based become apparent. Because problem solving is an ongoing challenge for the administrator, data collection and evaluation must be an ongoing priority for the administrator as well.

The process of data collection harbors challenges separate from applied problem solving, warns Deming. For example, collecting *too much* data or collecting *inconsequential* data can lead to riches of useless data that only confound and befuddle onsite problem management (Deming, 2000). When an organization collects too much data and adds some data that are inconsequential, management finds it difficult to make sense of the forest for the trees. Because problem solving is the reason administrators collect data, it is important to collect only data that help solve problems.

Collecting unnecessary data may complicate current problem-solving efforts and create new problems as well. Data collection and evaluation policy and protocols must be reviewed periodically for their simplicity, parsimony, comprehensiveness, and, most especially, utility. Data collection and review are more productive when all relevant stakeholders readily understand the operational utility of collected data. Utility is established by the data's driving role when addressing generally acknowledged problem sets.

Data collection and review are comprehensive and parsimonious when all relevant data are collected and there is no wasted effort or expense collecting irrelevant data. The whole rationale behind total quality management is to focus on operational policy through continuous review and use of relevant data. Data collection and all that goes with it must always be subordinate to institutional improvement.

The goal of data-driven management is to focus on the numbers that matter, not merely numbering all that *might* matter. People are very creative at delivering the numbers expected of them. If decision makers seek nonessential data, employees will work to deliver the numbers required even at the expense of the institution's mission (Walton, 1986).

Imagine a school where the only number that mattered was student retention. By making every school day one long party, an administrator might ensure student retention. But schools are about more than retention. One long party means that one or more of the four corners of educational purpose are neglected, as are a host of legitimate schooling concerns. The numbers matter. They matter so much that administrators must put much effort into identifying what numbers ought to be collected and prioritized in annual problem-solving challenges.

THE POINT OF POLICY: GETTING BETTER ALL THE TIME

Circumstances surrounding any organization are bound to change. As circumstances change, the numbers that best indicate optimal organizational performance may change as well. As mentioned earlier, sometimes data are collected without sufficient rhyme or reason. If the data seem irrelevant to further institutional improvement, the administrator should ask why such data continue to be collected. In the end, the key pragmatic question in the collection of data is, "What do these numbers indicate in the pursuit of our organization's shared purpose?"

In a well-working organization everyone is contributing. In a deficiently run organization there is a problem with organizational policy, planning, and protocols. Deming (1982) warns that data-driven evaluation of individual personnel can be a potent source of fear and ultimately destructive of the organization's congeniality and social milieu—properties we describe as making up much of the organization's relevant moral architecture. Unfortunately, in the legalistic environment in which many schools operate today, numerical data descriptive of individual productivity often seem to be the only leverage the administrator has for limiting liability in the wake of certain personnel decisions.

Dismissing subordinates to repair an operational glitch in an organization usually forces the appearance of another bottleneck somewhere else in the organization (Goldratt, 2004). Personnel dismissal seldom does more than hide a problem for a while. Instead of dismissing personnel at the first indication of organizational weakness, conscientious leaders are well advised to look instead at the organization holistically and then figure out what data-driven rearrangements of policy, process, or procedures can improve organizational function (Sergiovanni, 1996). Failure to identify malfunctioning organizational arrangements is a *management* problem. Failure to secure buy-in on necessary adjustments is a *leadership* problem. Together these two problem areas represent a central administrative challenge (Sergiovanni, 2005).

The administrator must have both the integrity and the moral courage to make difficult decisions, make amends when things go wrong, and always be prepared to step forward with a plan to make things right. Designating a "fall person" to avoid personal responsibility for an operational defect is ineffective over the long haul (Haybron, in press). Such behavior weakens organizational moral architecture by sending signals to employees that they each might one day be victimized as well. Of course, there are times when an employee may be adamant about not collaborating with the rest of the team. When this happens the administrator may reassign the person somewhere else in the organization. And in the worst circumstances, it may be necessary to let the person go all together.

NO CHILD LEFT BEHIND: A SOURCE OF EVALUATION AND ASSESSMENT BLUNDERS

As noted earlier, when personnel are evaluated by the wrong numbers, the organization suffers (Vohs, Mead, & Goode, 2006). In No Child Left Behind (NCLB), student scores on standardized tests are often used to evaluate individual teachers, administrators, and ultimately schools, districts, and even the state and national educational systems. As Deming predicts in all such cases, the target numbers demanded by NCLB programs will be delivered, but, again following Deming's caveat, at what cost to the overall educational product?

The evaluation practices of NCLB are far more commensurable with how one might imagine evaluating propagandists, salespeople, or marketing personnel rather than educators. Sales personnel and propagandists are properly evaluated by the attitudes, behaviors, and ideas they get others to adopt. It does not matter to such opinion makers how they get their target audience to adopt such attitudes, behaviors, and ideas. However, to educators it matters very much *how* students come about their attitudes, behaviors, and ideas. Unlike salespeople and propagandists, educators succeed in large part only when they bring together passionate, respectful, and critically thinking students into the Great Conversation (Wagner, 1997).

Whatever might be the best way to evaluate educators' success in *educational* undertakings, it surely cannot be by the percentage of student aggregate scores on standardized tests. McNeil (2000) has documented incidents of cheating and data manipulation from individual classrooms to the superintendent's office in districts throughout the country. Such dishonesty is not an ethical problem, properly speaking, but rather an ethical issue. The difference between the two is that in the case of ethical issues there is general agreement on what is right, but the difficulty lies in getting people to do what is right. In the case of ethical problems, there are grounds for substantial dissent on what counts as right-minded solutions to a moral challenge. Educators know there is little excuse to cheat for purposes of self-interest. Cheaters acting on self-interest alone should be fired. Their credibility as a role model to students is lost forever. But cheaters in response to NCLB sometimes believe they are cornered by unreasonable assessment and evaluation practices inexcusably harmful to them and to their students. For these cheaters, what is involved is an ethical problem for them and their administrators.

Even honest educators who would never technically cheat are, as Deming would predict, creatively changing their modus operandi for success on high-stakes, standardized tests. Such changes in modus operandi may include less attention to critical thinking and creative hypothesizing, diminished interest in apprehending truth, and less willingness to share in the unconventional understandings of others and many other features central to the Great Conversation. Does the effort to secure higher test scores warrant so much cost in these other areas?

QUESTIONING
THE AUTHORS

?

What would your response be to a teacher who admitted that she gave a recently traumatized student and a special needs student a few correct answers on a test so that each could graduate from high school? How do these cases differ from one in which a principal encourages teachers to "help" students score higher on standardized tests so the campus gets additional state funds? If you are the immediate supervisor overseeing the responsible administrator in each of these cases, what advice would you give?

No one ever got a Nobel Prize in any science simply because she knew a great deal of information. Nobel laureates are people who fall in love with a set of treasured questions. And their passion for truth leads them to persist in asking, "How do we know?," "What do we mean by that term, variable, or causal explanation?," and "How can we learn more or test this hypothesis or idea?" They persist in asking such questions until their investigations lead to somewhere no one else has ever been. Nobel laureates usually are considered some of the most conspicuous products of successful education. But where will future Nobel laureates come from if the schools show students that to the schools, only higher test scores matter?

The true value of education is that it leads participants further away from evident error and toward greater shared understanding of the world. This does not mean education will invariably lead to everyone seeing everything exactly alike. Indeed, the process of schooling students for success in high-stakes testing is far more likely to lead to such a result. Education or, as we say, the Great Conversation is an ongoing dynamic in which participants accept a role and a shared vision and discover ambition and respect for truth, all in light of their appreciation for the inherent fallibility of human epistemics (Tiberius, 2008).

Our current concern is not with any content school children may be learning. Rather, the concern is that some assessment policies may undermine the four corners of educational purpose and limit universal participation in the Great Conversation. The numbers NCLB requires are simply too narrow for comprehensive evaluation of educator success. Besides passing along information, successful educators **teach** students when and how to doubt. Successful educators teach students persistence and patience in search of further truths. Successful educators teach students the value of listening carefully to other truth seekers and the importance of sharing one's own apprehension of truth. High-stakes testing evaluates none of these, so there is little reason to applaud the numbers of high-stakes testing as a measure of educational improvement in our schools. Moreover, if onsite administration neglects evaluating these attributes of educational success, educational scope may be traded for an inappropriately narrow set of tactics and strategies, along with a diminished range of substantive information previously shared with students (Noddings, 2007). In contrast, Scheffler's emphasis on the plasticity of the human mind and his and Deming's emphasis on human betterment (Byrne-Jiminez & Orr, 2007; Gabor, 1986) militate against settling on assessment tools easily used if those tools are ill suited for evaluating a comprehensive range of educational success.

PRAGMATIC IDEALISM

By the term *pragmatic idealism* we mean nothing akin to what philosophers might imagine by such a term. In fact, to the professional philosopher such a term may look something like an oxymoron because pragmatism as a philosophical position developed largely in opposition to a 19th-century school of thought known as idealism. So by the phrase *pragmatic idealism* we mean to draw attention to the moral commitments of philosophers who largely abandoned hope of acquiring truth on any grand scale but remained committed to the possibility that a right approach to immediate problem solving exists nonetheless and leads, albeit by fits and starts, to the ideal of a better world (Dewey, 1938). Dewey's self-described intellectual descendants Hilary Putnam and Israel Scheffler described a better world in terms of universal acknowledgment of *fraternité,* or brotherhood (Putnam, 2004) and universal fulfillment of human potential (Scheffler, 1985) socially and in all of the sciences.

Pragmatic idealists believe people can develop in terms of moral proficiency (Dewey, 1908). Moral proficiency is a matter of acquiring dispositions accommodating to the moral commitments of others who also share a commitment to always be other-regarding as well. As Hilary Putnam explains, pragmatism must be seen not as an objection to principle-driven morality but rather as a tolerance for variability of nonuniform behavior and surface rules imposed by the local setting (Putnam, 2002; Tiberius, 2008). This tolerance for nonuniform behavior must be aligned with a sustaining commitment to *the fraternity of man,* and the alignment shows itself in an acquired attitude of promoting the well-being of all (Putnam, 2002).

Israel Scheffler also embraces the idea that moral concerns begin with a focus not on rules and principles but on local problems. But like Putnam, Scheffler (1985) also is equally unwavering in his endorsement of a universal commitment, a commitment he describes as the flourishing of human potential. In short, although both are sensitive to beginning moral reflection in the context of a locally framed problem set, each prescribes that further deliberations keep in mind a universal commitment to seek human benefit indiscriminately.

A Reflective Break

How do you develop schools where students and teachers pursue important intellectual and social questions despite the surrounding community's focus on entertainment and athletics? How should you focus attention on the Great Conversation when the attention of your evaluators is on quantitative data assessing strictly schooling achievements?

Local problem sets exhibit uniqueness, but this doesn't mean that moral right-mindedness is left solely to the accidents of history (e.g., whoever happens to be principal or superintendent at the time the problem set arises). The pragmatic idealist approach is far from being subjective or relativistic in any naïve sense. For example, Dewey (1938) made repeated references to educators' professional responsibilities as commitments clearly transcending local context and reflecting professional normative tradition. Scheffler (1985) similarly notes that the human species, adorned as it is by all its wonderful cultures, is still naturally of one mind when it comes to the idea that education (as well as many attempts at schooling and socialization) aims at the flourishing of human potential generally and through the pursuit of individual excellence especially. In short, though focused on the problem of the moment, pragmatic idealism is driven by a shared motivational commitment to make things a bit better for all.

Many administrators have become so fearful of making value judgments that the idea of seeking human betterment may seem somewhat daunting. (This fear is a fear that should be eliminated in an appropriately rich and elevated moral architecture.) But there is really no way around the challenge (Howard & Scheffler, 1995). Education by its very nature is an evolving and universal human institution. Its historic resiliency can be attributed only to the fact that it serves some enduring set of valued purposes for all of humankind. Conspicuously, education by its very nature sets out to make people different than they might become if left to their own untutored impulses and haphazardly formed social surroundings.

People can learn how to venomously express feelings of hate toward others, they can learn techniques for mutilating their own bodies and optimizing the pain they inflict on themselves or others, they can learn to manipulate corporate financial records for their own advantage, and they can learn to win athletic and academic events without regard for honesty or fair play. But surely none of this is the sort of stuff any educational administrator would openly countenance. These are all properly described as things learned. It is difficult to imagine anything that more evidently underscores the fact that education simply isn't about learning. Rather, it is about a much narrower realm of things that can be learned, namely, things of value. Pragmatic idealists may describe this value in terms of commitment to human betterment. Others may describe the value differently. But no one can meaningfully describe the range of learning appropriate to education as something of disvalue or value free (Peters, 1981).

Pragmatic idealists from the early Dewey, Pierce, and Ramsey (Dokic & Engel, 2006; Peirce, 1992) to the more recent Putnam, Quine, and Scheffler (1974) all emphasize that pragmatism isn't driven simply by satisfactory outcomes but rather by commitments to securing satisfactory outcomes for stakeholders, if not humanity more generally (as in the case of Dewey, Putnam, and Scheffler). For example, an occasional right answer produced through a Ouija board is a method pragmatic idealists would be unlikely to countenance because even if the method succeeded in this context, there is much historic reason to discredit the reliability of the method in any other context. Pragmatic idealists are not simple-minded advocates of whatever works. What works must methodologically prove itself to have at least some promise of serving the goal of human betterment beyond a single chance instance. This requires not only a realization of some human betterment but also some understanding of why a method holds some promise for this and similar problem sets.

Understanding may be the most difficult and educationally relevant ideal to grasp (McLaughlin et al., 2009). Understanding is not a matter of iterating information or exhibiting certain skills. Howard Gardner's (1993) theory of multiple intelligences and Gilbert Ryle's (1949) distinction between "knowing how" and "knowing that" both readily illustrate that knowing that certain things are true and how to grapple with a learning challenge are not all of one piece. Understanding is the ultimate pragmatic meta-achievement that brings multiple intelligences and skills of "knowing how" with "knowing that" together with some idea of why people initiate an undertaking in the first place (Sternberg, 2003).

The goal of pragmatic idealism is to imagine how the presentation of problem-solving tasks can lead to an immediately practical exercise of intelligence and from there to a more general understanding of problem-solving sets in general. These further problems will certainly include like problems, but presumably the pragmatic idealist seeks analogical transfer of learning as well. The range of accumulating learnings should enable people to understand how to manage local challenges and how to better understand one's place in the world and ultimately (here's where the idealism comes in) one's responsibility and potential to contribute to human betterment. Pragmatic idealism is so much more than a mere epistemic method. In the end it is a practical ethic and a theory of ideally lived experience as well.

MAKING THEORY RESPONSIVE TO PRACTICE

Educational administrators even more than policy specialists must remind stakeholders that education should never be seen as a set of tactics for solving randomly emerging problems at the moment. Tactics must embody strategies aimed at more general understanding. Education must reflect the best human efforts to keep alive in every student the dream of answering the unanswerable, imagining the unimagined, and discovering islands of truth, real truth in the opaque haze of prior speculations and inquiry. There are pragmatically fruitful steps schools can take to help students embrace such educational ideals. Some of these are as follows:

- Nurture respect for every participant in every aspect of the educational process.
- Demonstrate again and again that the pursuit of both knowledge and understanding is to be admired. This can be done by celebrating from classroom to district central offices the Nobel Awards, the MacArthur Foundation Awards, the Fields Medal, and the Templeton Prize. In short, emphasize that intellectual accomplishments are to be admired at least as much as aesthetic, cultural, and athletic feats.
- Teach students the epistemic foundations of various disciplines and fields of creative inquiry (Hirst, 1990). This means students must know more than facts. They must acquire the skills, attitudes, and dispositions characteristic of problem solving in the various disciplines and commensurate with the four corners of educational purpose generally (Snyder, Acker-Hocevar, & Snyder, 2004).
- Encourage teachers to move beyond the question "Why" to two additional questions: "How do you know?" and "What do you mean by the term ___?" These two questions prompt far more rigorous reflection than the undisciplined conversation that often follows in the wake of simple "why" questions.
- Ensure that students come to understand that when they make public claims to know, they undertake an obligation to justify and offer grounds for such claims when asked by fellow truth seekers.
- Create motivational programs bringing teachers into the library to read or study during the school day. Teachers reading in the library can become role models to students and even other teachers.
- Encourage principals to sponsor "principal seminars" on a regular basis in order to demonstrate to faculty, staff, and students that they live a life of thinking and learning. These seminars could be after school and open to all students who want to wrestle with genuine intellectual topics. These seminars show that the principal or superintendent is committed to lifelong learning and sharing in the Conversation with others.
- Include in everyday announcements some intellectual, artistic, scientific, or physical fitness achievement by a person on the national or world scale. Again, the idea is to draw attention to adult role models.
- Nurture "teacher circles," discussions of either subject matter content or pedagogical technique. Members of the circle might be considered "on call" so that other circle members can contact them about a special problem. There should probably be no money associated with the discussions if the intent is to stimulate and internalize the need for ongoing professional growth.

- Develop motivational schemes for showing students that intelligent and novel questions are as important to the advance of the Great Conversation as is sharing acceptance for a bit of newly justified data.

All stakeholders from students and parents to professional personnel should be encouraged to imagine, share, and implement additional ways of realizing the goal of participation in the Great Conversation. Because the purpose of this book is to explain the moral demands of educational leadership and management, one should expect a disproportionate emphasis on the educational ideals as opposed to all the other legitimate ideals of schooling, training, and socialization. Still, we would be remiss to omit commitments to these other areas, and so we suggest a few nonspecific schooling recommendations as well.

- Ensure civil decorum as people move throughout school and district facilities and on district transport (Anderson, Rungtussanatham, & Schroder, 1994).
- Extracurricular activities should be respected by all, in part because they often lead to participation in civil society more generally.
- Teachers must prepare students to meet high-stakes testing requirements in order to minimize subsequent interference in the students' more comprehensive education.
- Teachers and staff should generally feel free of fear when innovating in order to better serve professional standards.
- Learning is something that must not be forced.
- Ensure safety by any means necessary. Most importantly, students should be socialized to cooperate with others and to look beyond satisfaction of self-interest and fear of those in power.
- Evaluate teachers on more than student scores on standardized tests. Find ways to evaluate them on their ability and commitment to hosting the Great Conversation.
- Identify and focus on a handful of the right numbers for assessing institutional effectiveness. Those numbers may change over time, but identifying the wrong numbers or overwhelming staff and faculty with a demand to address too many numbers only hinders institutional agility and robustness.
- Demonstration of personal integrity and all the other virtues secures organizational integrity and must be especially evident in managing budgets, administering protocols for personnel evaluation, leading broad-based strategic planning, and so on.
- Both sets of recommendations just listed—in addition to the management principles of Deming for institutional effectiveness and the leadership principles of Scheffler and Putnam for educational fulfillment and purpose—show how theory may lead to pragmatically ideal circumstances.

DISCUSSION QUESTIONS

1. Policy emanates from several sources. There are state and federal mandates. There are also principles and traditions of the local, state, and national communities and the worldwide heritage of the profession itself. With all this in mind, how should

school and district policy be developed, and what should be its aim? How should a superintendent go about advising her school board in the making of policy? What ethical considerations should be noted?

2. Psychologist Barry Schwartz (2002) warns repeatedly that behavioristic approaches to education are dangerous to student development. He says behavioral techniques focus solely on external rewards and not on what is good to do. This focus subordinates education to the goal of attaining external reward every time. Moreover, rubrics define what is good enough for the reward, and concerns for true internally desired excellence are neglected. Schwartz and others (Baron, 2005; Berliner & Biddle, 1995; Kohn, 2004) are concerned that such procedures distract from the perennial educational commitment to help each student "reach for the stars" and "become all that he or she can be." Do you think there is any merit to these concerns? How will you develop a responsibly data-driven organization in light of Schwartz's concerns?

3. Israel Scheffler believes the human mind is quite plastic. What happens in schools can dramatically shape how students come to see the world. How should administrators want students to see the world?

4. If the Great Conversation is eliminated from school missions, what is left of those missions?

CASE STUDIES

Case Study 4.1. Holding Teachers Accountable for Test Scores

As a principal, you know you and your staff will be held accountable for student test scores and that these scores will be used to make decisions about the distribution of money to so-called high-performing schools and teachers' merit pay. Because you understand statistics better than many in your district, you argued against the proposed, and eventually approved, district plan. Knowing that there are implicit moral caveats in the plan, do you point them out to your advisory committee and staff and encourage them to reject the funds, or do you distribute the funds according to the district's plan? For example, knowing that the principle of regression to the mean results in weaker students doing better on subsequent administrations of a standardized test and higher-performing students drifting toward the mean, do you give merit pay to the teachers who have larger numbers of weaker students (because their scores rose modestly) and withhold merit pay from teachers with larger numbers of stronger students (because their scores dipped slightly)? Do you accept money for being classified as a high-achieving school, or do you attempt to get the district to spend the money on schools that have great educational challenges and needs? What risks are you willing to take with your supervisors and staff in situations of this nature?

Case Study 4.2. Great Conversation of Humankind Versus Unsatisfactory Test Scores

For the last 2 years, you have been working with administrators, staff, parents, students, consultants, and others to simultaneously raise test scores in your school and place a greater emphasis on getting students more deeply involved in the Great Conversation. Test scores have improved modestly in social studies and literacy but have fallen in mathematics and science. District personnel and many parents tell you that they want more attention given to raising test scores and less attention given to debate clubs, second languages, the arts, civics, and extracurricular activities. They think chess and international affairs clubs should be abolished in favor of after-school tutoring and academic mentoring programs. A number of parents also add that the Conversation emphasis has been too focused on Western ideas and neglects the contributions of people of color, women, and Eastern ideas.

What should your response be? Should you drop your emphasis on the Conversation and focus instead on raising test scores? Should you develop the Conversation more fully to ensure that it is inclusive of the human pursuit of truth? Should you generate an argument for continuing the emphasis on the Great Conversation, appropriately inclusive, while ensuring continued improvement in test scores? What kinds of data and evidence might help you make a cogent argument for continuing to give attention to both realms? Would you suggest a revised or compromise plan for a few years, with a more inclusive look at a broader range of student outcomes and not just test scores? Should you abandon the idea that the two goals can be achieved in today's educational climate?

ACTIVITY

Activity 4.1

Create a slide presentation that you can share with your teachers to show them how to feature and emphasize adult academic achievement. Specifically, draw attention to recent winners of specific Nobel Prizes, Fields Medals, or Templeton Prizes. Show children that intellectual achievement is an admirable and ongoing adult motivation and not just a school-based, childhood activity.

FURTHER READING

Fullan, M. (2003). *The moral imperative of school leadership*. Thousand Oaks, CA: Corwin.

Hare, W. (1993). *What makes a good teacher?* London, ON: Althouse.

Jazzar, M., & Algozzine, B. (2006). *Critical issues in educational leadership*. Boston: Pearson.

Marsch, C., & Willis, G. (2007). *Curriculum: Alternative approaches, ongoing issues* (4th ed.). Upper Saddle River, NJ: Pearson Merrill Prentice Hall.

Maxcy, S. J. (2002). *Ethical school leadership*. Lanham, MD: Scarecrow.

Pellicer, L. O. (2007). *Caring enough to lead: How reflective practice leads to moral leadership* (3rd ed.). Thousand Oaks, CA: Corwin.

CHAPTER 5

The Costs and Benefits of Inclusion

ACCOUNTING: THE META-LANGUAGE OF COSTS AND BENEFITS

Morals are a small subset of human values. Many values have little or nothing to do with morals and are generally regarded as simple projections of subjective preference. For example, having red as a favorite color or strawberry as a favorite flavor usually has nothing at all to do with morals. Favorite colors and tastes are values simpliciter; that is to say, they are simply preferences. Morals are quite different. They are not simply preferences but preferences people typically think they *ought* to hold and to share with others (Fiske, 1992). Paradoxically, people may also feel morally obligated, which means they may feel compelled to act and speak in ways that differ at times from their most immediate desires. All morals may be values, but clearly not all values are morals.

Setting aside for the moment the distinctive characteristics of morals as a subset of values, consider instead how the entire range of public values can be studied. As economists note (and as we discussed in Chapter 3), where we put our money shows much about what we value. Of course, the expenditure of funds doesn't tell the whole story. For instance, morals are about what we say we *ought* to value, not what we in fact value. Moreover, common sense tells us we often do not value what we think we ought to value (Audi, 2005). There are many economic and psychological reasons for this apparent disparity (Ariely, 2008), but here it suffices simply to note that the disparities exist and that they are especially apparent when the values under consideration are morals. Nonetheless, public commitment of wealth does indicate much about the prioritized importance of public values.

In an extraordinarily insightful book titled *The Myth of Ownership,* Liam Murphy and Thomas Nagel (2003) explain, in an analogous manner consistent with the aforementioned theme, that there is no element of tax law that does not rest on a foundation of moral commitment. Murphy and Nagel explain how all aspects of ownership and property emerge from the nature of community and its foundational moral architecture. Most notably, they make it clear that a society's distribution of wealth is the most poignant and practical reflection of its *immediate* ideals. For example, how much a country values education as a public good can be determined by how much of the taxable wealth is redistributed for that purpose. Analogously, at the local level the distribution of wealth within a district's schools similarly reflects much about community understanding of educational and schooling purpose. In short, the details revealed in accounting audit sheets are the meta-language of institutional and community commitment to their moral ideals and other values. We will illustrate Murphy and Nagel's more general point by reviewing an incident of wealth redistribution that occurred in a single high school. In addition to being simple and indicative of situations the reader is likely to encounter, the example will also reveal something about leadership style and highlight moral concepts especially important in the ideal practice of educational leadership. In short, the example sets out the pragmatic necessity of addressing questions such as "What do we really value?" and "What *should* we value?" "How should we address and honor personal, professional, and other shared moral principles and values?"

This example was described to us by the principal himself. Throughout his discussion of the situation he did not realize that there were moral issues involved until we pointed out to him that leadership style and shared vision are matters of morally responsive relationships and compatible ideals, respectively. He was a new principal at a large high school. He eliminated department-based budgeting shortly after assuming office. He claimed that he was trying to secure a better cost–benefit profile for the entire school. Critics accused him of micromanaging, paternalism, and demeaning the professionalism of departmental staffs. On the other hand, the budget revealed in dollars and cents that the current system led to a disparity of wealth between departments. Some departments were accumulating inventory, whereas others were becoming increasingly impoverished. The new principal thought the disparities reflected an ongoing unfairness in the process of wealth distribution and a failure to fund appropriately all that the school claimed to value. Critics complained that even if there were grounds for the principal's concerns, he did things the wrong way. (Note that the grounds acknowledged here clearly are moral grounds, as Murphy and Nagel might predict.) Supporters argued that for the first time in years there would be a more equitable distribution of wealth and that is sufficient to trump any lapse in leadership style. The issue is one of social justice and nothing more. But are things really that simple in this case?

A PRACTICAL ASSIGNMENT

What advice would you offer the new principal about changing budgetary responsibilities if he asked? Would your advice focus more on operational efficiency, leadership style, stabilizing moral architecture, or perhaps some combination of the three?

Pause to think about this example for a moment. At least five major moral challenges are evident in this situation. What appeared initially as nothing more than a simple change in accounting procedure and a change of administrative style shortly revealed itself as a challenge to democratically based moral architecture and competency in addressing openly the question, "What should we value?" In retrospect, to use the technical language of moral analysis, the animating source of this crisis centers on the moral issues of paternalism, educational and schooling purpose, and autonomy. These moral concepts must be drawn on to answer the context-based question, "What higher-order principles *should* we value?" Presumably we must at the very least value an equitable distribution of wealth, but the issue of equitableness is a richly textured moral concept for even the most morally alert and professional administrator to consider. To clarify the **equity** issues involved, the administrator must reflect a whole range of moral commitments.

The principal in this case acted paternalistically. But he did so on behalf of the students and faculty he believed were underserved. Presumably, he saw his decision as direct and to the point, distributing wealth in accord with his idea of what we should value in the school. We will stipulate that he was neither capricious nor self-serving.

Sometimes an administrator must act courageously and alone on behalf of others, especially minority populations of all types, particularly those most unempowered in a given situation. Because the moral rightness of the redistribution is not at issue, all that is left is the complaint that the administrator's manner of redistribution showed too little respect for the input of others. In short, critics charge, he acted in an inexcusably authoritarian way.

As we have already noted, administrators must at times act alone on behalf of others. At the same time, acting in authoritarian fashion when the circumstances do not justify the need to act unilaterally leads to the development of a type of moral architecture most administrators probably would rather avoid. It is in the nature of the Great Conversation to be inclusive, to value and develop the autonomy of others. Consequently, an educational leader should not act paternalistically as a matter of administrative style but rather only when forced to do so by professional and moral obligation. Even then, however, unilateral action need not be pursued in a manner that undermines a democratic institution's moral architecture. The set of five competing moral concerns—respect for others, developing autonomy, fairness, democratic cooperation, and equity—merge as a single foundational matter and not as a mere list of issues that can be addressed one at a time. To address a set of competing moral concerns requires that an administrator have not just a rule at hand but rather an entire moral theory in order to bring all relevant considerations together. Moreover, the institutional moral architecture under which disparate parties are operating must have sufficient elevation in order to afford perspective to all competing stakeholders. *Sufficient elevation* is the term we use for principles, ideals, and virtues that in the eyes of all involved supersede any immediate disputes and temper the emotional intensity of those who are at odds with one another. To be sufficient, the elevation must allow competing claims to be viewed at some remove, that is, in light of some higher-order principle, ideal, or virtue that stakeholders agree should always moderate how social engagement should proceed within the organization. Furthermore, the administrator's deference to such principles, ideals, and virtues not only models for others how contentious decisions should be addressed but also can further elevate the institution's moral architecture by furthering such tradition. The more stakeholders recognize and adopt such lofty traditions, the easier managing dissent becomes. In contrast, if dissent is handled badly, respect for operating under higher ideals and principles will decline, deflating the architecture more generally. As the architecture deflates, future challenges become more difficult to overcome as a consequence of the residual loss of stakeholder respect and support for previously esteemed principles, ideals, and other decision-making referents. In short, decisions and procedures of the moment are more than transiently relevant to the institution's destiny. Those that honor ideals raise cooperative standards and expectations for future collaborative engagement. Those that dishonor ideals lower expectations for future collaborations and lower standards to everyone just getting by or just following along.

When grounds for shared moral commitment are made explicitly clear and further developed in an organization through day-to-day operations, a robust moral architecture emerges that affords organizational resiliency over the long haul. With this in mind, the administrator should see each moment of potential turmoil as an occasion to lift the institution's moral architecture to new heights, reflecting the realization of ever more lofty ideals.

A PHILOSOPHICAL QUESTION

Whether an administrator is seen as paternalistic, authoritarian, or democratic has ramifications for the direction of an evolving moral architecture. To what lengths should administrators go to narrow any gap between staff perceptions and administrative intentions in matters particular to moral commitments? How do staff perceptions and administrative action affect the organization's evolving moral architecture?

EDUCATION FOR INCLUSION

The preceding case shows just how challenging it can be to acknowledge respect for the autonomy of others and yet still secure equity in meeting the needs of all. Autonomy, paternalism, and equity seemingly lead to conflicts of duty whenever the development of one is pursued to excess and inevitably at the expense of the others.

Achieving the right balance in such matters is what one might call the general challenge of inclusion. By contrast, what we shall call the *specific* or the *technical* challenge of inclusion begins with the focus on the needs of special populations. For many people, their first encounter with a clearly articulated sense of the challenge of inclusion began through awareness of the special or technical challenge of inclusion. For instance, in the United States a historic moment involved passing legislation, PL 94-142. Attention to the specific challenge of inclusion is an ongoing affair with a plethora of judicial decisions accumulating around the successors of PL 94-142, the Individuals with Disabilities Education Act of 1990 (IDEA) and the Individuals with Disabilities Education Improvement Act of 2004 (**IDEIA**). This series of legislation and accompanying court cases break new ground in education in ways akin to *Brown v. Topeka Board of Education,* the Civil Rights Act of 1964, and subsequent legislation. Each of these initiatives represents an expensive national undertaking showing specific commitments of value on the nation's audit sheets. More importantly, each represents an extension of a more general value, or what we have called the general challenge of inclusion. To couch the general challenge of inclusion in terms already familiar to the reader, think of inclusion grandly as one of the defining elements in the Great Conversation. *Inclusion* in this sense means inviting everyone into the shared quest for truth and understanding. Inclusion in this sense honors the most important goals of multiculturalism and the goals of PL 94-142 and other special population initiatives simultaneously. Each initiative is about bringing together an ever wider body of voices to share in the Great Conversation. And as noted several times previously, this is a central meaning of education: the open, shared search for truth and understanding. Education is about bringing together minds. Education brings together people not so much to ensure everyone is of one mind (such concerns are more germane to schooling and training initiatives) but to ensure that minds are engaged interactively (Lipman, 2003).

Exclusions from the Conversation were numerous in the past (Gardara & Contreras, 2009). Things are now better, but few would say educators have fulfilled their professional ambitions in this area of human betterment. The costs to humanity of any continued failure to address the general challenge of inclusion are enormous. Perhaps the costs are higher now because the world is increasingly becoming something of a global village (Barry, 2001). Because humans can no longer ignore one another, there is a desperate need to use all the intellectual resources available to the species. Human talent squandered in the past can no longer be neglected (Snyder, 1994). For example, racial exclusion may have prevented the great American inventor Booker T. Washington from contributing even more to the developing technological society. Gender exclusion may have partially silenced Nobel-winning geneticist Barbara McClintock, ethnically exclusionary practices may have largely silenced Nobel laureates Albert Einstein and Ramon y Cajal for a time, and religious exclusion may have appreciably silenced atheist Charles Darwin or the devout Sir Isaac Newton. It is only by good fortune—and courage—that physical handicaps, race, gender, ethnicity, and religious exclusionary practices did not completely silence any of these voices, but these people are more likely to be the exceptions rather than the rule.

A REALITY CHECK

Inclusion questions often take on a profound local flavor. What inclusion issues in your area are likely to be the most challenging over the next 5–10 years? Have the challenges been "officially" identified? What steps and missteps have been made in addressing them? Boards often have legal counsel present during their deliberations. How would districts benefit from counsel by professional ethicists, as hospitals often do?

Although discussing the details of the general challenge of inclusion is beyond the scope of this chapter, it is important to sketch the broader parameters of the general challenge. For example, will inclusion apply to generational populations as fully as genders, races, and ethnicities? Will inclusion recognize the voice of religious and nonreligious alike, gays and straights, evolutionists and design theorists, strict constructionists and critical theorists, communists and capitalists? Clearly, the general challenge of inclusion in the Great Conversation is an unending responsibility for schools and districts. This task is not an easy

Figure 5.1 What Policies and Practices Will Help Address the General Challenge of Inclusion as Districts and Schools Involve Multiple Voices in Informed Decision Making?

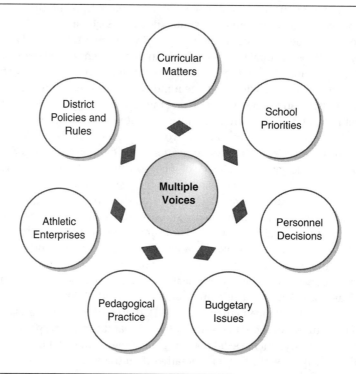

one given the previous record of exclusionary policies and practices characterizing schools and society. If things are to change productively, then institutional moral architectures must continue to evolve in order to foster the full development of the Great Conversation. Figure 5.1 illustrates some of the complexities of this task for site-driven school management and leadership.

One of the most widespread and challenging general inclusion concerns at present is meeting the educational needs of students whose primary languages differ from the majority's. Strides seem to have been made in some areas; for example, making more Spanish-based courses available to students has been an important step forward, but think of the host of languages represented by all those who immigrate to this country. The conscientious educational administrator must make the case to all stakeholders that sometimes it costs disproportionately more to bring people from diverse and special populations into the Great Conversation. Support for inclusion in the Conversation is an inherent professional ideal that no educator can ignore.

Fairness is a foundational principle many of the theorists discussed in Chapter 2 acknowledge animates surface-level moral issues. The notion of fairness is often drawn on to arbitrate between competing claims of groups seeking full access into the Great Conversation. There are times when the most unfair thing one can do is treat everyone as equal. For example, it is one thing to say everyone is welcome to attend a community college, but without ramps and other accommodations for special populations they are as a de facto matter precluded from full access.

The obligation to ensure fairness as opposed to mere equality is much more challenging and often places the administrator at risk of criticism for **favoritism** or for being *too* paternalistic. "Everyone gets the same treatment" is not a principle of fairness. It is a principle of equality and nothing more. Equality is somewhat uncomplicated. By contrast, fairness can be complex and difficult to apply. Fairness sometimes requires that some people be treated differently from others. However, when treating people differently the goal should always be to ensure fairness and to optimize the range of participant inclusion. In the end, getting it right and treating all fairly is something morally alert thinkers must focus on even when the majority of stakeholders may lobby for mere equality of treatment instead.

Every administrator ought to know that there is a host of legislation and court renderings making inclusion (in the technical sense of IDEIA) a very challenging concern for administrators. More than half of all litigation and arbitration involving schools is associated with IDEIA matters (Zirkel, 2002). An earnest and responsible administrator may try to become knowledgeable about each little detail of the law. But one should ask, "For what purpose?" There is no way to nail down every detail of relevant law, and besides, the laws of inclusion are in flux. And what if one could become knowledgeable about every detail of case law involving inclusion in the technical sense. Would that make a person a more effective administrator or just better at crawling under a barbed wire fence of legalities hoping to save a few dollars or otherwise avoid bothersome legal inconveniences?

Professionally, goals of inclusion should be at the heart of every administrator because such goals are also at the heart of the Great Conversation. The law shouldn't be necessary as a means to force administrators to do the right thing in such cases. First and foremost, the most professional administrators should be naturally inclined to act in the spirit of least restrictive environments and find in the law guidance on points not to overlook. In cases of IDEIA or any other issue of inclusion, the principle of fairness, interpreted as extending opportunities to those compromised by the misfortunes of nature or society, should nearly always be the administrator's guide.

Pragmatic considerations alone counsel that proactive leadership do more than contrive maneuvers to avoid inclusion costs. Public institutions are meant by law to be open and responsive, which is to say they are meant to be inclusive and fair in every way. Any attempt to avoid inclusion costs could lead to much more costly litigation (Zirkel, 2006). However, more important is the fact that inclusion in every way is part and parcel of the professional educator's moral ethos.

RESPECT FOR PERSONS AND THE ASSAULT ON INCLUSION: BULLYING, SEXUAL HARASSMENT, SEX EDUCATION, AND RELIGIOUS AND ETHNIC TOLERANCE

Many forces are working against the general challenge of inclusion in the public schools. These forces are not just those of political division and budgetary constraint. Bullies and other sources of harassment also lead to exclusion of some students, faculty, and staff in the more subtle arena of daily school activity.

Once upon a time **bullying** was largely neglected as simply a matter of leadership style when it occurred among adults (bossiness) and more often than not even when it occurred among students ("kids will be kids"). Certainly on moral grounds and in the face of recent school tragedies, bullying must be recognized as both wrong and potentially costly to the district whenever and wherever it occurs, at any level of district life. Ignoring bullying in any form these days is reckless and irresponsible on the part of administrators.

CLARIFYING THE CONCEPT

Can you think of an example of administrator or staff bullying that has occurred in your school or district? How was it addressed? What related problems have subsequently occurred? When parents, unions, students, and even some politicians become a source of bullying, how should the administrator handle matters?

It is not much of a stretch to imagine a litigant claiming he dropped out of school because school authorities failed to protect him from ubiquitous bullying and that he suffered grave economic and psychological difficulty as a consequence. It is not much of a stretch that juries may become increasingly sympathetic to such claims as they hear more news reports about the harm caused children from others' violent bullying. And under the pressure of high-stakes testing one can also imagine teachers removed from the classroom for poor performance filing suit against an administrator who, they claim, bullied them into unproductive practices, leading to lower test scores on the part of their students. These potential situations may be exacerbated even further in the future by the fact that bullying will have increasingly more venues than it did 50 years ago (Wilder, 2007). For example, technology has made it possible to stalk a victim almost continuously without even being in the victim's immediate vicinity. Frightening threats can be made anonymously, and reputations can be destroyed by bullies who have mastered the Internet. And what of district liability if school hardware is used to initiate threats, slander, and libel and otherwise bully innocents?

Bullying of any kind contaminates moral architecture. And, as noted earlier, bullying isn't limited to the actions of schoolyard thugs. Wherever bullying is tolerated and at whatever level, it alters the covering etiquette and even the very scaffolding of the institution's moral architecture. The main reason bullying is so intolerable is that it aims at the destruction of another person's self-respect and that person's exercise of autonomy. In the educational community, bullying is tantamount to pushing the victim away from participation in the Conversation. In short, bullying is an exclusionary activity, and as such it stands in absolute opposition to the inclusive nature of the Great Conversation.

The more timid among those bullied may drift from institutional participation, but some may initiate lawsuits or form unions or other interest groups, all in an effort to erode the exclusionary forces they think are keeping their voices from being heard by those who are bullying them. Bullying destroys the elevation of moral architecture. Bullying leads toward "might makes right" type of thinking. As its scaffolding crumbles under the pressure imposed by acts of bullying, the covering etiquette of the institution's moral architecture dissolves, and then its superstructure begins wearing away as well. Eventually, something approaching a Hobbesian state of nature emerges. Recall that in a Hobbesian state of nature each person is emotionally and socially isolated from each other person and all feel abandoned, left to fend for themselves. The district or school approaching a Hobbesian state of general disruption is in great peril, and to varying degrees so are many of its stakeholders, both as groups and as individuals.

Harassment is another tactic by which some people distract others from full participation in an organization and from participation in the Great Conversation. Although harassment (other than sexual harassment) is often seen as a lesser offense because it aims only intermittently at distracting others from the exercise of autonomy, over the long run recurring harassment can separate the victim from the organization or the Conversation as completely as the more acute experience of being bullied.

Nothing distinguishes humans, some claim (Englehardt, 1986), more from other animals than the exercise of autonomy. Autonomy realized is the crown jewel of the human spirit. Whether in the classroom or the superintendency, leaders should work to inspire the exercise of autonomy in others. Each person who finds fulfillment through autonomy is more likely to contribute to the Great Conversation, and each contribution is a benefaction to nearly all others. Clearly autonomy and a willingness to accept the general challenge of inclusion go hand in hand.

A REFLECTIVE BREAK

Respecting the autonomy of staff and students without creating an environment of "anything goes" is sometimes challenging. What ethical principles or virtues are important to understand and practice in order to nurture autonomous staff and students?

The protection of others' autonomy or developing autonomy in the case of students is a prima facie duty of administrators and their districts. The duty to protect autonomy is entailed by the concept of the Great Conversation and its focus on the general challenge of inclusion. Consequently, each educator has a profession-defining duty to protect and enhance the autonomy of others.

The protection of autonomy, though always a priority for administrators, is not always easy to defend, much less develop in others (Clark & Mills, 1979). As explained in Chapter 3, administrators may at times be duty bound to act unilaterally and even paternalistically. In each case, this may mean limiting the autonomous behavior of others, especially when allowing such behavior might lead to exploitation and inequity. In short, an administrator may be duty bound at times to abort the protection of autonomy out of genuine and responsible compassion for others. For example, a teacher who has a drug crisis caused by the interaction of prescribed drugs for epilepsy and over-the-counter drugs for sinus congestion may need to be removed from the classroom for a few hours for both his and the students' protection, although it is contrary to the teacher's protestations. Failure to act unilaterally and promptly in such an unusual case would be a grave moral error from the perspective of nearly every moral theory. Such neglect would also expose the administrator and the district to possible litigation if anyone in the classroom were harmed as a result of the teacher's condition. In sharp contrast, the boss who acts unilaterally and abruptly as a matter of administrative style (again, bossiness) is guilty of paternalistic abuse and assaults proper stakeholder autonomy.

In so many ways, the First Amendment of the U.S. Constitution (and similar laws in other nations) can be thought of as the autonomy amendment. The First Amendment protects all sorts of self-expression. In the school the evolving range of self-expression for students and staff has become a matter of considerable legal activity. Especially since *Tinker v. Des Moines* (393 U.S. 503, 1969), when the U.S. Supreme Court famously declared that students don't leave their rights on the schoolhouse steps, administrators have had to keep guessing where in loco parentis (the paternalistic expectation that schools will act in place of parents) ends and the students' established rights begin. For example, court cases have sustained an African American student's right to wear a hat indoors to celebrate her cultural heritage even when such apparel violates the school's formally articulated dress code (*Isaacs ex. rel. Isaacs v. Board of Education of Howard County,* 40 F. Supp.2d 335 [Md. 1999]). In general, however, the courts have upheld dress codes for both students and teachers, denying that the obvious limitation on autonomy is a significant violation of the Constitution's guarantee of self-expression (*Long v. Board of Education of Jefferson County,* 121 F. Supp.2d 621 [Ky. 2000] aff'd, 2001 U.S. App.Lexus 18103 [6th Cir. 2001]; *East Hartford Education Association v. Board of Education of East Hartford,* U.S. 562 F.2d 838 [1977]). Neither autonomy nor paternalistic responsibilities (in loco parentis) are given free rein by the courts in adjudicating appropriate administrative action of any kind. Even student, faculty, and staff self-expressions of affection for the divine are never fully free of limitations. Court cases such as *Epperson v. Arkansas* (393 U.S. 97, 1968) and *Santa Fe v. Doe* (530 U.S. 290, 2000) increasingly limited the autonomy of self-expression in cases of public prayer in order to be sensitive toward those offended by such display (Nussbaum, 2008).

Any effort to keep up with the courts' drift in these turbulent legalistic seas may seem overwhelming. More often than not the court's reasoning in most jurisdictions has exhibited great common sense, but that does not mean that the law has become firm or that trends are easily detected. Consequently, there is good reason for administrative feelings of unsettledness (Nussbaum, 2008). The best way to navigate the perils of unexpected judicial interference in a school or district is to recognize that what the courts intend most, generally speaking, is that *no harm* is done to those placed under the school's charge (Wagner & Benavente, 2008). In this, the courts and the good administrator should be of one mind. After all, the kind of harm anticipated throughout this section of the chapter is the harm of excluding people from autonomous participation in the Great Conversation. Avoidance of this harm should serve as a dependable guiding light for administrative practitioners.

CONFLICTS OF DUTY

In Chapter 3 we noted that education properly speaking is not simply about learning. There exists a fundamental distinction between learning simpliciter and learning tasks relevant to education. For example, we may say that a stomach *learns* to increase production of certain enzymes needed to digest acidic liquids if it has recently become habituated to the daily onslaught of highly concentrated lemon juice. The learned response to sharply increase enzyme production with the first sip of lemon juice on subsequent occasions is truly an instance of learning. Perhaps to some behaviorists all learning is of this fundamental sort. However, for most psychologists (Churchland, 1995) and for almost all visionary thinkers about education throughout history, the learning that serves as the ideal of education is substantively different from organ or simple biochemical responsiveness.

The learning that is the focus of education leads to things that somehow improve human existence. A skeptical reader may protest that learning that prime numbers seem to go on forever bakes no bread and so is of no practical import to human betterment. Consequently, either such learning is out of place in the schools or, the critic may charge, we need a broader definition of what learning is educationally valuable learning. Clearly, there is a benefit to be had from extended linguistic analysis of the term *education*. More must be said to sustain philosophically the claim that learning esoteric truths about prime numbers or cosmic subatomic entanglement is a worthy end in itself. Indeed, such analysis has taken place intermittently throughout human history (Peters, 1983). For our part we will skirt the challenge to further elaborate on an airtight, linguistically complete analysis of the term *educationally valuable learning*. Such analysis is not critical to the pressing fact of the moment, namely that conflicts of duty dealing with professional commitments to education will confront the administrator at every level.

Policy must at times prioritize the importance of various learning tasks. Policy that prioritizes learning tasks is every bit a moral prescription as is policy prescribing taxation objectives and practices. The seriousness that stakeholders exhibit when prioritizing reflects stakeholder intuition that there is a profound sense in which one can get such matters wrong. Intuitively at least, more seems at stake than the simple aggregation of individual, subjective preferences. Not just anything goes in prioritizing learning tasks or taxation objectives.

Unfortunately, no aggregation of data can ever bridge the gap to become a recommendation from what simply happens to be the case to what ought to be the case in the quest for human betterment (Hare, 2000; Hume, 1739/2000; Murphy & Nagel, 2003). David Berliner (2005) makes this explicitly clear in describing recent attempts to describe and then assess teacher quality.

Prioritizing learning tasks is something that can be done well or not so well. Prioritizing can eventuate in conflicts of duty, not just differences of subjective preference. To prioritize well and in the near absence of subjective preference requires great administrative self-discipline, but it can be done. For instance, administrators are often asked to consider what does more for students: learning tasks aimed at aesthetic development, learning tasks aimed at discrediting a particular political party, or learning tasks aimed at learning the function of, say, the periodic table? Things may look pretty subjective at first glance. Should society's benefit determine priority? If so, then what benefits society the most: appreciation of beauty, political savvy, or taxonomic arrangements of atomic elements?

Should what's most likely to be on a standardized test determine priority? Should what develops student autonomy determine priority? In addition, no matter how one answers questions such as these, interpreting answers in the practical exercise of assigning priorities to the sets of learning tasks under consideration is another demanding and complex challenge.

When done well, prioritizing learning tasks should lead away from conspicuous error and toward intellectual insight (Lynch, 2004), social justice, and human betterment (Scheffler, 1985). Of course, sizing up what counts as intellectual insight, social justice, or human betterment is a critical meta-ethical task to be completed before evaluating the success of any prioritizing procedure. And even when all goes well, some doubt about the right-mindedness of priorities may still remain (Lynch, 2004; Tiberius, 2008).

Morally upright administrators will seldom have a sense of absolute certainty when prioritizing learning tasks. What matters most in all such perplexing situations is that administrators truly recognize the seriousness of the task and the difficulty of the challenge and remain resolute in not settling for good enough when excellence in service to others should be the educational leader's driving motivation.

A PHILOSOPHICAL QUESTION

Friedrich Nietzsche is what is called a moral nihilist. A nihilist believes there is no meaning to moral discourse. For him all of morality is benchmarked by the power that lies behind this or that rule. For Nietzsche morals lie only at the surface, and there is no deep structure. How should schools respond to the prospect of moral nihilism creeping into their moral architecture? What kind of moral architecture is evident in schools that shy away from asking and answering questions pertaining to what ethics should drive school and district life?

Perhaps it was the timid administrator Lao Tzu had in mind when he had the master in his tale admonish the young student obsessed with surface-level rules, "You don't understand the point of morality." Putting a more Western spin on these same words of caution, Blaise Pascal declared in the 17th century, "The heart knows what the mind knows not." In short, in every apparent or potential conflict of duty, theory and intuition must be brought into equilibrium to satisfy the conscientious administrator's needs in her quest to get things right. More importantly, the administrator cannot settle for not trying to get things right.

EDUCATION, EVALUATION, AND FUNDING: PUTTING MONEY WHERE IT BELONGS

As noted at the beginning of this chapter, accounting ledgers track how a society distributes wealth. In this sense accounting practices serves as a meta-language for what a district or school values. The ledger is not a sociological aggregation of what individuals say they value or think they ought to value. The ledger may reflect no one's values specifically, but there can be no denying that the ledger stands as resolute testimony to the district or school's tangible commitments.

Ideally planning should drive budgeting, and ideally professional and moral commitments should drive planning. But such ideals are often limited to theorizing. In practice, substantial budgetary commitments reflect determinations made in different ways by people separate from both school and district. Nonetheless, once a record of value is determined, common sense dictates that administrators track whether their school and district are getting their money's worth. Administrators must identify measurement criteria that accurately reflect whether institutional efforts are succeeding. If the administrator identifies the wrong numbers, she will never know whether she and those she represents are truly getting what they are paying for; moreover, even the right numbers are likely to change over time, and so an eye to continuous improvement must be maintained.

Assessment is about measuring and counting observables. Evaluation, more broadly speaking, focuses on making sense of progress toward what is valued. As Michael Scriven (1976) explains, evaluation always begins with an act of valuing. Once what is valued is specified in terms of budgetary commitments, organizational assessments and evaluation procedures can be more usefully employed for purposes of ongoing planning.

QUESTIONING THE AUTHORS ?

In business some theorists talk about "value-added" activities. These activities cannot be directly measured by improvement in the bottom line but nonetheless are thought valuable because they help secure customer commitment to the organization. Would such a concept make sense in education? Who are the customers in education, and what do they value? What should the customers of education value? Should value-added commitments be supported by school or district budgetary commitments? What are examples of such educationally based value-added commitments, and how should they be evaluated (if at all)? Must everything that is legitimately valued in education be assessed and evaluated using only quantitative data? (See Case A.4 in Appendix A.)

District ledgers tell very specific things about what is valued in the district. For example, how much money is spent on instruction as opposed to athletics or monitoring personnel reveals which is valued more: instruction, athletics, or monitoring personnel. Evaluation and assessment should be tied proportionately to what is valued. However, for better or worse, this is not always the case. In actual practice, more time may be spent on assessing matters that are easy to assess rather than on matters difficult to assess, even when the latter matters are more critical to evaluating the educational mission of school and district. Disparities of purpose do not end with assessment practices alone. Again, in actual practice, it is often the case that data collected are subject to only a cursory evaluation before consequences are distributed and further planning ensues (Ariely, 2008). All this makes it ever more difficult for matching together all that should be valued with what is budgeted, assessed, evaluated, and planned for each year.

The story of each district's values begins with its ledger sheets. Because there are as many different stories as there are ledgers, we will focus in more general terms on what big purposes educational institutions are meant to serve. For example, education presumably should be of central importance to educational institutions. This may sound almost too trivial to mention, but think for a moment of all the totalitarian regimes such as Nazi Germany, Stalin's Russia, and Pol Pot's Cambodia. Recall the educational institutions in those states,

> ## — A GROUP DISCUSSION —
>
> If learning to read, write, and think helps make students "better people," shouldn't how it makes them better people be evaluated? If learning to be fair, responsible, caring, and tolerant makes "better people," shouldn't there be some effort to assess and evaluate just how much better people can become? If learning to respect people, the rights of others, and their autonomy makes people "better," then shouldn't there also be assessments and evaluations of just how much better people are becoming? How would you tie all these skills, attitudes, and dispositions together in a comprehensive notion of human betterment? Do we assess and value what is most important, or do we assess and evaluate simply what is easiest or most convenient to evaluate?

and you will immediately recognize that they had far too little to do with education and far too much to do with a strictly and morally corrupt schooling focus. What they valued was evident, and it was not education as traditionally conceived.

Whereas professional educators presumably know the difference between education and schooling, many stakeholders responsible for funding schools may not have such a clear understanding of the distinction. Consequently, to the extent that district funding is channeled in part by external stakeholders, allocations may reflect stakeholder clout as much as or more than conscientious budgeting on the part of an able educational administrator. What is valued by the schools is determined largely by who controls the budget; consequently, what is valued may drift far afield from the purposes of education, reflecting the realities of monetary control.

The term *education* denotes (as well as connotes) an ideal of human achievement (Lipman, 2003). Based on the four corners of educational purpose, the idea of education as the Great Conversation is clearly a moral challenge to improve the human condition. The very idea that education itself may be improved through evaluation, assessment, and planning is a pragmatically misleading concept. Education, properly understood, cannot be improved. It is in itself an ideal, not a means to some other end (Peters, 1983). Only our *efforts* to educate can be made more proficient through assessment, evaluation, and a commitment to continuous improvement of effort.

Education is not simply an assortment of things that happen to go on in schools. This is no mere semantic point. There is real consequence that follows from recognizing education as an ideal and recognizing schools as the public's vehicle for bringing people into the Great Conversation. There is real consequence to balancing such concerns against legitimate schooling concerns for which public schooling is responsible as well.

When all is said and done, every district ought to be able to look at its district ledger and see that what is valued most is reflected in its district budget.

WHAT DOES IT MEAN TO ASSESS EDUCATION?

We can—and should—assess elements of *educational practice*. The guide to assessment should not be based on the ease of extracting a quantitative data base (Nichols, Glass, &

Berliner, 2006). Instead, assessment should be based on what truly shows educator progress in bringing students ever more deeply into the Great Conversation. This may mean that at times assessment and evaluation practices may have to be based on indirect data and go beyond the simple measurement of information retained by students. Student persistence in following a line of inquiry must also matter and be measured. Student commitment to investigate a subject further without reward or punishment should also be measured and evaluated again, however indirectly. Student regard for fellow participants sharing in the quest for truth must be assessed and measured. Educational progress cannot be responsibly measured by taking merely one or two easily assessed traits from one corner of educational purpose and drawing an inference about the state of education generally (Nichols & Berliner, 2005). Finally, comprehensive measurement and evaluation of educational progress must always be managed with a degree of tentativeness because the possibility of error consequent on indirect measurement will always exist in bringing data together (Darling-Hammond & Snyder, 2000). Nonetheless, it is more important to increase the likelihood of getting things right than making it look *as if* one is getting it right. Presumably every conscientious administrator would agree with such dictum regardless of his or her underlying commitment to one or another moral theory.

Ordinarily people are likely to say that a Nobel-winning physicist is testimony to the effectiveness of his or her previous educational experience. If the physicist subsequently spent her life creating devastating weaponry, some might be less inclined to praise the effectiveness of that education. However, there may be conceptual confusion lurking about in such evaluation. The physicists' knowledge of physics may indeed stand as relevant testimony in favor of high-quality education, but the educational institutions that prepared the physicist also had certain schooling commitments. One of those schooling commitments may have been to prepare students to be defense-minded, and so the physicist's accomplishments score as a success on two levels. However, both of these judgments may also reflect a failure to grasp fully the idea of education as the embodiment of an ongoing ideal and not merely a record of transient accomplishment. A distinction between training (an aspect of schooling) and education might be illuminating in order to avoid such misconceptions.

Nobel Prize–winning physicists are clearly well trained in physics. Such training is something that can be assessed easily. Moreover, schools are certainly the right place to provide for such training. But being well trained is clearly not the same as being well educated, and schools must address student education as well as provide training and other developmental services. Training wedded to education should have caused the physicist to ask many questions about physics along the way, but it should also prompt the physicist to consider what use might be made of advances in physics. For significant involvement in the Great Conversation students must eventually attain not only a depth of *valuable* knowledge and understanding but also some breadth of knowledge and understanding. They must become more than well-trained technological assets in a community's defense or economy; in addition, they must embrace an ongoing commitment to participate in some aspect of the Conversation for the rest of their lives. This is not to say that physicists working on weaponry are not educated. They may be. But whether they are is a separate question from whether they are well trained or whether their education came up short, limiting some corner of educational purpose.

A PRACTICAL ASSIGNMENT

Schooling practices lead to much that is good in nearly every society. Schooling practices can also distract from the good inherent in participation in the Great Conversation. At what point should the administrator subordinate schooling interests to education? At what point should educational interests be subordinated to legitimate schooling interests?

What counts as valuable knowledge or as ongoing commitment to participate in the Conversation is intentionally left undefined here because such definitions are tangential to the immediate point at hand: Training and other schooling tasks are easily assessed, whereas the fruits of education are not so easily assessed and evaluated. Nonetheless, both schooling and education must be assessed and evaluated regardless of how challenging it may be to do so.

Deming (2000) warned that those responsible for product output will inevitably find clever and inventive ways to deliver the numbers as asked. This is as true in the schools as anywhere else. In the current social milieu we find schools focusing on an increasingly narrow range of subject matter and on an increasingly narrow range of students, namely those most at risk for failing a high-stakes, standardized test. Standardized tests typically emphasize passive recollection and little more. The administrator who lets high-stakes testing drive the curriculum abandons a more professional concern for assessing, evaluating, and planning polices conducive to educational development of students (Schmoker & Wilson, 2005).

Focusing on what is easily assessed leads to an overemphasis on behavioral approaches to learning (Townsend, 1995). Behavioral models limit attention to what is discrete and can be summarily aggregated. Whether behavioral models do or do not produce the best or most important assessments and evaluations is a question too seldom asked (Baron, 2005).

Barry Schwartz (2002) claims that behavioristic approaches to learning are inherently damaging to students because they lead students and teachers to view learning as simply right output in the right context. In addition, because the reward is tied to merely producing the expected output under the right circumstances, subjects of behavioral models learn to aim at what is good enough to be rewarded and nothing more. Finally, according to Schwartz, behavioral approaches make the reward what students seek and learning tasks a mere tax that must be suffered to achieve what is truly rewarding. Behaviorism mitigates against developing dispositions, skills, and attitudes that accompany learning and participation in the Conversation as an end in itself (Sternberg, 1997, 2003). In other words, some skills and dispositions associated with educational purpose (e.g., search for truth) and nearly all educationally central attitudes and dispositions (e.g., quest for excellence and demands for justification, respectively) are neglected when attention settles on good-enough behavioral output required to secure a reward beyond education (Baron, 2005). At best, within the behavioral paradigm only one and maybe two corners of educational purpose are addressed adequately. At best behaviorism teaches that learning is only of instrumental value and that good things to have are separate from educationally valuable learning tasks.

To illustrate Schwartz's point, recall that before 1962, Catholics went to masses wherein the liturgy was in Latin. A Catholic may have known both how and when to say a certain Latin phrase and therefore probably would pass most behavioral criteria for knowing the Latin of the mass. Nonetheless, most Catholics of that time report not having any idea what the words meant; they just knew how and when to say the words. As Schwartz would point out, these Catholics met standard behavioral criteria for learning. Yet these very Catholics admit that they didn't understand what they were saying, and all too often when they didn't have to go to mass, they found little reason to do so because they understood so little of the ritual.

Educationally valuable learning should lead to understanding and not just the acquisition of information (Baron, 2005; Lipman, 2003). It is certainly easy to assess and evaluate information stored in a file cabinet, but file cabinets do not engage one another. A file cabinet model of learning success does not lead to active student inclusion in the Great Conversation. Schwartz is not alone. Other notable psychologists, such as David Myers (2005), Martin P. Seligman (1996), and Howard Gardner (1993), also warn against the dangers of behavioristic approaches to evaluating learning for reasons similar to those mentioned earlier. Despite such expressions of concern from some of the nation's leading learning theorists, the country's move to high-stakes testing regimens has rejuvenated behavioral distractions from educational purpose. Behaviorism's sole value seems to be its ease of assessment and reliance on simplistic reward structures (Ariely, 2008).

When funding is tied to what can be easily assessed rather than to what is most important in education (admittedly a morally complex value decision), it is tempting to imagine school performance drifting from a focus on education to a focus, by employees at least, on generating data and securing rewards and continued employment (Nichols & Berliner, 2005). More noble causes such as the well-being of students can fade in importance when funding and evaluation send a different message, deconstructing what really counts as important (Amrein & Berliner, 2003; Darling-Hammond, French, & Garcia-Lopez, 2002).

BOARDS, UNIONS, POLITICIANS, PARENTS, AND COLLEAGUES

At the beginning of this chapter we made the case that district accounting practices are a meta-language for describing what is really valued in a district, and accounting ledgers track the unfolding story. This story may not be one any administrator or group of stakeholders would like to tell. Nonetheless, the ledger is undeniably a de facto tale of the district's priorities. In addition, the annual budget exerts pressure on all stakeholder groups to reshape their respective values, and so the ledger influences many smaller stories along the way as well.

District and school budgets are not pots of gold to be divided up onsite. Much of the distribution of wealth is determined by federal and state legislation. Expenditure of funds is also constrained by earmarked private grants, board policy, litigation costs, union contracts, and so on. No district or school administrator gets to look at all funds and then budget from them as he or she sees fit. Moreover, district wealth that is available for administrative apportioning seems to grow smaller each year in comparison to funds committed by external obligation. So although the episode described at the beginning of this chapter is real enough—it is important to distribute available wealth in accord with the best professional sentiments—overall district budgets inevitably reflect many demands that must somehow be assimilated into a common narrative. The larger the fiscal disparity between a

Figure 5.2   Satisficing Considerations

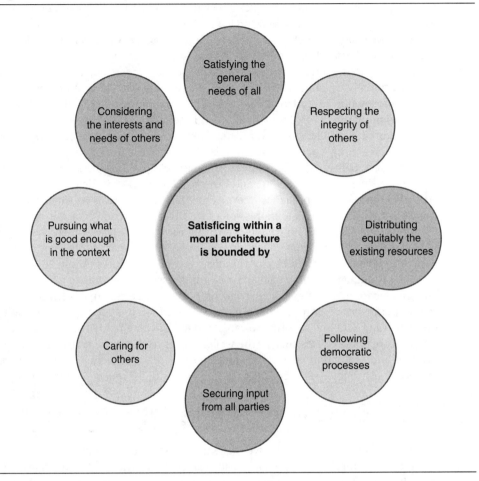

well-funded *schooling* function and any specific *educational* function, the more often the schooling function becomes a hurdle to fulfilling educational ambitions.

The best administrators bring together stakeholders by reinforcing a shared vision of education and its balance against responsible schooling obligations. Details will change, but the manner in which all groups are brought together remains the same: administrative integrity in the effort to secure the most "satisficing" options free of any wholly exclusionary practices (Nida-Rumelin, 1997). *Satisficing* is an economic term for planning that sacrifices gambles aimed at securing optimal reward for practices much more likely to be successful at securing at least a minimally satisfactory reward for all. Given the budgetary options open to today's administrators, it would be difficult to imagine any other way to go.

The economic planning practice of satisficing is commensurate with most of the moral theories discussed in this book, except perhaps for some forms of moral realism. Satisficing is also compatible with our recommendation to seek that path least likely to offend the moral sensibilities of others. Finally, satisficing seems most compatible with moral architectures that are inclusive, cooperative, caring, and democratic and, most importantly, exhibit generalized, individual integrity. Figure 5.2 illustrates the range of satisficing considerations likely to challenge administrators.

District ledgers tell a story of constraint and challenge. Budgeting practices and subsequent planning protocols reflect much of the character of school and district moral architecture (Fiske, 1992; Vohs, Mead, & Goode, 2006). Given less than free rein over budget and planning, stakeholders' hopes for optimality are inevitably dashed; nonetheless, no stakeholder group should settle for anything less than something that is at least satisficing to one and all among groups of legitimate stakeholders. By seeking modest win–win solutions for everyone through satisficing, the administrator shows his or her integrity and commitment to cooperate with all and within the operative moral architecture.

DISCUSSION QUESTIONS

1. Educators should be idealistic. One of our most cherished ideals should be the inclusion of our students in the Great Conversation. How does the concept of satisficing responsibly temper idealism in this context?

2. Describe your idea of a data-driven school or district. What steps can you imagine would advance your school or district toward your ideal?

CASE STUDIES

Case Study 5.1. Imposing Values on Children

Children of recent immigrants from diverse cultural heritages are increasing in number at your school. You are the principal. A few parents accuse the school of teaching Christian values. More specifically, they charge that although the school is not teaching religion, its imposition of Christian values on students offends their Muslim and Buddhist beliefs. How would you address their concerns? How would you seek to show respect for diverse religious beliefs and ensure that the limits and freedoms of religion are maintained?

Case Study 5.2. The Bully With a Coach's Cap

As a new principal, imagine that you have inherited a school culture that evidently neglects matters of social justice. The school seems dominated by an intimidating coach. His football and baseball teams have won three state championships and eight district championships in 14 years. Given his physical size, strength, intimidating personality, and coaching accomplishments, few publicly question his "over-the-line" demands and behaviors. The superintendent is content to coast for 3 years until retirement. The former principal routinely acquiesced to the coach's dominating ways. Several teachers complain that the coach is undermining them by reassuring his star players that if they are having a problem in a particular class they should come and see him. His athletes tend to intimidate and bully other students, evidently with some sense of impunity. Your leadership and management of the school will hinge on how you address the bully who wears a coach's cap. What factors and considerations would you make a part of your plan?

ACTIVITY

Activity 5.1

At school or through some private group in which you are active, take the lead and create a service project for some weekend. After the project is completed, write an essay describing how you came up with the idea. Specifically, explain how you think the project contributed in some small way to human betterment. Explain what you did to get others involved and explain the challenges you faced in getting others to participate. Describe your feelings in completing the project. Finally, describe how you imagine this same process having a role in your idea of educational leadership.

FURTHER READING

Gutmann, A. (1999). *Democratic education.* Princeton, NJ: Princeton University Press.

Haydon, G. (2000). *Values, virtues and violence: Education and the public understanding of morality.* Oxford: Blackwell.

Howe, K., & Miramontes, O. (1992). *The ethics of special education.* New York: Teachers College Press.

Strike, K., Haller, E., & Soltis, J. (2005). *The ethics of school administration* (3rd ed.). New York: Teachers College Press.

Yell, M. (2005). *Law and special education* (2nd ed.). New York: Prentice Hall.

CHAPTER 6

Factors to Consider When Making Judgments About Controversial Issues

TOLERANCE FOR ZERO TOLERANCE

Throughout this book we have talked about leadership in the context of moral architecture. In the last chapter, we spoke directly about leadership bringing people together in a shared vision ripe with moral implications. We stressed that the truly successful administrator cannot long survive simply by trying to juggle competing interests. In this chapter, we examine ethical conundrums such as zero tolerance policies and the differential treatment of students as other sources of potential turbulence disrupting the administrator's dreams of smooth sailing.

Ethical issues surrounding special populations, school safety, hate speech, and related questions are addressed in this chapter in the context of building and sustaining moral architectures suitable for schools intent on preserving the Great Conversation. The inquiry in this chapter focuses attention on prescriptive morals (surface-level rules) that might successfully or unsuccessfully serve as a *covering aesthetic,* completing a school's or district's moral architecture.

In the end humans cannot get far without a set of morals at hand (Scanlon, 1998). Morals create the final shape of a moral architecture. Morals are lifted above the level of human whim and capriciousness or "might is right" thinking by the virtues and higher-order principles that ground detailed, prescriptive morality and define its failure as **immorality**. As noted previously, elevation in moral architecture depends on there being higher-order principles and virtues that provide criteria for adjudicating between conflicts of duty that are inevitable when decision making rests on surface-level rules alone.

These higher-order virtues may look like the feminist sense of bonding, Hume's social sympathy, or biologically grounded instincts for cooperation. Higher-order general principles may look something like Kant's, Rawls's, or Strike's recommendation to treat

103

humans as ends and never as means; Mills's, Bentham's, or Strike's recommendation to bring more pleasure into the world while minimizing displeasure; or Hobbes's and Deming's recommendation to drive out fear. In any case, effective moral architectures are sustained by something more than a set of surface-level rules, each reflecting the same moral force and upheld by the same commitment to power. Effective moral architectures are elevated and deserving of awe and reverence only to the extent that the higher-order principles, ideals, and virtues are truly honored by an overwhelming majority of stakeholders.

The educational leader must help identify and articulate these virtues and higher-order principles to secure buy-in from all stakeholders. This must be done in advance so that when the inevitable conflict of duty arises there is some **intersubjective agreement** between stakeholders, making possible a resolution of differences based on something more than **psychological egoism.** The search for intersubjective agreement requires leaders to bring people together to be largely of one mind, at least in matters of just and mutual regard.

Especially in the case of public or institutional morality, advocates of utilitarianism, rule utilitarianism, and reflective equilibrium often press their strongest arguments on grounds that their respective theories give general form to all surface-level rules covering a moral architecture. When conflict arises at the surface level—that is, the aesthetic skin of the moral architecture—sturdy and lofty scaffolding makes deference to virtue or higher-order principles more relevant in resolving conflict than the exertion of force by one person or group against others. See the box below.

The Dimensions of a Moral Architectural Model

The Covering Aesthetic of Moral Architecture
The prohibitions and prescriptions that can be fairly applied in complex situations (requires collaboration between those of great pragmatic sense and those of great aesthetic sense).

The Scaffolding of Moral Architecture
The structure creating a hierarchy with more general principles (requires collaboration between those who have an uncommon sense of the human condition and those with an eye to rigor and soundness of thinking)

The Moral Foundation of Moral Architecture
Virtues and sympathies that frame and animate moral behavior (requires those who are scientifically minded working in close collaboration with those who most deeply have empathy for the phenomenology of human moral experience)

Plato identified the highest forms of truth, beauty, and justice with one another. Certainly there seems to be something intuitively satisfying about the notion that whatever is just must be true in some sense and that whatever is true must be just in some sense. After all, how often do people refer to divine harmony of some sort or the idea that "what goes around comes around"? Pushing the Platonic intuition a bit further, it is also appealing to think that genuine truth and justice possess an important and unique beauty. Without fear of becoming too reckless with metaphor and analogy, it seems reasonable to assert that moral architecture, like any other architecture, is always something of a work of art. Thus, the moral architectures of schools and districts must be developed and maintained at least in part by moral artists. By the term *moral artists* we mean people who know how to create novel structure out of the raw material of rules, principles, and raw intuitions without distorting the functionality of the overall structure. In short, there is much that goes into building and sustaining serviceable moral architecture. One need not be a **metaphysically** minded Platonist to appreciate the idea that there is indeed something beautiful about truly serviceable moral architectures.

Taken together—foundation, scaffolding, and skin—an effective moral architecture should reflect the diverse talents and skills of school and district communities to answer questions such as "Who do we want to be as members of this community?" This answer requires attention to more mundane and specific questions, such as "Whom do we each owe?" "What is it we owe to those to whom we have a debt?" "How do we know when we have successfully lived up at least minimally to our commitments toward self and others?" "How should we express concern and compassion for one another as individuals and as collectives?" "What conventions do we wish to encourage and discourage, and to what lengths will we go to informally institutionalize such things?" and "What should we tolerate in ourselves and others, and what do we find intolerable in ourselves and others?" See Table 6.1.

Table 6.1   Key Questions in Building Comprehensive Moral Architecture: Whom Do We Want to Be Members of This Community?

To whom do we have a moral responsibility in the school?	Which ethical principles do we want to promote?
What do we owe to one another?	What ideas, attitudes, and behaviors will we tolerate?
How do we know when we have met our minimal moral duties to one another?	How do we determine which ideas, attitudes, and behaviors we will not tolerate?
What virtues do we wish to encourage?	How will we nurture freedom as well as fairness?
How will we nurture a caring community?	When is it obvious that the moral architecture of a school or district is ill suited to educational purpose?

Suggestion: As you think about these questions, compare your answers with those of another person with whom you naturally sense a sort of shared bondedness and then again with someone whom you suspect sees community very differently from you. How and why do your answers overlap and diverge in each case? Can building shared moral architecture accommodate diversity of perspective? To what extent does shared moral architecture protect diversity of perspective?

Moral scaffolding and foundation have received much attention throughout this book. However, even the most cursory review of Chapter 2 reveals that moral theorists in general recognize the imperative that ***ought* implies *can*** must guide every attempt to implement our moral theorizing. This means that erudite and lofty principles (scaffolding and foundation) that lead to good wishes but can never be fully realized through surface-level rules and aesthetics offer no guidance to leaders when guidance is what is most needed. So, it is time now to consider a bit more reflectively some of the characteristic surface-level rules common in many schools today. We do this in order to reflect on the extent to which such surface-level rules and aesthetics (virtues and courtesies) support or weaken the ideals of a robust and functional moral architecture.

Zero tolerance prohibitions seem as good as any other place to begin to reflect on the surface-level rules currently in fashion in many schools and their commensurability with the ambitions of administrators to build and sustain lofty moral architectures throughout schools and districts. Zero tolerance policies are becoming ubiquitous as means for encouraging and discouraging certain types of behaviors. (See Case Study A.2 in Appendix A.)

Bringing weapons, poisons, and hallucinogenic drugs to school should surely be discouraged. Bullying, beating, and mauling classmates are the sorts of things all are likely to agree are bad things and to be eliminated from school and district terrain. Regardless of the communities involved or the diversity and nature of supportive moral architectures, disgust toward these sorts of behavior is probably a near universal among professionals most responsible for developing institutional moral architecture. In light of the presumed offensiveness of such behavior, is it reasonable to assume that a one-size-fits-all set of prohibitions to end such behaviors is the right way to go?

What seems simple enough on the surface can prove a bit more problematic in practice when people examine these surface policies or rules in light of their school's or district's normal operations (Shealy, 2006). Here in particular, unwavering mandates perhaps should give way to the guidance of pragmatists and the more artistically minded in moral matters. Not only pragmatists but most other theorists discussed in Chapter 2 are likely to balk at the unbending insensitivity that accompanies many zero tolerance policies. Zero tolerance's obsession with *behavior* instead of *actions* often leads to uncompromising stances. At such times administrators and other responsible stakeholders may believe that the constraints imposed by zero tolerance policies leave those charged with implementation feeling guilty at times for having to impose what seem to be irrationally harsh penalties in a given context. Other stakeholders may feel justifiably irate at the imposition of a zero tolerance policy in cases where mitigating circumstances are clearly evident. In the end, nearly everyone associated with implementation of zero tolerance policies will feel uncomfortable much of the time.

In a televised *Dateline* episode airing in 1996, John Stossel was aggrieved at the fact that an honor student and Eagle Scout with a congressional appointment to West Point was being expelled from school just days before graduation for violating the district's zero tolerance policy with regard to weapon possession. The student's expulsion would mean that he would not be admitted to the nation's military academy at West Point. The district superintendent looked into the camera and explained, "Zero tolerance means zero tolerance! If people are not happy with my administration of the rule, then they need to go to the school board and get the school policy changed." At first glance the superintendent's position seems somewhat reasonable. No one wants weapons in the school. So why were people so disturbed by this consistent disciplinary action?

A REALITY CHECK

The authors imply that school leaders sometimes need to be artistic as well as pragmatic when it comes to wording statements or creating documents related to moral matters. Is it really possible to say, "Drugs, firearms, and gang identifiers are not allowed on campus under any circumstance"? What does that mean about the wearing of yarmulkes, rosaries, and the like? What does it mean about carrying scissors or knitting kits with needles in them? Is Midol akin to crack? What can be done, if anything, to create an aesthetic covering the kinds of actions and only the actions all agree are truly inappropriate in the schools?

If the student had brought to school an AK-47, surely people would have sided with the superintendent. Most probably, they would have sided with the superintendent if the weapon had been a pistol, a straight razor, a switchblade, or some other obvious tool of aggression. The student had indeed brought a knife to school, but not just any knife. The student dressed late the morning of the incident. In addition to proudly wearing his Eagle Scout shirt, he had quickly slipped into the same jeans he had worn to an Eagle Scout meeting the night before. In those jeans he had his Eagle Scout pocket knife. Imagine. Here is an Eagle Scout wearing a variation of his Eagle Scout uniform and having his Eagle Scout pocket knife still in his pocket. This is a clear and present danger, wouldn't you agree?

A school police officer noticed the bulge in the student's pocket and asked him to empty his pockets, whereupon the knife was discovered. The process of enforcement rolled downhill like a snowball gaining speed and with no way to stop. This model student and Eagle Scout was expelled, and with the expulsion his hopes for West Point were ended by the zero tolerance rule. Certainly the student, and maybe even the nation, has lost much here because the young man may have become an exemplary military officer. What is wrong here?

Quite possibly every moral theorist you have read about in this text, with the remote and possible exception of Jeremy Bentham, would agree with Stossel's exasperated, "Give me a break!" Here we have an administrator who can apparently see no further than an insensitively managed regulation. His apparent approach to leadership is based on surface rules alone. He seemingly has given little thought to what his school stands for or what moral architecture should sustain the kind of community he is trying to lead. He is adeptly covering his own flanks, but he is doing little else of merit for the school, society, this student, or any student for that matter. If students see that administrators have little ability to distinguish an innocent mistake from malicious behavior, then what respect are they likely to have for the administrator or his directives?

Admittedly, a pocket knife in the hands of a gang member is prima facie a weapon of aggression. But as any fan of Robert Ludlum, Tom Clancy, Stephen Coonts, or another mystery or adventure novelists knows, anything can be a lethal weapon in the wrong hands. Pencils, cafeteria utensils, or a lipstick container can be used to murder another person. In short, each *can be* a weapon of aggression. And in sharp contrast, a knife in the hand of a surgeon can be life saving, a very good thing indeed. Maybe, just maybe, a knife in the hands of an Eagle Scout who is also an exceptional student with a record of meritorious behavior may be a good thing. At the very least, a knife in his pocket is probably benign. Where is it truly reasonable to draw a line of demarcation?

Pragmatists will undoubtedly be the first to urge reflection on the immediate context when advising where to draw lines of demarcation between the permissible and the impermissible. The details of intent and context must be considered because each situation is unique. Other moral theorists will urge reflection on the grounding principles of the school district's moral architecture. Their point will be to inquire into how this or that surface-level moral rule advances the cause of human moral experience generally, realizing in practice what conceivably ought to be done.

In the previous illustration, John Stossel explained, the district superintendent knew of the Eagle Scout's commendable academic and behavioral record. If the administrator knew all this, then how could he ignore it when he upheld a decision to expel the boy? Does the administrator's action suggest a flat moral architecture where *transient* surface-level rules dictate every decision rather than some higher-order commitment to human betterment?

QUESTIONING THE AUTHORS

?

The authors refer to transient, surface-level rules. How can leaders help staff and students distinguish between practical rules for school operation and ethical principles for school and life? Does confusing the two types of rules flatten or elevate a district or school's moral architecture?

The superintendent's answer was to insist that if he made an exception for one student, he would have to make exceptions for others. In other words, this administrator either confused fairness with the principle of equality or believes that equality of treatment trumps fairness. (One can only imagine his thoughts about affirmative action, special appropriations for special education students, etc.)

Surely there is nothing conspicuously errant about making similar decisions *in similar circumstances*. But determining similarity of circumstance is often a challenge, one no morally sensitive administrator has a right to avoid.

Think here of the analogy to common law. In common law each case is decided in light of the last case most like the present case. The task of lawyers is to identify past cases most similar to that of their clients and with an outcome favorable to the client. The court then must decide which precedent truly seems to be seamlessly binding between past and present circumstance. The task can be quite daunting at times, but such practices of precedential thinking and adjudicative action have served the courts well over the centuries. In short, similar thinking in the context of similar circumstances may serve well in the complexity of school operations, and when the circumstances differ those responsible for adjudicating such matters must make appropriate adjustments.

In summary, the Eagle Scout example shows that the initial zero tolerance rule is too narrow and crude to be effective in developing a robust moral architecture for serving the school and district communities. School authorities need rules sufficiently complex in order to be universally and *fairly* applied in a variety of situations. If the task is to deprive thugs or irresponsible people of tools to be used as weapons, then there must be evidence of the tool's prima facie use as a weapon and the culprit's disposition to use it in a careless or malevolent manner. The task itself is justified not simply by some surface-level rule in place but more generally by such deeper principles as the Hobbesian or Deming principle of driving out fear, the utilitarian principle of maximizing pleasure, universalist convictions to optimize cooperation and collaboration, and so on.

An administrator who enforces a rule while dismissing all contextually relevant and mitigating circumstances is creating a "might makes right" moral ambiance (Searle, 1995). Rather than developing an elevated moral architecture of principle, he may well be nurturing the seeds of bullying. That is, the message he is role modeling may be that when you have the power—the juice, as kids like to say—you get to do things your way. In the end, this sort of thinking is far more compatible with the way gang members and fascists think than the thinking of effective school administrators concerned with building a moral architecture sustaining the Great Conversation over the long run.

Press accounts have weakened school and judicial reliance on zero tolerance policies in some parts of the country over the last few years, but in other areas of the country they are as prevalent as ever. In Florida 10 years ago there was a famously reported case of a 5-year-old boy expelled from kindergarten on grounds of sexual harassment for kissing girls. (The authors each remember such a boy in the kindergartens they attended decades ago!) And there was also a widely reported case of a teenage girl expelled for sharing an over-the-counter analgesic with another girl suffering severe menstrual pain. Moral architectures that are unable to accommodate childhood innocence or compassionate sharing cannot do much to prepare students for shared participation in either the Great Conversation or democratic processes. These sorts of zero tolerance policies are an affront to student moral development inasmuch as they mitigate against the search for higher-order moral principles and virtues that make moral architectures robust.

An administrator who governs solely by surface-level rules without reference to an overarching moral architecture shows no understanding of or tolerance for the individuality of circumstance or the uniqueness of persons (Zagzebski, 2001). Such displays of intolerance are unlikely to prepare students for collaborative participation in democratic communities. Such environments are more likely to create an us-against-them instinct for survival. For example, imagine an administrator who hates gays and lesbians. Imagine how such an administrator might apply rules limiting affectionate behavior on campus. Zero tolerance could easily become an excuse for hidden bigotry. Imagine that district rules then change in a direction more favorable toward affectionate behavior on campus. The administrator will reliably abide by the new rules, just as he did for the previous rules. This is because for him the rules are all that matter, not the underpinning structural sympathies, virtues, and principles. However, if the administrator was homophobic before, will anyone be fooled by his adherence to the new rules? His attitude of intolerance will still probably be evident. His moral leadership will remain apparent and unchanged regardless of his compliance with any shift in rules. Moreover, given more latitude to interpret the appropriateness of certain behavior, he will probably shed the responsibility given him, as the unempowered may prudently fear, and instead take the opportunity to vent his **chauvinism.** In any case, the point is that regardless of the rules, prejudice or bigoted authorities will wreak havoc on a community's moral architecture, lowering its allure in the eyes of stakeholders.

QUESTIONING THE AUTHORS

?

The examples the authors give seem to imply that there is an important contrast between being ethical and reflective on one hand and being unthinking and unethical on the other. Is this the case? How might a reflective disposition help an administrator be ethical? How might a commitment to stable rules help an administrator be ethical?

No set of prohibitions can rid communities of the problem of cowardly scoundrels in positions of power. If the moral architecture of the school or district is to include tolerance toward gays and other groups of students such as religious fundamentalists, Green Party advocates, and so on, then attention must be given to more than just the strict adherence to rules. The moral architecture must manifest an appropriate ambiance or moral ecology (Goodlad, 2004). The feel of the place must be filled with honor and reciprocal respect.

Schools cannot be places of character formation and democratic understanding if they are situated in a moral architecture without a solid foundation, scaffolding, and consistently derived, surface-level moral rules. Wishful thinking and a smorgasbord of disparate rules expressing sheer administrative power will never prepare students for the responsibilities of democracy, citizenship, parenting, and so on. An important schooling function in democratic societies is that students learn what it means to live within a moral architecture conducive to shared community. In addition, schools committed to fostering the Great Conversation must be similarly predisposed to developing and sustaining inclusive and respectful communities free of even transient **rudeness** and devoted to the search for and sharing of human understanding. School and district moral architectures expressive only of social power can neither teach nor model necessary democratic commitments and sensibilities.

Strength of leadership need not be associated with despotic practice. Quite the contrary may well be true: Strength of leadership focuses not so much on control as on the development of autonomy throughout the organization (Mangin, 2007). The truest strength of leadership is exhibited through the ongoing construction of an environment where reflection, caring, freedom, and fairness are honored and where the stifling effect of "might makes right," "policy is policy," and "make the easy choice" management is minimized or eliminated (Noddings, 1992).

RACISM AND HATE SPEECH: FRAGMENTS OF SCHOOL AND DISTRICT CULTURE

In the last section, zero tolerance policies are shown to inhibit effective educational leadership and at times possibly destroy moral architecture. The cause of such policies' inhibitory character was shown to be an unyielding insensitivity to context and to the individuality of person. The unyielding rigidness of zero tolerance policies should not be defended strongly on grounds of consistency and **equality** unless one is willing to elevate equality as a moral principle above fairness. No one major theorist seems willing to do that. It is generally acknowledged from Aristotle to R. S. Peters (1983) that treating everyone equally may be the most unfair consequence that can result from any policy. For example, not everyone should be inoculated against a minor chronic disease if there is good reason to believe some people may be fatally allergic to the vaccine.

Educational policies such as **disparate impact** considerations and the **Equal Access Act** often require disproportionate expenditures of resources on students with special needs. It would generally be considered *unfair* to insist that an equal dollar amount be spent on each student regardless of special needs and circumstances. Fairness and equality have never been equated with one another in moral theory. The closest the two concepts come to one another may be captured in Aristotle's (1958) recommendation that equals should be treated equally and unequals unequally. More pointedly, in the educational context some students may need unequal resources in order to secure the same access to educational success as most other students. The acknowledgment that fairness may demand a differential treatment of students under varying circumstances brings us back full circle to the problem with zero tolerance policies. How are administrators and policy makers to tell under what conditions differential treatment is fair? This is certainly a problem, and the problem is only worsened by one-size-fits-all planning.

The problem of differential treatment of others often threatens the stability of an organization's moral architecture when leaders fail to recognize the difference between surface-level rules (the aesthetic covering) and the deeper principles, virtues, and sensitivities (the foundational and structural values) that make for a more robust and resilient environment. When there is good reason for differential treatment of individuals, differential treatment is in order. When there is no good reason for differential treatment, such treatment would be arbitrary, capricious, and unfair.

Some, if not all, advocates of almost every moral theory discussed in Chapter 2 would find racism and hate speech horrific. In every moral theory, there are grounds for despising racism and hate speech. There is good reason to conclude that there should be no tolerance for either racism or hate speech in a nation's schools. Does this settle everything a school leader needs to know about racism and hate speech? Probably not.

In the daily operations of school districts, specific rules applying penalties and punishments must be administered to ensure awareness of and respect for prohibitions against racism and hate speech. This is where the realities of leading touch the realities of living in a complex world. Consider the matter of hate speech. It is reasonable to conclude that it is something to be intolerant of, but can hate speech always be so easily identified?

CLARIFYING THE CONCEPT

Some discussions are said to be merely about matters of semantics, and others are said to be about important meanings. Are there important differences between hate speech, racist remarks, offensive names, and out-of-date vocabulary? If so, how should a school deal with these differences in surface-level rules and its overall moral architecture? Considering consequences of implementation, how do "ought implies can" considerations matter here?

The "*n*-word" is a common example of a word reflective of hate-filled attitudes and denigration of people because of their race. Yet some young people embrace the name when used by one another within their own culture or racial group. What about the words *honkey* and *cracker?* Are those as much a part of hate speech as the "*n*-word"? How does a community of morally sensitive people decide? What about *fatty, four-eyes, ho,* and so on? How do we know where to draw the line? Again, the difficulty of the problem is no excuse for avoiding the challenge. Hate speech should be eliminated from the nation's schools, and somehow as a democratic community devoted to respecting the rights of individuals stakeholders must figure out where to draw lines and when and how to amend lines already drawn.

Finally, at what point do hate speech and innocent insensitivity part ways? For example, there is all the difference in the world between a student who turns to a classmate and accuses, "*You* people usually . . ." and a student of conspicuous good will and earnestness who clumsily and unwittingly asks, "Well, why do you people always . . . ?" In the first case, the student may be presumed to be speaking hatefully even though no "hate words" are used. Should such deliberate insensitivity be considered so offensive as to deserve punishment usually reserved for the deliberate use of hate words? That is, should students who derogatively use the "*n*-word" and *cracker* be treated the same way as people who sneer "*You* people . . ." in an open discussion? And should people who sneer "*You* people . . ." be treated the same or differently from others of presumed good will who clumsily ask or say, "You people . . ."?

It is one thing to find across the board or at least postulate that moral theory condemns hate speech. But it is an altogether different affair to craft enforceable rules that are consistent with the direction intended by the moral architecture of the school. The difficulty of addressing hate speech should not entice administrators to adopt a relativistic stance, make simplistic but politically correct decisions, or acquiesce in the blind application of punishments to every technically described episode of hate speech. Administrative moral responsibility requires more. Defining that further responsibility is not at all easy, however. There certainly are no algorithms at this level of moral discourse to crank out truth at every turn. Nonetheless, there must be punishments for acts of hate speech, but both punishments and accurate identification of hate speech violations must be adept. The management of punishment for hate speech violations must be deftly handled with an eye to underlying principles, virtues, and sensitivities to be exhibited and modeled in the context of the encompassing moral architecture. Again, there is no fail-safe system of moral management, but that is no excuse for management to be less than vigilant and morally alert to the challenge. There may be no fail-safe prescription for success when addressing matters of hate speech, but in schools that successfully meet the challenge, the covering aesthetic of the moral architecture is, as Plato would predict, evident as a thing of beauty. And again, as it is easy to imagine what Plato might predict, schools that fail to meet the challenge of tempering hate speech are conspicuously ugly institutions. Their failure is no secret; their failure in this regard cannot be hidden, no matter how oppressive the exercise of administrative power.

PROVIDING A SAFE ENVIRONMENT: AT WHAT COST?

Other surface-level moral rules that make up the covering aesthetic or skin of school moral architectures address matters of student and staff physical and psychological safety. It is routinely assumed that if children do not feel safe at school, they cannot learn (Simmons & Black, 1991). And if staff feel unsafe, they cannot teach or perform very well other professional duties.

Rules, separated from some coherent and comprehensive moral architecture, are unlikely to relieve students and staff of the need for what some feminist theorists describe as communal cooperation and care. Students and staff feel most secure not because police, metal detectors, and an elaborate system of rules and punishments are in place but because there is a sense of community, making such protections unnecessary or at best an incidental distraction. There is a significant difference between leadership that focuses on the apparatus of control and leadership that focuses on the development of community. In the former case, the moral architecture is deflated and diminished in importance by the apparatus of control and its vigilant deployment. In the latter case, the apparatus of control may still be necessary, but its presence is deliberately subsumed under a more focused concern for the building of a genuine sense of community.

A genuine sense of community, that exemplar of Platonic beauty and feminist ideal, is one in which the moral architecture is built on honor, bondedness, and shared appreciation for higher-order moral principles and virtues. Schools that serve as zones of safety for student learning and teaching excellence are most evident in schools and districts with elevated moral architectures. Schools with minimal moral architecture feebly try to provide some modest safety through the deployment of a showy array of fortifications and enforcement strategies. In some schools there is so much focus on safety from student aggression that learning resources may be squandered and children's opportunities to learn diminished (Gellman & Delucia-Waak, 2006).

One reason for administrative overemphasis on fortification and enforcement where it does occur may be administrative fear of litigation. Vulnerability to litigation is an ever-present distraction to school administrators today. In today's litigious society fear of liability is hardly unreasonable, but it should be minimized—along with other fears—in a district that has a strong and vital moral architecture. Conversely, no administrator should ever be reckless, inviting litigation. But a conscientious administrator cannot simply focus on avoiding litigation. Her range of responsibilities is far greater. If she focuses simply on avoiding litigation, the school or district's architecture will flatten and become little more than a hodgepodge of rules and consequences. Administrators serve their constituencies best by addressing the entire range of safety, support, and moral architecture that makes learning and creative exploration central to the school and district social milieu.

Ongoing and ineffective management of student aggression is a sign that the school has an ineffectual moral architecture. The addition of more campus police, metal detectors, cameras, and so on serves only as a stopgap measure, slowing encroaching assaults on safety. Such stopgap measures are no solution to what is clearly a more endemic problem. They may be necessary in times of transition, but they do not solve safety problems in the long run. The competent administrator implements such measures as needed but only to the extent that they are necessary. In the face of problems with student aggression, schools and districts must be careful to avoid role modeling anything leading students to think that all social interactions revolve around the exercise of force and might. Schools should be institutional role models (Gardner, 1991) not of coercion and oppression but rather of democratic responsiveness fostering participation in the Great Conversation. In addition to advancing conditions conducive to effective administration, such institutional role modeling is the only plausible way schools and districts can prepare students for the responsibilities of genuine participation in democratic structures as adults.

A PRACTICAL ASSIGNMENT

Assume that you are a new principal in a school with serious safety problems and a deficient moral architecture. Consequently, as one might imagine, there is little emphasis on the Great Conversation. What steps would you take to address these matters? Describe your priorities for addressing these concerns. Whose support would you need in order to create a more functional moral architecture fostering inclusive participation in the Conversation?

Onsite administrators know that details (the skin of moral architecture) get all the attention in daily practice, and this is as it should be. But what daily attention to detailed prescriptions and prohibitions ultimately reveal is how effective a school or a district is in moving forward in its primary mission. That primary mission of course is to create in students and staff a universal inclination to participate in the Great Conversation for the rest of their lives, one way or another.

PARTICIPATION IN THE GREAT CONVERSATION OF HUMANKIND

Preparing students to participate in the larger communities that surround them may legitimately lead to encouraging patriotism as part of the *schooling* function. But as our world grows ever smaller, the relevant communities of which students should all see themselves grow ever larger. Consequently, it is an inherent part of the *educational* function of schools to open students' eyes to the world's various nations, cultures, demographics, physical characteristics, and immigration patterns. It is also part of the educational function of the schools to show students the world's sciences, laws, humanities, and arts. When schools effectively invite students into participation in the Great Conversation, they lead students in the direction of mutual respect for one another, a passion for truth, and a more general understanding of the four corners of educational purpose.

> **A REFLECTIVE BREAK**
>
> What are the educational and ethical responsibilities of a principal who hears that one of her teachers is dogmatically and one-sidedly discussing economic, political, and historical ideas and even **grading** on students' grasp of the teacher's opinions? How should she carry these responsibilities out?

Ever present in the conscientious administrator's mind is the fact that in carrying out noneducational schooling duties the school is always at risk of becoming a tool by which a segment of society's power brokers hope to gain control over the future. In every historical or sociological account of demagoguery, scholars and social scientists make explicit the intent of malevolently and benevolently intentioned demagogues to control society by gaining control over the schools and the media. It is the duty of every educator but especially of administrators to never serve as an extension of any group currently in or seeking disproportionate power. As Paulo Freire (1998) observes, schools—though they cannot be neutral—should not capitulate to the ideological and economic orientations of the powerful, regardless of whether they are leftist or rightist dogmatists. When schools promote ideologies and dogmas, they abandon their duty to develop in students the skills, attitudes, and dispositions of critical assessment and tarnish students' developing passion for inquiry and truth.

SUMMARY RECOMMENDATIONS

It has not been our custom throughout this book to make explicit recommendations about surface-level rules of application. So if you were hoping that in this chapter we might break from that pattern, you are undoubtedly disappointed. Nonetheless, we do hope we have made you aware of some very important considerations worthy of reflection when deciding what prescriptions and prohibitions might best fill out your school's or district's evolving moral architecture. Certainly, keeping in mind that moral architectures for *educational* purposes must always reflect diversity and intellectual ideals proper to the Conversation is a good place to start every time.

DISCUSSION QUESTIONS

1. Martin Luther King Jr. demonstrated the importance of tolerance and moral intolerance. On moral grounds, he was unrelentingly intolerant of racism. Can you think of an issue today that ought to prompt an administrator into intolerance? Once the line is drawn separating grounds for intolerance from tolerance, courage becomes a necessary moral virtue for effective educational leadership. Explain why this is so.

2. Delineate a list of priorities and responsibilities you think an effective administrator ought to address. Explain the grounds that you think justify the hierarchy you have created.

3. The administrator owes a moral duty to society in general. She also owes a duty to students, teachers, and professional staff, other employees, parents, the school board, fellow administrators, the law, the academic disciplines taught at the school, the community (national, state, and local), and the tradition of the Great Conversation. Prioritize with appropriate individual weightings this list of stakeholders as best you can. Explain your reasons for the assigned priorities.

CASE STUDIES

Case Study 6.1. The Teachers Gone Wild Blog

As Ms. Alvarez walked into Superintendent Goldstein's office, she observed him holding his head in both hands and looking down at a sheet on his desk. He didn't even look up when she entered and approached his desk. She asked whether he was feeling okay or whether there was some problem. Goldstein looked up and then finally spoke: "You have to ask Jenkins to resign, or else I will suspend him." The superintendent lamented, "It's difficult. As you and I both know, Jenkins has been through this sort of thing once before."

In the previous incident Goldstein referred to, Jenkins was accused by two senior girls of attempting to kiss them at a post-graduation party, and a third girl claimed he fondled her. He was arrested and formally charged with sexual assault the next day.

As things turned out, the girls recanted their fabricated stories when they realized the damage about to befall Mr. Jenkins. One girl admitted instigating the story with her friends after Mr. Jenkins rebuffed her advance that evening. All charges were dropped, but Mr. Jenkins had already been pressured into resigning his position at the school where he was then teaching.

A string of questions shot through Ms. Alvarez's mind as she asked, "So, what has happened this time?" (The Mr. Jenkins she knew was a model teacher and citizen. He was an excellent biology instructor and a contributing member to the "Volunteer After School Learning Community.")

Mr. Goldstein said a blogger had created a site called "Educators Gone Wild" to warn parents and students of sexual predators in education. On the blog, one of the stories was about Mr. Jenkins and the earlier accusations. Parents and school board members were pressuring Mr. Goldstein to dismiss Jenkins. The fact that the previous charges were dropped and the accusers recanted their stories was of little interest to anyone. And these developments were not mentioned on the blog. The superintendent explained that the district could not afford that sort of publicity. "It's unfortunate," he claimed, "but Mr. Jenkins must go. As his principal I want you to tell him his contract next year will not be renewed, but if he resigns we will give him the most favorable recommendations we can. I am sorry to place this burden on you." Assuming you are Principal Alvarez, what other alternatives might you imagine pursuing to preserve and enrich the integrity of what you believe to be the district's moral architecture when addressing this case?

Case Study 6.2. The Terrors of Bluegrass High School

You are the new principal at Bluegrass High School. You have been told by the former principal, the superintendent, and several board members that your job will be a breeze as long as the girls' basketball team continues doing well. This should be no problem because most of the girls in the first string are returning seniors from last year's state championship team. Moreover, many of the girls' parents are board members or otherwise prominent members of the community. All seems right with the world—at least on the surface. Within the school community itself, the team is colloquially called the Divine Diablos, divine on the court and diabolical everywhere else.

Having to deal with a team of arrogant bullies was one thing; now, however, photographs of the players in various suggestive poses wearing articles of their team uniforms showed up on the Internet. Subsequent stories in local and major newspapers were creating large-scale public scandal for both the school and the district. You get a phone call at home from the school board president. He tells you that his call is off the record and asks you not to mention it to anyone, including the superintendent. He advises you that the board expects you to act quickly, quietly, and—most importantly—charitably in dealing with the situation. His final words are, "Think of them as your own daughters."

What options would you consider in addressing the behavior of the team members? What might this situation say about the school's and district's moral architecture? If you remained at Bluegrass High School beyond the current school year, what priorities and plans would you work toward in future years?

ACTIVITY

Activity 6.1

To get an idea of what the skin of a moral architecture looks like and consider how it can be shaped, adopt a courtesy that you don't currently use and keep a journal for a month indicating how the new courtesy has affected your world. For example, if you overlook thanking bus persons or waiters for filling your glass or removing your plate, make it a point to make eye contact when they do, smile, and thank them. Or if you do not now write thank you notes for little courtesies extended toward you, begin doing so. For this activity, don't use e-mails. Instead, use formal thank you cards and personal handwriting to show not only your appreciation for the courtesy but your respect for the other person. This may seem like a small matter, but try it and see how those receiving the cards respond to you and act toward you in the future. This is a surprisingly effective way of distinguishing yourself from the crowd as a person who appreciates others and what they do. There are a host of courtesies to choose from, and most of us overlook one or another of them. Note in your journal the accumulating things you notice as this new courtesy becomes habitual in your life. Courtesies are but one small element in the skin of a moral architecture, but this exercise might draw your attention to how small things change an environment. Also, take notice of the courtesy you chose. It may reflect something of your foundation or structural sense of how the moral world should be.

FURTHER READING

Applbaum, A. (1999). *Ethics for adversaries*. Princeton, NJ: Princeton University Press.

Beck, L. G. (1994). *Reclaiming educational administration as a caring profession*. New York: Teachers College Press.

Buzzelli, C., & Johnston, B. (2002). *The moral dimensions of teaching: Language, power, and culture in classroom interaction*. New York: Routledge Farmer.

Campbell, E. (2004). *The ethical teacher*. Maidenhead, UK: Open University Press.

Freire, P. (1998). *Pedagogy of freedom: Ethics, democracy, and civic courage*. New York: Rowman & Littlefield.

Katz, M., Noddings, N., & Strike, K. (Eds.). (1999). *Justice and caring: The search for common ground*. New York: Teachers College Press.

Noddings, N. (2003). *Caring: A feminine approach to ethics and moral education* (2nd ed.). Berkeley: University of California Press.

Rebore, R. (2001). *The ethics of educational leadership*. Upper Saddle River, NJ: Merrill Prentice Hall.

Salomone, R. (2000). *Visions of schooling: Conscience, community, and common education*. New Haven, CT: Yale University Press.

Sergiovanni, T. (1992). *Moral leadership: Getting to the heart of school improvement*. San Francisco: Jossey-Bass.

CHAPTER 7

The Pragmatic Value
of Justice for All

THE PRAGMATICS OF JUSTICE

Even in the hands of a master moral theorist such as John Rawls (1971), the concept of justice may seem all but impenetrable to grasp and master in application. Nonetheless, every educator committed to the Great Conversation recognizes immediately that elements of justice are needed simply to ensure universal participation in the Conversation. For example, the Conversation could not occur in the absence of respect on the part of each participant for each other participant. In addition, the Conversation by its very nature is committed to inclusion and extending an invitation to everyone to participate. Any exclusionary practice is immediately evident as an injustice. These matters are all quite practical and not at all ethereal. They are matters demanding pragmatic attention to immediate detail and context, not abstraction and lofty speculation. For example, in the collective search for truth it is a transparent, pragmatic commitment that each participant is given a voice, and each opinion and claim to know is given a *just* hearing. Just hearings are realized only when there is an unmitigated tradition of participants thinking critically and honestly about the utility of every new idea and alleged fact. In short, justice is an essential and pragmatic element of any moral architecture suitable for supporting the Great Conversation.

It is no oxymoron to say that there is an unwavering, pragmatic value to respecting both truth and fellow truth seekers in the Great Conversation. Indeed, what makes the Conversation so fulfilling and of such high utility to all participants is that its scope and ambitions extend beyond mere classroom conversation or any conversation that languishes as a result of its being wholly contextualized in the immediate environs. In short, there is good pragmatic reason why the concept of justice in particular deserves extended treatment in a book on the ethics of educational administration.

JUSTICE: A LINCHPIN CONCEPT IN MODERN THEORIZING

Today the term *justice* is used in many ways. Theorists talk of distributive justice, social justice, retributive justice, transitional justice, compensatory justice, restorative justice, and more, and it is not always clear—certainly to the practitioner—how one theory of justice is effectively intended to be of more narrow focus than another (Braithwaite, 2002; Walker, 2006). An extended meta-analysis of justice talk might be a very useful exercise, but in a book more intended to direct administrators toward practical action the meta-analysis will be sacrificed. In its stead, the notion of justice used will be a popular rendering of Rawls, focusing attention on securing minimal benefit for each person as if the rules and policies contrived were created without anyone knowing in advance what social role he or she may have in the future. This Rawlsian sense of justice protects the need for differential treatment in order to secure fairness when context necessarily creates an uneven playing field.

Differential treatment in the name of social or distributive justice should never be confused with granting **license** to some to treat others disadvantageously. Quite the contrary. When creating rules and policies from behind an imagined "veil of ignorance," as Rawls (1971) recommends, there is too much risk involved for rational, self-interested agents to create situations that may turn out to be disadvantageous to them once the veil of ignorance is lifted and each person is confronted with the realities of the world and daily practice. In contrast, the license to treat others differentially through policies is based solely on grounds of securing fairness. That is, differential treatment is morally authorized and may even be obligatory in cases where failure to institute such differences because of context or circumstance would strike most ordinary people as patently unfair and wholly counterintuitive.

Endorsing a concern for justice does not involve a further commitment to embrace a universalist position of some sort or entail the abandonment of all other moral theories. Indeed, a concern for justice may be regarded as an integral virtue. Justice may also be deemed a consequence of the feminist commitment to bondedness or even a derivative from a theory of providence. Justice may also be deemed simply an intuition or consequent sense of social sympathy (Baron, 2000). In short, a concern for justice is compatible with many moral theories, and certainly it is basic to the needs of every educational administrator's intent to build a moral architecture sheltering students for participation in the Great Conversation and for able participation in other democratic communities as well.

JUSTICE, PROMISE, AND THE RELEVANT ORIGINS OF ENDURING MORALITY

In *The Evolution of Morality,* Richard Joyce (2006) offers an evolutionary account of moral origins. The fact of morality's universal character he takes as established from languages around the world. Human languages of even the most elementary sort are designed for cooperation, blame, altruism, guilt, compassion, and a host of other human practices and emotions necessary for a weak, slow, and land-based mammal to survive. While avoiding questions of origins, both psychiatrist Robert Coles (2000) and psychologist Lawrence Kohlberg and his colleagues (Power, Higgins, & Kohlberg, 1991) find evidence of universal concerns with matters of justice from all over the world as well. So without too much fear of being wrong about the importance of justice in moral practice, justice will be stipulated from this point forward as a proper concern of every administrator. Coextensive with this administrative commitment to justice, Joyce's linguistic and evolutionary argument for the origin of morality leads to acknowledgment of promising and promise keeping as central to morality generally and leadership morality especially.

As Hacking (1975) notes, without language and especially the language of morality (Hauser, 2006; Joyce, 2006) and all it represents, humans could have never developed as self-conscious stewards of the world. Humans deliberate across cultures about matters as diverse as global warming, racial discrimination, just war, oppression of the poor, human rights, fair employment practices, proportioning aid in the wake of catastrophe, possible extinction of other species, superiority of one religion over another, and the list goes on. The species' current disproportionate ability compared with other species to sustain a flourishing world is not a consequence of sociologically localized, moral systems but is rather a function of the human capacity to build personal and group character as well as moral commitment through promising, and the justice of such select causes. Promising may be the greatest of all human inventions, and it is simply and undeniably an element of human moral experience generally. The moral institution of the promise has given humans a unique opportunity to cooperate across vast regions of geography, culture, and history.

Note for just a minute how intimately matters of justice and promising are linked. It is generally said to be unjust not to keep promises, and yet matters of justice are sometimes relied on to excuse a person from holding to a promise. Promise keeping and justice are important ethical issues. Knowing when to abort a promise in the name of justice is an important moral dilemma. Such issues will command the attention of every morally alert educational administrator day in and day out. With such importance evident, one might hope for an equally evident algorithm for ensuring moral success each day.

BOOTSTRAPPING PRINCIPLES AND VIRTUES AND THE GREAT CONVERSATION

However human language and promise making emerged, they are clearly among the most foundational ethical developments in history. Schools and their principal goal of education as the Great Conversation realize their ideal destiny most appropriately in a curriculum supported by a moral apparatus featuring promising, justice, cooperation, commitment to duty, and shared responsibilities. In addition to the genuine search for truth, the never-ending focus on morality comprises nearly everything that education as the Great Conversation needs to proceed productively. Simultaneously, the Conversation itself draws attention to and makes ever clearer to all what the shared moral principles, ideals, virtues, and evaluative observations of humans ought to be. Thus there is always a symbiotic bootstrapping effect between human moral ideals of the moment and further participation in the Great Conversation on one hand and between general language development and human moral experience on the other.

This tandem development of language and morality suggests that the Great Conversation unfolds in the manner of a double helix. Each developmental strand bootstraps further the development of the other strand. This double helix metaphor places the *ideal of education* beyond the whims and fancy of local schooling interests because the Conversation and the moral support it requires are constantly pushing toward the frontiers of universal inclusion and shared general truths, moral and otherwise. In other words, education is best understood as a human phenomenon and not as a local social institution (Tiberius, 2008). In the case of schooling practices, however, things are altogether different.

Schooling and its component socializing and training missions often properly reflect a strong local component. In contrast, the educational function of schools is inherently *transcultural* both in content (search for truth) and ideally in process as well (i.e., the Great Conversation). This transculturalism is consequent to the human desire in the best of moments to understand the world and to share what is learned with others. To exclude anyone from the Conversation either deliberately or through negligence is an assault on the sense of social justice all educators ought to share.

QUESTIONING THE AUTHORS ?	For education to be transcultural, should schools in all cultures be required to study the same curricula and subject details (e.g., history, music, art, civics)? If not, how should the local context figure into the curriculum of the Great Conversation?

Education as the Great Conversation must forever open horizons for participants to see and consider all the world has to offer. Surface-level moral rules aimed solely at operational efficiency specific to the local level are unlikely to fulfill the most important purposes of the Conversation. The search for truth and inclusion in shared inquiry requires specific moral protections such as respect, social and distributive justice, and a network of implicit reciprocal promises between all participants. Advance in the Conversation requires the broadest and most global vision possible, both in terms of subject matter and in terms of moral consideration.

Ideally, laws should never be necessary to force an educational leader to reach out (Johnson, 2008) and bring others into the Great Conversation. However, laws may be necessary to free administrators from local prejudice in order to act responsibly in matters of inclusion and social justice, especially in the case of children of undocumented workers. Educators are, or at least should be, professionally unrelenting in their commitment to extend an invitation to the Conversation to all. This commitment should be evident in each school's and district's moral architecture, from the foundation up to the architecture's skin. (Recall that the architecture's "skin" is composed of surface-level rules prescribing or prohibiting specific actions.)

PROPERLY WORKING MORAL ARCHITECTURES

In the most functional moral architectures, the highest-order moral principles (the scaffolding) help adjudicate conflicts of rules and duties created by incommensurable surface-level prescriptions and prohibitions of behavior and actions (architectural skin). The virtues supporting the scaffolding define the collective character of the people whom the scaffolding protects and gathers together.

By contrast, the least functional moral architectures have fewer applicable higher-order principles (less scaffolding, and the principles that do exist are at best of modest inconvenience to saints and sinners alike). In these *flat* architectures, all rules, regulations, rights, policies, and laws tend to stand on equal ground with all other rules, regulations, rights, policies, and laws; all are aimed at doing little more than articulating specific actions and behaviors to be pursued or avoided. In flat architectures little more than brute power typically arbitrates competing claims and interests. Flat architectures are based on brute exercise of power and tend to be unstable and fluctuating in their priorities. In contrast, more elevated architectures, supporting mutual respect and freedom, tend to be more resilient and awe inspiring to stakeholders than are the less elevated architectures, limited to the close monitoring of behavior through surface-level rules alone. To paraphrase Aristotle's well-known dictum, it is better to be ruled by principle than the transient whim and capriciousness of those in power. More important, perhaps, is the likelihood that when the architecture is flat, the administrator's leadership is illusory because many stakeholders may be only following along rather than committed, loyal followers who together with the administrator subordinate themselves to shared moral ideals.

A REFLECTIVE BREAK

What does it mean to say that moral architecture and the Great Conversation bootstrap on one another? What does it mean to say that language and human moral development bootstrap on one another? How does an appropriate moral architecture advance participation in the Conversation in a specific school?

One reason schools are valuable to society, as Gunter (2001a) observes, is their special potential to develop compassion and cooperation in school employees and students. Districts, schools, and the societies and cultures affected by them don't evolve by accident (Blasé & Anderson, 1995). Other-regarding students, graduates, and employees bring other-regardingness into the surrounding communities through their daily practices in and out of school. The reader may recall Kant's belief that a good person is identified by a good will. Analogously, we believe that a good district is best identified by its collective good will, as evidenced in its moral architecture. The moral architecture of a good district conspicuously manifests inclusion, virtue, social justice, and reverence for the Great Conversation.

Responsible leadership does not leave the development of moral architecture to chance or to wholly external controls (Prawat, 1992). Responsible leadership requires not just moral vision but idealism in moral vision. Idealism in moral vision sets an agenda beyond individual self-interest (Fullan, 2004). In the absence of shared idealism, an institution's moral architecture flattens and risks disintegration. The characteristics of flat moral architecture versus elevated moral architecture are as follows:

Flat Moral Architecture	Elevated Moral Architecture
• School leadership limits attention to obedience, applying penalties and punishments. • Shared vision is seen as necessary only at the top of the hierarchy (others are meant simply to follow along). • Any deep ethical structure in humans is denied.	• School leadership clarifies and cultivates ethical understanding and appreciation throughout all district and school undertakings, based on lofty ideals and commitments. • Leaders focus on developing a social learning community that is characterized by thinking and acting ethically and developing virtues protective of different voices. • Elevated structure reflects a shared moral vision of professionalism and idealism.

MAKING COMMUNITIES BETTER THROUGH BETTER SCHOOL AND DISTRICT ARCHITECTURES

In an important way, moral architectures are part of hidden curricula through which students, faculty, staff, and administrators all learn to share in community and to become more other regarding. The hiddenness of moral architectures stems in large part from the ubiquitous character of moral architecture. It is not unusual for people to look past that which is most common and on to the unusual. There is no community without moral architecture, but just as people are typically not self-consciously aware of being in a community even while in its midst, they are not self-consciously aware of the moral architecture that permeates every aspect of that same community.

When something is seemingly everywhere, whatever it is, it seems to lose something of its identity. For example, whatever the specific moral architecture of a community or organization, it permeates every aspect of social life. As Campbell and Russo (2001) aptly anticipated, once inside the organization or community it is very difficult to gain perspective and observe the operational features of the architecture. Cognitive scientist Douglas Hofstader (1979) captures this idea very nicely with the observation that studying our own minds or community structures of which we are intimately a part is akin to a hand trying to grasp itself.

A member of a community is a part of the community's moral architecture, just as the community's moral architecture typically becomes a part of the character of each constituent member. Although the intimacy of the dynamic seems nearly complete, alert participants can still recognize on sustained reflection many or most of the elements of the architecture in play.

In a sense, being morally alert within a moral architecture is akin to being deeply in love. At first, lovers seem to have great perspective on the other, noting many details of the beloved as they stand at the threshold admiring one another. But as time advances the bond between them so deepens that the resulting intimacy obscures many details of the relationship. The lived experience, the gestalt of it all, becomes more than anyone typically notices. This is not a bad thing; it is just what happens when people move ever closer together, creating new social, economic, and moral units that never before existed. With the right cues, however, lovers can be prompted to step back and again recognize details of one another and of the bond they share. Similarly, as feminists would be especially quick to note (Noddings, 1992), even in the schools the bonding reflected in the presence or absence of indices of care and so on is obscured to those accustomed to living together in that way. It takes effort and alertness to appropriate cues to step back from time to time and examine the details of the school's or district's architecture and review whether it is continuing to be all that the administrator and stakeholders intend.

More often than not it is the administrator's responsibility to initiate ongoing review of the moral architecture. Also, periodic focus on school or district architecture should remind participants as explicitly as possible of the importance of moral architecture in curriculum and operational success at every level. Moral architecture (no more than lovers) should never be taken for granted—at least not for long.

To push the analogy with lovers just a bit further, a stable and well-structured moral architecture is meant to bring students into the Great Conversation, just as a stable and loving relationship is often meant to bring lovers into a robust and resilient marriage capable of supporting a family. By fostering the Conversation, the architecture broadens the collective and collaborative horizons of student and faculty experience. And finally, just as families depend on internal moral architectures fostering a network of responsibilities, duties, caring, and compassion, so too moral architectures compatible with the Conversation should presumably extend students' and the faculty's sense of responsibility and sense of social justice, appreciation of global world order, and sense of responsive beneficence to all peoples. In short, the moral architecture of schools should lead students and faculty alike to a cooperative and participatory mindset when entering and participating in other institutions beyond the school.

A GROUP DISCUSSION

There is a fourfold agenda for administrators when building a vibrant moral architecture in schools and districts: (1) cultivating a view of faculty, staff, and administrative responsibilities, (2) nurturing student participation in a sharing community, (3) broadening student views of global welfare and human betterment, and (4) encouraging schools to model moral qualities and behavior for other societal entities. Should schools undertake this agenda? Why or why not? What constraints might hinder a school or district from taking on such an agenda?

SUSTAINING MORAL ARCHITECTURE IN THE FACE OF CHALLENGE

A constraint on the bootstrapping effect between the Great Conversation and moral architecture comes in the form of intrusions and influence from sources external to schools and districts. These intrusions can be small and local or huge and reflect national priorities. Local intrusions usually can be managed well onsite by capable administrators. Larger intrusions resulting from federal legislation or agency law must be accommodated, and this may strain the entire resources of a school's or district's moral architecture. Two examples of such sweeping intrusion into current school operations can be found in No Child Left Behind (NCLB) legislation (No Child Left Behind Act of 2001; PL 107-110) and Career and Technology Education (CTE) legislation.

Imagine an urban high school in California bringing students together from various backgrounds in the immediate network of feeder middle schools. The students typically are not ready to be together with one another, and that sets the stage for tension and potential disruptions throughout the year if the transition is not managed well (Simmons & Black, 1991). The administration feels it is barely hanging on, underbudgeted and continuously under siege from stakeholders both inside and outside the institution. In addition to campus police and metal detectors, drug-sniffing dogs are routinely brought to campus, distracting students from the four purposes of education. Teachers may even fear for their own safety and have little sense of community with one another (Gellman & Delucia-Waak, 2006). Imagine further that the administration is nobly struggling to make a difference, and indeed, some small advances have been made. But add to this scenario all the detailed imperatives from various government entitlement programs, IDEIA, civil rights mandates, prescriptions for tolerance, and demands for zero tolerance, and the challenge may overwhelm even the most talented administrator.

The additional effort and resources needed to address constraints as intrusive as those imposed by NCLB alone may be the proverbial straw breaking the spirit needed to address all such challenges. Instead of being directed to developing a moral architecture featuring a shared sense of social justice and conducive to pedagogical mission, administrative attention may be diverted to meeting schooling imperatives. Administrators may desperately strive to meet external schooling mandates while teachers close their doors, keep their heads down, and deliver what is most likely to ensure that they have a job the next year. Authentic concern for inviting students into the Great Conversation will probably dwindle in proportion to the external demands and associated sanctions for failure to deliver expected numbers (Shealy, 2006). Moral architecture exists even in this imaginary scenario, but it is likely to be flattened to the point of being little more than a network of surface-level rules and associated penalties and punishments. And imagine this already overburdened system saddled with CTE legislation as well. The first function of schools such as the imaginary one described here may well become filling out reports with the "right" numbers (Vogel, Rau, Baker, & Ashby, 2006) while all else is left to chance and to the individual conscience of mavericks such as the venerable Jamie Escalante.

In *California's Consolidated State Performance Report: Amended Part II,* submitted to the U.S. Department of Education, the condition of all schools is summed up in 58 pages of numerical documentation. Somewhere in that mass of data, presumably, is the measure of each school. By implication there should be some indirect indication of the success and educational value experienced by each student (Darling-Hammond, 1998, 2004). After all, the policy is titled No *Child* Left Behind. But summative numerical data are not sufficiently sensitive to warrant inferences about each child. Summative data say nothing about the heroic performance of good teachers and administrators in the most challenging environments or bad teachers and administrators in the most advantageous environments. Ironically, NCLB is about *no child* at all! It doesn't even speak to the sorting out of good teachers and administrators suitable especially for children of certain types.

In contrast to the heavy-handed approach of NCLB, onsite moral architectures fostering inclusion in the Great Conversation are about the well-being of each child, not about summative data describing a bunch of children. Presumably, the most professional educators are meant to focus attention on each child's success. Professional educators do not fulfill their most important professional responsibilities by focusing exclusively on summative test scores that tell only how widely distributed some alleged minimal competency may be (Haladayna, Nolen, & Haas, 1991). Summative test data have their place, but the data should not be used in a way that subordinates three of the four elements of educational purpose. There is more to educational purpose than the acquisition of information. Where does all this leave the imaginary school described earlier and so many other schools just like it? More importantly, where do such intrusions fit into the most truly professional commitment of educators to focus on the well-being of *each* child through attention to each of the four corners of educational purpose?

Recall the story of Jamie Escalante. Escalante worked miracles for about 20 students each year by teaching calculus. But such miracles would matter little in a school of perhaps 5,000 students and driven by the summative data required by NCLB. In addition, because the summative data required by NCLB focus only on minimal success, excellence goes unnoticed; the extraordinary achievements of a mere 20 students don't matter to NCLB. In NCLB terms, 20 students performing well enough to get past the high-stakes testing requirement matter as much as Escalante's "miracles." Ironically, as Nichols and Berliner (2007) mention in *Collateral Damage*, 1,000 students barely getting by a standardized test matters 50 times more in terms of summative data than Escalante's 20 champions of excellence. Among the thousand students, many may be underperforming, yet in summative terms of reported test data, that doesn't matter. If students get by the state's standardized test, as Nichols et al. (2006) explain, there is no reward to the schools for seeing them through to their highest level of excellence because NCLB focuses solely on the widest distribution of minimally satisfactory performance. In short, the educational success of schools and districts cannot be effectively summed in an annual compendium of numerical data (Popham, 2001).

To take a page from Aristotle's *The Politics,* education should be about self-actualization (not to be confused with the self-esteem movement, which many [e.g., Hirsch, 2006] accuse of focusing too much attention on feelings and not enough on performance). For Aristotle, self-actualization meant that the individual learns to use her excellencies excellently. In other words, increased student competence (excellence) leads most naturally to increased confidence, not the other way around (Wagner & Benavente, 2006). This is another example of the bootstrapping effect discussed earlier.

Increased competence leads to increased confidence, and increased confidence normally leads to further competence, and on and on. Truly professional teachers understand this bootstrapping process as inherent in the Great Conversation, and they recognize their moral duty to assist every student in the bootstrapping opportunities available in his or her own life. The schooling distractions created by summative data-driven reports and the associated harsh impositions, threats, and penalties that often accompany such data-driven management are an assault on the very professionalism of educators (Nichols & Berliner, 2005). The moral architecture of schools already under stress is likely to be reduced even further by NCLB's emphasis on managed data at the expense of involving students in a Great Conversation.

A PHILOSOPHICAL QUESTION

Think of a school you know well. What indications are there of a flattening moral architecture? What would you suggest to strengthen and elevate the moral architecture? How can all surface-level rules associating penalties and punishments with specific violations be conspicuously tied to higher-order moral principles, virtues, or moral sensitivities?

The second influence on the moral architectures of schools imposed from without and mentioned earlier is the CTE legislation. As with NCLB, the ultimate cost of CTE may be that it places too much focus on managed data at the risk of limiting each student's self-actualization (Amrein & Berliner, 2003). Some may also complain that it focuses too much attention on vocational development of the individual for the sake of the economy and too little on individual flourishing (Brighouse, 2006).

In the case of CTE, each state must comply with federal directives by creating a state CTE plan in order to qualify for the federal government's Perkins funds. On paper, state plans may look wonderful. They each speak to personal development and developing talent for the needs of a more robust economy. For example, in the *Texas State Plan for Career and Technology Education, 2005–2007,* as required by the Texas State Education Code (Public Education Career and Technology Goals, Sect. TEC 29.181–182), there are seven directives and supporting action recommendations for each directive. The recommendations for each directive seem to offer something for everyone and take away nothing. However, it is still up to the district and schools to bring staff together to accommodate the new demands with those already being addressed at the local level.

Admittedly, improved worker skills lead to improvement of available human capital in the future and to better economic standing of individuals. Seemingly everyone is a winner. But higher income alone does not guarantee workers and citizens greater happiness, and nowhere is this more apparent than to educational leaders onsite in local contexts. Training for high-tech careers and education for personal flourishing are bound to conflict for resources in a standard 7-hour school day (Spring, 2004). Curricula and instruction must be appropriately balanced to secure economic goals, social justice, and a better education (Gardner, 1991). This is fundamental.

Brighouse (2006) is cautiously sympathetic to the idea that economic advance can be meaningfully pursued as long as schools sustain the importance of developing student autonomy, respect for truth, and human flourishing generally. If graduates become a bit wealthier but have no idea of how to make their lives better as a result, Brighouse warns, they have benefited little. The promise of CTE plans sounds exciting, but will the execution of the plans, complicated by mass data collection, create pockets of individuals who fit into an economy but have no sense of why that should matter to them? It is the administrators onsite who take lofty dreams and turn them into robust, operational activities.

In light of so many mandated schooling initiatives, there is much to worry an administrator holding to the dream of bringing together everyone in a Great Conversation. At this point, however, something must be said about how best to deal with the world as it is and not how well-meaning professionals may want it to be. To accommodate schooling intrusions such as NCLB and CTE in the school's educational mission, the wary and responsible administrator is advised to consider the following heuristic sequence of planning steps and actions. Step 1 is obviously to take note of the economic resources available in school and district to meet new demands and continue to meet ongoing responsibilities. Step 2 is to take inventory of the strength of the operative moral architecture for bringing all stakeholders together to address the new demands collaboratively. Step 3 is to draw everyone's attention to the highest-level principles in the school and district architecture that have made it resilient in the past and, through renewed commitment, will ensure robust survival in the future. Revitalization of moral architecture must precede the effort to place new demands on staff and other stakeholders. Finally, Step 4 is to implement protocols and procedures to bring everyone together in a shared commitment to respond to new demands while preserving what already serves current stakeholders successfully.

ELEVATING SCHOOL AND DISTRICT MORAL ARCHITECTURES

Administrative wisdom begins operationally with a vision beyond personal self-satisfaction and reward. That vision must conspicuously involve other-regardingness, that is, a commitment to

A REALITY CHECK

In what sense might vocational education, NCLB, and CTE initiatives lead to inequities and social injustice in society? How should an administrator incorporate such programs into a moral architecture that keeps open always the universal invitation to participate in the Great Conversation?

the well-being of all (Goodlad & Lesnick, 2004). In contrast, administrators who unwisely boss people about with ever-changing surface-level directives stay in place only on the flimsy contention that might makes right. The idea that might makes right holds up only on grounds of moral relativism, wherein it appears evident that there is nothing outside the power structure to look to when considering action or policy. Bosses operate out of a very low-level moral architecture, and subordinates typically do little more than follow along for the time being. In contrast, administrators of wisdom want all stakeholders to know that they honor and look up to the highest-level principles of the school's or district's moral architecture and subordinate themselves to such principles, just as they expect other stakeholders to do. This wisdom is the difference between the professionally inspired vision of an educational administrator leading followers and the contrivances of a boss to stay in power, with others forced into following along (Schmoker & Wilson, 1993).

Foundational principles, sensitivities, and virtues are heuristically helpful in sorting new external demands into the operational function of district and school without loss of educational purpose. By treating NCLB or CTE as shared challenges to be accommodated rather than rejected within a moral architecture of lofty perspective, stakeholders show good will toward all, both internal and external to the schools. Once again this reliance on moral architecture illustrates that shared organizational vision can be transiently fragmented, but organizations can still survive. Organizations survive in the face of fragmenting organizational vision when wise administrators draw attention to the (presumably) lofty moral architecture that makes stakeholders a community and that will see them through the challenge of forging a new organizational vision suitable to the community served.

SOCIAL ENGINEERING, SCHOOLING, AND THE FOCUS OF EDUCATION

Horace Mann is famous in American history for his leadership in establishing publicly supported education. According to Mann and many since, it is good public policy to bring people into schools to become better citizens. Because of further innovative legislation, more students now graduate from high school than ever before, and more go on to college than ever. And although there is some unevenness between some racial and ethnic groups, advances in the social justice of inclusion are being made. For example, since 1998, 60% of postsecondary students have been female. Unfortunately, the continued disproportion between male and females among minority populations is not an advance but a failure to more effectively extend the invitation of inclusion to all (Sommers, 2000). Attrition rates at colleges have declined, often as a direct consequence of institutional responsiveness to legislation, and this seems a good thing, although many employers complain that those who now graduate are more poorly prepared than at times when retention rates were lower (Gross, 2000).

> ### A PRACTICAL ASSIGNMENT
>
> How can an administrator ensure that statistically sound, empirical generalizations do not lead faculty and staff to stereotype groups of students and their parents? What stereotypes are most common in your community? How do they affect schooling practices and educational opportunities?

With more and more people seeing the schools as tools for reengineering society, despite the admitted good that has resulted, legislative pressures have also limited the educational leader's opportunity to fulfill strictly educational objectives such as inclusion of all in the Conversation. Perhaps the alleged deterioration of educational purpose within the schools is exaggerated by people outside the schools looking for a cause in order to advance ambitious political careers (Berliner & Biddle, 1995). In any case, the schools will continue to be venues for society to tackle social challenges and develop educational opportunities. Therefore, it will be the continuing challenge of the educational administrator to attend to society's legitimate needs and demands while preserving the focus on educational purpose in each district school.

THE PRAGMATIC VALUE OF JUSTICE

Building the right moral architecture for a school is an immediate and practical problem for school and district administrators. Sometimes it is easy to think the problem is less immediate than, say, figuring out the district's transportation schedules and transportation needs for the next year. In some ways it is less immediate; nonetheless, building the right moral architecture cannot be left on the back burner for long. Neglected moral architectures have a way of becoming flat architectures. The following questions should be considered when focusing on building a rich moral architecture in a school:

- Do administrators, staff, and students understand and appreciate the basic moral commitments and values that are being promoted in the school? Why or why not?
- Can staff and students distinguish between and discuss the occasional overlap of ethical principles and practical operational policies and rules? Do staff discussions and developmental activities ever include these topics?
- Do the school's professed basic intellectual and ethical commitments (e.g., equal respect of persons, fairness, diversity, freedom of thought, intellectual engagement, and respect for evidence and cogent arguments) permeate all aspects of school life?
- Do staff and administration understand the nature of professional obligation and shared moral vision?
- Are there localized fiefdoms of control in the school or community? Do they interfere with the effort to share a common moral vision throughout? Where are they located, and why are they allowed to exist?
- Are pedagogical practices examined for their ethical import as well as their efficiency and effectiveness?
- Are values and moral commitments consciously addressed in curricular matters?

- Do administrators, staff, and students see themselves as members of a democratic learning community akin to the Great Conversation, or does everyone do her own thing?
- Are the goals of the school supported by the moral architecture of the school?
- Is the Great Conversation a public relations item or a genuine set of activities and experiences of the school?
- Are there other questions that you would add to the previously stated ones? Are there some you would revise or restate? Are there any that you would want to delete? How do these and other shared commitments lead to a more productive and resilient educational institution?

Consider the following analogy. Many people wish to get into better physical shape. Wishes alone don't work. Neither do plans and protocols—at least not alone. To become fit, one needs commitment. The commitment that counts the most is commitment that leads to action (Ionesco, 1962), in this case commitment to exercise nearly every day or commitment to invite a group of students every day to search a bit for truth together.

Unexpected obligations may interrupt fulfillment of the most unwavering commitments. Imagine a newly committed runner descending the stairs one morning for the first of a lifetime of daily runs. The runner's dog, Duchess, is relieving herself in the kitchen. There is prudent reason to abandon all other tasks and quickly remove Duchess from the house and subsequently clean the residue from her mishap. The emergency trumps the runner's intention to exercise that day because there is now less than an hour to get to work. The run must be aborted—but for how long?

Committed people don't allow unexpected obligations to become a routine excuse for neglect. Exercise may not be the most immediate need at a moment of crisis, but if it continues to be a high priority that day there is a good chance that the truly committed will find a time to complete a run before bedtime. This is analogous to how it is with the commitment to build a moral architecture. Moral architecture is not built at a planning session one day and acted on the next. The styles and practices of leadership build the community's architecture each and every day through role modeling, an accumulating array of promises, and shared trust between stakeholders. When neglect to the details of such matters becomes *routine,* the architecture will inevitably weaken, and institutional resiliency will deteriorate.

Say it is early August and district transportation needs and schedules must be finalized. Late in August this may become a matter of immediate and pressing concern. A boss can act now and rush off to the next task, and that is all there is to it. That appears efficient, but is it?

By bringing together representatives from accounting, the district council, the parent–teacher organization, and the motor pool, a senior driver or two, and the transportation director, the administrator shows that although the need for closure is urgent, she is making every attempt to include as many stakeholders as possible to secure shared commitment and show a sense of other-regardingness to all. She may have to put strict limits on the length of discussion given pending deadlines, but the courtesy extended to all stakeholders shows she is truly committed to other-regardingness and not just as a transient practice for sharing possible blame. The time spent including everyone now may save time over the year repairing things that went wrong because not everyone had input at the front end. Moral architectures emerge from and are sustained by extending simple courtesies (e.g., saying "please" and "thank you," especially in thank you notes), holding annual faculty retreats, showing an interest in others' celebrations and tragedies, and in general fostering an environment of honor, duty, respect, and virtue. Ultimately each of these things reflects a further commitment to some higher-order principle or virtue. They are not just sustained through chance; it is the daily actions that make moral architecture more than lofty speculation about morality.

There have been many great and famous lawyers and doctors. Be that as it may, no profession has a heritage to match that of education. From Socrates, Plato, Aristotle, Moses, Jesus Christ, Mohammed, and Maimonides to William James, John Comenius, Richard Feynman, Maria Montessori, Jacques Barzun, Ella Flagg Young, Elsie Clapp, Marva Collins, Jonathan Kozol, Jaime Escalante, Paulo Freire, Paul Goodman, Stephen Carter, Leon Kass, and so many others, all have been known as great teachers. To be a leader within such an extraordinarily noble profession is a great thrill to those who truly understand what they are getting into. And it is appropriately humbling as well. Not one of the people named here or any other great teacher lacked a vision for human betterment. Not one of these people entered the temple of learning with a solely self-interested agenda. Each recognized the other-regarding essence of bringing people into the Great Conversation. Each recognized that it takes courage to press forward, bringing the Conversation to all without resorting to the tactics of power politics.

In many ways the future is being carved out by society and its schools now (Searle, 1995). The words of John Dewey in a speech given in 1929 are as resoundingly true now as then: "The challenge of the future is moral, not technological." Think of all the technological innovations that have come about since 1929. Is there any reason to believe the future ahead will be any less dependent on the moral than in Dewey's day? Is there any reason to think that educational leaders can be less concerned with the moral architectures of their schools and districts than in times past?

CLARIFYING THE CONCEPT

What leadership styles and personalities do you think are most helpful in cultivating an elevated and richly textured moral architecture in schools and districts? What character traits are most important in developing a shared vision of the school's or district's moral architecture?

DISCUSSION QUESTIONS

1. What does it mean to be other-regarding in practical reasoning? Give an example illustrating what the term means to you.

2. What does it mean to be an idealist in moral thinking? Is it possible to think about morality and not be an idealist of some sort? Explain why or why not.

3. David Hume said that all the sentences describing how the world is will never tell us how it ought to be. Some administrators like to describe themselves as practical people who let the facts speak for themselves. Of course, we all know that there are no talking facts. Pragmatists, in particular, note that every fact is a fact only in the context of some story. What ideals should drive your thinking about educational policy? What ideals should be reflected in every community's goals when creating school policy?

CASE STUDIES

Case Study 7.1. Sex Education: Considering Conflicting Opinions and Promoting Educative Learning

Two groups of parents have demanded to speak with the principal about the school's plan for ninth-grade sex education. One group demands that respect for virginity be advocated and mention of alternative lifestyles omitted. The other group wants children to be taught every aspect of how human copulating machinery works and how people can best protect themselves from disease. The two groups are convinced they are at odds with one another. Is this dispute a moral issue? Can a disputed issue be both moral and curricular? What is the most pragmatic way for an administrator to address this issue? (Be careful to distinguish between cowardly strategies and avoiding adversity on the one hand and doing what is most responsible on the other.) There are socially skillful ways of addressing the matter, and of course they should be used. More important, however, is the fact that effective leaders want to do the right thing. So what is the right thing to do in this case?

Case Study 7.2. A Request for a Letter of Reference

Ms. Palacio, an assistant principal, asks you to write a letter of reference for her. She is applying for a principalship in a diverse urban school district. Shortly after mailing a very strong letter of support for her, you are told by one of the school's cheerleaders that Ms. Palacio made an anti-Semitic remark in the school cafeteria in front of several students. You know that Ms. Palacio is a strict disciplinarian. You also know that recently she had to discipline two cheerleaders for violating the school travel policy. The cheerleaders both seem to be of Middle Eastern descent. Could the current report be the product of some conspiratorial act of vengeance against Ms. Palacio instigated by the rebuked cheerleaders? You now wonder why you didn't just stick to district policy and let the personnel office answer all questions related to Ms. Palacio's performance.

As you reflect on these matters you recall that several years previously Ms. Palacio was accused of making a strong anti-Muslim remark in the presence of both students and staff. Upon investigation, however, you found no evidence that she made such a remark. With all this still working on your mind, upon arriving at your office you find five notes awaiting your attention. The first is from the superintendent and states that she wants to discuss a personnel issue. The second is from the education writer for the local newspaper and indicates obliquely that he's heard a rumor that he wants to discuss. The third note is from Ms. Palacio herself and warns that she has an emergency she needs to discuss with you immediately. The fourth is a phone memo from the personnel director of the school district to which Ms. Palacio has applied and concerns "a person you have recommended for a position." The fifth note is from a parent of one of the two suspended cheerleaders and asks that you return her call immediately.

As you ponder which message to respond to first, you are reminded that a school ethics consultant has a meeting with you in 10 minutes. You had planned to discuss a series of professional development activities with him, but now you consider using the time to discuss what looks like an emerging firestorm involving Ms. Palacio. Which should you do first: return the phone calls, meet with Ms. Palacio, or beg off all five until you have more time to think and maybe discuss the matter with the ethics consultant? Is your decision in this case purely strategic, driven by legalistic concerns, or motivated by some concern to do the morally right thing while preserving the integrity of the school's moral architecture? In short, what do you think is your first and primary responsibility at this point in the unfolding set of circumstances?

ACTIVITY

Activity 7.1

Kierkegaard (2000) talks about communion with God as something that only knights of faith can recognize in one another but can never articulate. Similarly, Douglas Hofstader (1979) has observed that the mind trying to understand itself is akin to the fist grasping itself. We have observed similarly that those within a moral architecture cannot grasp all of its details. Jot down a few notes to yourself on the moral architecture of your school or district. Go to a couple of people who you think see the world largely as you do. After explaining the idea of moral architecture to them, ask them to describe a few features of the architecture you share. Do they see elements you overlooked?

FURTHER READING

Blasé, J., & Anderson, G. (1995). *The micropolitics of educational leadership.* London: Cassell.

Fullan, M. (2004). *Leadership & sustainability: System thinkers in action.* Thousand Oaks, CA: Corwin.

Glickman, C. D. (2002). *Leadership for learning: How to help teachers succeed.* Alexandria, VA: Association for Supervision and Development.

Gunter, H. (2001). *Leaders and leadership in education.* London: Routledge and Kegan Paul.

Johnson, S. M. (1996), *Leading to change: The challenge of the new superintendency.* San Francisco: Jossey-Bass.

Katz, K. A., Noddings, N., & Strike, K. A. (Eds.). (1999). *Justice and caring: The search for common ground in education.* New York: Teachers College Press.

Knapp, M. C., & Talbert, J. (2003). *Leading for learning: Reflective tools for school and district leaders.* Seattle: Center for the Study of Teaching and Policy, University of Washington.

Kowalski, L. T. J. (Ed.). (2004). *School district superintendents: Role expectations, professional preparation, development and licensing.* Thousand Oaks, CA: Corwin.

Murphy, J. (Ed.). (2002). *The educational leadership challenge: Reforming leadership for the 21st century.* 101st Yearbook of the National Society for the Study of Education. Chicago: National Society for the Study of Education.

Sizer, T. R., & Sizer, N. F. (1999). *The students are watching: Schools and the moral contract.* Boston: Beacon.

Starratt, R. J. (1994). *Building an ethical school: A practical response to the moral crisis in schools.* London: Falmer.

CHAPTER 8

The Role of Law in Moral Evaluation

LAW AS PUBLIC MORALITY AND SURFACE TO MORAL ARCHITECTURE

As we approach the end of this volume, there are several ideas we want to discuss that we think will help you build a strong school and district moral architecture. We begin by noting how school law is related to ethics and the practical art of leading in a school. Second, we briefly delineate how understanding the nature of law can illuminate both its general intent as a community moral resource and its immediate goal of restricting, defining, or prescribing educational and schooling practice. Third, we introduce the idea that being ethical may require that we occasionally challenge certain laws because they run counter to some fundamental moral principles and virtues. Such challenges obviously require courage, wisdom, social acuity, an understanding of professional ethics, and more. Fourth, we describe the relationship of the school administrator to very specific prescriptions and prohibitions and the human need to sense what is just in specific circumstances. In particular, we examine the administrator's need to think reflectively and make judgments about what is fair, wise, and humane in actual situations as they present themselves and not just in some pristine and abstract way (Tiberius, 2008). Finally, we conclude that the wisdom of leaders is as critical to developing the moral architecture of schools as it is to developing prudent law. These ideas and others are summed up in Table 8.1.

JURISPRUDENCE, PHILOSOPHY, AND PRACTICAL STUDIES

Jurisprudence is the study of the nature of law (Gather, 2004). Oddly, many nonlawyers imagine the law is somehow free of philosophical speculation and especially free of moral commitments. Yet no discipline is free of philosophical speculation. Philosophy stands at the crossroads of all other disciplines. If a person asks serious questions about the epistemic foundations of any discipline long enough, one begins to do philosophy. This is certainly

Table 8.1   School Law and Ethics: The Relationships and Implications

Factors	Emphases	Leadership Questions and Implications
Law	The legal is embedded in the moral and vice versa.	How do we know when the law is based on sound ethical grounds?
Legal intent	The legal intent goes beyond the literal rendering of written law.	What are the explicit implications and implicit intents of the laws and judicial renderings?
Empowerment	The law can and often does protect the powerless.	Whom is this law or policy designed to protect? Does it simultaneously disempower others? Does the law promote an equal respect for all persons? If not, what must be done?
Justice	The fair decision treats equals equally and unequals unequally.	How do equality and fairness overlap? How do they differ at times? Is this law-and related policies-fair and equitable? What role, if any, should feelings play in deciding what is just? What does it mean to have a feel for the administration of the law? How do you ensure that punishments and entitlements are fair and not just equal?
Wisdom	The wise decision is based on multiple considerations.	Why is wisdom important in the administration of the law and related policies? How are being wise and being ethical related? How do we know when we are administrating wisely? Describe how a decision might be just but on some grounds be unwise. What might count as a legitimate reason for letting mercy overrule the requirements of justice? Judges occasionally show mercy; should school administrators do the same? Why or why not?
Courage	The virtue of courage is needed to ensure that justice and wisdom are balanced with renderings of the law.	Under what circumstances will an administrator probably need to marshal courage to question the wisdom or justice of district policy? What can a district and school do to foster a moral architecture that values courage?

true of the law. Moreover, in law, questions of moral philosophy are also inevitable. And what is true of the law in this case is probably true also of every practical discipline focusing on human, social behavior and action. For example, management texts in business reveal references to many moral terms and imperatives (Kouzes & Pozner, 2006; Shriberg, Shriberg,

& Kumari, 2005; Walton, 1986). In short, when one is dealing with the practical aspects of human social life and behavior, as does the law, moral reflection is unavoidable.

Educational leadership is also a practical study. Consequently, its scholars and practitioners are inevitably drawn to moral philosophy and epistemology, respectively. For example, moral questions such as, "What counts as an ethical leader?" and epistemic questions such as, "How do we *know* we are ethical as leaders?" are commonly considered. The foundational moral theories sketched in Chapter 2 have immediate implications for both questions. But knowledge of foundational theories does not constitute sufficient understanding. The administrator needs to know more if she is to serve as a role model and sustain an appropriate moral architecture. The administrator needs to understand educational law because it (including court precedent, legislation, and administrative policy and regulations) contains an abundance of applied community moral wisdom.

Law in any form is fallible. That is, it doesn't always achieve what lawmakers wish. But in a democracy especially, it represents fragments, at least, from a broad range of stakeholders of a shared sense of human betterment. And, keeping in mind the practical, even when the law is misguided its impositions and guidelines must be addressed and accommodated in one way or another.

In short, responsible educational leaders must consider the purpose of law and its particulars in a given case when examining school issues. Finally, without serious reflection on the nature of law itself, it is easy to envision it as artificially limited to little more than its formal loci of origin, that is, the law as written in law books. But there is more to the law. For example, the law extends well beyond what legislatures prescribe. For most people, the law that governs their lives is court-made law: precedents covering years, decades, and sometimes even centuries. Court-made law may also be as recent as the first tests of newly written law from legislatures, or it may be centuries old, as is often the case in property law. Both legislatures and the executive branch of government may also create agencies to carry out their respective responsibilities. The policies and regulations of these government agencies make up **administrative law.** It should be noted that administrative law is especially relevant to school administrators.

The regulative policies districts create for their own administration are only artificially distinguished from administrative law. In fact, the courts often demand that a district live up to its policy when a litigant sues because the district seemed to arbitrarily shift from its own written policy. Obviously, the power to sanction and enforce sanctions varies greatly in the case of all these different sources of law and policy, but that does not make the rules and regulations under consideration any more or less prescriptive or less focused on matters of human betterment. In the end, administrators must take time out not just to understand the particulars of this or that law or legal rendering but also to consider the nature of law, its purpose, its realm, and its metatheory or jurisprudence.

A Group Discussion

How do you know when a law needs changing? If you could change a current law that influences your work as a principal or superintendent, what would it be? What are the morally relevant elements of this misguided law as you see it? In the spirit of Henry David Thoreau, under what circumstances (if any) do you think civil disobedience could ever be a professional duty for an educational leader?

THE NATURE OF LAW

As we indicated earlier, every realm of law is full of moral implications. From property and tax law (Murphy & Nagel, 2003) to the law of evidence, criminal law, and contract law (Stein, 2005), moral implications abound. And what is learned from the law can be both directive and something of a moral asset to administrators.

What is meant by the statement that the law can be a moral asset? It means that the law can be an aid to the principal and superintendent as they make ethical decisions. The idea of law as moral asset is not always appreciated by practitioners, and there are a couple of good reasons for this. The first and most obvious reason for the failure to appreciate the law as a moral resource is that the law is sometimes wrong-headed. Clearly, sometimes the law aggravates rather than improves situations in either education or schooling. Even so, there is an important sense in which the law is self-correcting over time, and so we see the law evolving (presumably) away from deleterious social consequence. By observing how the law is guided away from contaminating social error, the administrator gets a sense of community understanding and its convergence on a sense of the common good (e.g., what should be done in schools for the well-being of students and society). Laws enacted to better serve students of color, students with challenges, and students whose first language is not English are all examples of a move toward the betterment that is achieved through universal education.

The second reason some practitioners fail to see the law as a potential *moral* resource is that they see the law as just a set of prohibitions and prescriptions fancied by those in power. This cynical and hardened view can diminish practitioner respect for the accumulated wisdom often evident in the law. Some legal theorists are themselves somewhat responsible for this dismissive attitude toward the underlying soundness of law. The full history of how these theorists contributed to such a jaundiced view of the law is too complex to describe here. And, of course, these theorists may be right and the law is just a set of rules in a game of life, but we think not. In any case, a more positive view is necessary if school administrators are to avoid creating a negative, self-fulfilling prophecy about the law's proper influence on educational and schooling ideals. A brief sketch of how the law came to be viewed as a very important sort of game—but a game nonetheless—may prompt some useful understanding of current cynicism about the law (Dworkin, 1988). Indeed, such a sketch may help open the door, allowing the reader to see the law as an appropriate moral resource in school and district moral architectures.

Linguistic origins and convention played a role in recent thinking about morality (as indicated in Chapters 1 and 2), and such considerations also had an effect on jurisprudence in the mid-20th century as well. Philosophers and linguists at the time had become largely convinced that there was no necessary connection between how things *are* in the world and how language *portrays* the world. If language allows people to get things done satisfactorily, then that is all that can be hoped for when it comes to grasping the meaning of a word, phrase, or sentence (Sapir, 1921; Saussure, 2002; Whorf, 1964; Wittgenstein, 1967). When applied to the law, this philosophy eschewed all cognitive import to moral theorizing and postulated instead that the law is simply a nonmoral set of sentences, imperatives, and hypothetical conditionals that serve as rules in a grand sort of game. These sentences (laws) dictate which moves are allowed in the game of life and which moves are prohibited. These sentences also specify enforcement against violations of the law. In short, people are required to obey the law simply because without the conventions imposed by rules and sanctions, the resulting pandemonium would devastate all social organization. In other words, law's virtue is solely that it ensures civil stability (Hart, 1963; 1997).

Presumably communities and organizations will sink into anarchy without enforceable, surface-level rules and sanctions. But is soul-searching reflection on moral right-mindedness really unproductive? Is the law really only about who plays the better game (as the television attorney portrayed by James Woods in *Shark* often proclaims, "Justice has nothing to do with a judicial decision. Justice is God's problem, winning is my problem")? If law is justified solely by ensuring civil stability, what nonmoral or amoral justification is there for securing civil stability? Without such justification, aren't civil and school anarchy just as good an option as civil and school stability?

Certainly some see no purpose or justification whatsoever in law. Anarchists such as Peter Kropotkin, Michael Bakunin, and Noam Chomsky (Bakunin, 1970; Chomsky & Pateman, 2005; Kropotkin, 2002) argue against all such justifications. Why shouldn't they? If there is no grounding for sentences identifying right and wrong, if laws are only accidents of history, why should anyone be bound by them? Even in the classroom it seems there are anarchists who see little reason for standard prohibitions and prescriptions for appropriate behavior (Neill, 1995).

A REALITY CHECK

A person may argue any theoretical position she wishes (e.g., anarchy). In actual life, one of the tests of the seriousness of a person is whether she actually practices or lives on the basis of what she professes. Why is it unlikely that you will have a genuine anarchist visit your office, criticize your language game rules, and argue that students should be allowed to do whatever they please? In what ways do parents sometimes get close to an anarchist position? How should you address their concerns?

When all is said and done, many legal scholars, such as Murphy and Nagel (2003) and Stein (2005), argue plausibly that the law can never escape its moral moorings. Indeed, most arguments for change in law reflect allegations that the moral moorings of current law have grown loose and are *morally* indefensible. In essence, law becomes nothing more than the "set of morals [prescriptive sentences] those holding the sovereignty of state wish to endorse and enforce" (Kierstead & Wagner, 1993). Although this definition of the law seems true enough in that it doesn't subordinate either law to morality or law and morality to the will of those in power, it doesn't quite go far enough. Although the definition reflects that the law cannot be separated from morality, it does not reveal anything about the fluid nature of law and its quest to improve civil society. However, administrators must consider the normative and developing social wisdom of the law when reflecting on the appropriateness of school and district moral architecture. Therefore, the law understood in this sense becomes a legitimate *moral* resource for school leaders rather than an impediment or constraint.

Although it is naïve to suggest that convergence of morality or its subset of enforceable implications through law *always* leads toward human betterment, there are historically powerful examples of law forcing policy accommodations in schools and districts that have indeed led to human betterment. Consider the example of the well-known cases the U.S. Supreme Court bundled together to address the practice of school segregation (*Brown v. Topeka Board of Education* 347 U.S. 483 [1954]; *Briggs v. Elliot* 342 U.S. 350 [1952]; *Davis v. County School Board of Prince Edward County* 103 F.Supp. 337 [1952]; *Gebhardt v. Belton* 33 Del. Ch. 144,87 A2d862 [Del. Ch. 1952]; *Bolling v. Sharpe* 347 U.S. 487 [1954]). These cases will be referred to collectively as *Brown,* following the convention of the Court.

A century before *Brown,* African Americans and certain other minorities were prevented from enjoying any benefits of public education in some states. Clearly this practice affected the members of said minorities, but one can also easily imagine how they affected the moral architectures of districts, schools, and classrooms throughout these states. The 13th, 14th, and 15th amendments were intended in part to end these exclusions. In the wake of such progressive legislative efforts, many states began providing public education to previously excluded minorities in schools separate from schools with all-white populations of students. This maneuver should not surprise us in retrospect because the amendments forcing a change of behavior could not by themselves overcome attitudes of prejudice and bigotry that had been nurtured in the exclusionary moral architectures then existing in districts, schools, and classrooms before the change in law.

The equal rights amendments represented an advance in moral thinking about what should happen in the nation's schools. They made more palpable the claims of the U.S. Constitution that all are created equal. They forced a change in behavior, but as one might expect, change in moral attitude lagged behind, given the many exclusionary moral architectures that existed throughout the country's school system and the country itself. In *Plessy v. Ferguson* (163 U.S. 537 [1896]) the U.S. Supreme Court affirmed the technical conditions of the equal rights amendments and thereby affirmed at least some of the moral advances these amendments represented. Unfortunately, in its ruling in *Plessy* the Court failed to recognize that their "separate but equal" doctrine was still a de facto violation of the intention of the equal rights amendments cited in the Court's own decision.

Plessy remained the law until the U.S. Supreme Court reversed itself in *Brown. Plessy* was a timid and morally deficient interpretation of the equal rights amendments. However, it did represent confirmation of a moral advance in attitudes and practices 50 years previously (Zirkel, 2004). Today there is little doubt that separate but equal is insufficient for ensuring genuine equality of opportunity. And this convergence toward a more inclusive spirit in education should be expected in light of both universalist moral tendencies and an ideally pragmatic move toward convergence, as we outlined in Chapter 2 and described as a principle of minimizing substantive moral error.

Precedent was cited for *Brown,* but many knew that the decision was in fact made on progressive moral grounds. Certainly few today would argue that *Brown* was wrong to reverse *Plessy.* Few today would disagree that *Brown* advanced universal principles of public morality. *Brown* remains an important aspect of American moral architecture. More importantly for the purposes in this book, the law created by *Brown* became an animating force in bringing about a more inclusionary moral architecture in districts, schools, and classrooms across the country. Clearly, *Brown* is an example of how law outside the classroom, school, or district can affect the moral environment within each and do so positively.

As *Brown* illustrates, there are very positive reasons administrators should seek the counsel of the law. Regardless of whether it's legislative law, administrative law, or judicial renderings, the law often embodies the collective understanding of common betterment. Also, although the law as in *Brown* may not always articulate what people favor at the moment, it is often close enough to minimizing substantive moral error such that people are willing to live under the architecture of its progressive movement.

Although there is a case to be made for the law's convergence toward principles supportive of human betterment, there is also the ever-present reality that the law, like other human institutions, is always fallible and always vulnerable to error. Consequently, given the inherent and morally responsive nature of law, educational administrators must be prepared to learn from the law and perhaps, at other times, to have the courage to challenge it when it seems gravely in error.

Trying to lead by relying on the dictates of the law alone is at least as risky as trying to lead with only grand moral theories in mind. Educational leaders need to take guidance from many relevant sources. The law is clearly one such source.

Communal wisdom, as reflected in the law, is often a closer approximation of our highest-level moral principles than what might be anticipated by any one person alone. Admittedly, there may be times when a law truly fails and impedes educational development or associated schooling goals. Detecting fault lines in the law may challenge an administrator's acuity of understanding and comprehensiveness of imagination. When genuine fault lines in the law are detected, the administrator may be called upon to marshal sufficient courage to challenge appropriately a destructive legal dictate.

MORAL COURAGE, PRUDENCE, AND THE LAW

Much thought, deliberation, collaboration with fellow professionals and other stakeholder groups, and planning should precede any decision to challenge a law. Nonetheless, no conscientious educator should ever think of the law as an unimpeachable or exhaustive force dictating clear and precise directives in advance of all imaginable circumstances. For example, the law in most states requires educators to report to the state's child protective services instances of suspected child abuse. Child abuse is surely wrong, morally wrong, so there ought to be laws minimizing its occurrence. Moreover, state immunity statutes (under Section 6736 of the No Child Left Behind Act, "Limitations on Liability of Teachers," the federal government extends immunity to educators in certain cases when hitherto that had always been left to the states) and case law (*Hennessy v. Webb,* 264 S.E. 2d 878 [1980]; *Truelove v. Wilson,* 285 S.E. 2d 556 [Ga. 1981]) both protect administrators and faculty from liability if a premature report, made in good faith and without malice (*McLaughlin v. Tilendis,* 253 N.E. 2d 85 [Ill. Ct. App. 1969]), turns out to be ill founded. The disproportionate protection of reporters as opposed to those likely to be investigated is deliberate so that the unempowered child may be protected. The unempowered in this case, at least in the eyes of the law, are children needing protection from neglect or powerful, menacing familial predators. (Most states follow the guidelines issued in 1977 by the U.S. Department of Health, Education and Welfare, which created the Model Child Protection Act with Commentary.)

A PRACTICAL ASSIGNMENT

What does an administrator need to understand before challenging the surface-level precedent established by a court decision? What could justify an administrator's claim that she knows a better way to go than that dictated by the law? Consider the reasoning of people throughout history who are noted for rightly challenging certain laws as you answer these questions.

Yet are we really so sure that the poor and various people of color (who may be disproportionately reported in certain districts) are not themselves unempowered, even as adults, when confronted and potentially challenged by university-educated administrators, teachers, and welfare and child service workers? There may well be degrees of unempowerment to which the law in this case is somewhat insensitive (Gardara & Contreras, 2009).

The law is clear, and the intent of the law is clear. But where the rubber hits the road, much is still unclear. For instance, under what conditions should an administrator suspect abuse or neglect? This is no simple matter. A careless report can lead to an unwarranted investigation. An unwarranted investigation may cause internal disruptions and fear within the family unit that last years afterward. These effects can be detrimental to the child who no longer enjoys strong family discipline, and they may be detrimental to genuinely responsible and well-meaning parents who, after an investigation, feel compromised in their ability to raise their children. In such cases an overzealous adherence to the intent of the law, especially while ignoring nuances of moral responsibility, may be as damaging to children as the possibility of caregiver neglect the law was meant to address. Ethically, parents also need to be treated fairly and caringly. It's best for them, and it is best for their children.

CLARIFYING THE CONCEPT

How should an administrator handle a teacher's report of suspected child abuse? How complete should the report be? How much evidence should the administrator require of the person making the report? Consider the meta-ethical question, "What exactly counts as a case of suspected child abuse or neglect?"

There is a growing body of litigation exposing districts and administrators to liability for failing to report suspected child abuse (*Pesce v. J. Sterling Morton High School,* 830 F.2d 789 [7th Cir. 1987]). Seemingly any reticence to make a report seems imprudent inasmuch as administrators are generally protected if they make the reports in good faith in carrying out their professional responsibility (*Picarella v. Terrizzi,* 893 F.Supp. 1292 [Pa. 1995]; *Landstrom v. Illinois Department of Children and Family Services,* 892 F.2d 670 [7th Cir. 1990]). Yet it is precisely here where the administrator may need to muster courage.

The safest strategy for the administrator is to report anything that comes her way. But wrongful reports can hurt. As noted earlier, wrongful reports can hurt children, their caregivers, and others. They can isolate and intimidate a certain sector of stakeholders in the school or district moral architecture, and this is likely to compromise what all intend to accomplish (Wagner & Benavente, in press). Beyond concern for liability and bothersome litigation there are always additional moral concerns with which the administrator must deal, and deciding what counts as a case of suspected child abuse is one example. For instance, the administrator must ask whether child abuse reporters' biases toward certain ethnic or economic groups plays a role, either consciously or unconsciously, in their noticing grounds for suspicion.

Another consideration for the school leader is that some divorcing parents are willing to accuse an estranged spouse of child abuse. They even try to co-opt school personnel in their attempt to assault one another through the courts. School administrators carry a heavy burden of responsibility when deciding whether they are witness to suspected child abuse or neglect in these and all cases of alleged suspected abuse. Administrative consideration of such matters must always begin with consideration of the welfare of the child.

QUESTIONING THE AUTHORS ?	An example of moral convergence is the principle to respect all people equally. Making a call to Child Protective Services may place a parent at risk of unjustified suspicion and possible investigation. Not making a call when suspicion is in order places a child at risk for continued abuse or neglect. Are parent and child each fully autonomous? Can one person be said to be more important than another when it comes to allocating risk? What does it mean to say someone is unempowered? In allocating risk, how might considerations of empowerment be relevant? Would you consider poor, uneducated adults unempowered when confronted by college-educated evaluators?

LAW, ORDER, AND THE FEEL OF JUSTICE

In his book *The Politics,* Aristotle (1958) pointed out that if society does not live by moral tradition, including its constitution and the law, then all that is left to live by is the whimsy and capriciousness of those in power. History has often vindicated this observation. Aristotle also acknowledged that tradition, convention, and the law may at times be in error and should be changed. In short, for Aristotle, the wisdom of the ages is to be respected but never mindlessly.

The Aristotlean idea of government by law and not by men remains an important principle even in today's modern democracies. Social stability is best served when the administration of justice is predictable. This is true not only for countries but for schools and districts, too.

Zero tolerance policies probably have their origins in a misunderstanding of recent jurisprudence and the Aristotlean argument for predictability. That is, such policies secure predictable consequences for explicitly defined violations. But, critics ask, just how well defined can a description of a violation be?

Zero tolerance policies are a recent development presumably representing the belief of some that states' administrative school laws, district policies, rules, and regulations were too often administered capriciously or with prejudice. Certainly, if disparity of penalty and punishment between adjudicated cases runs rampant, then supervisory moral authority is compromised and the school and district moral architecture weakened as a result. The penalty or punishment for the same offense should be equal. But what counts as the same offense or the same penalty?

The term *equality* is sometimes mistakenly equated with terms such as *fairness* or *justice*. Similarly, inequalities are sometimes mistakenly assumed to be instances of injustices. Consider the following example. Johnny complains it is *unfair* that he has to go to bed at 8:30 each evening but his brother does not. His parents explain simply, "Johnny, you are only 6, and you need your sleep. Your brother is 32." The implication is presumed to be so obvious that nothing more need be said even to a 6-year-old. Treating two brothers equally is not the same as treating them fairly. In this case the brothers are certainly treated unequally, but it would surely be unfair to make a 32-year-old man go to bed at a certain time just because his 6-year-old brother is required to do so. And it would be irresponsible to let little Johnny choose his sleeping time as might a middle-aged man. Sometimes treating everyone equally is the most unfair thing one can do.

Arguments about affirmative action revolve around the distinction between equality and fairness. Similarly, arguments about disproportionate expenditures on public school students revolve around the same distinction. Those who favor disproportionate spending or affirmative action argue on grounds of fairness. Those who oppose either argue that equality is the linchpin of fairness. Both are right to an extent, and that fact is probably the cause for much continued debate. Aristotle and, more recently, R. S. Peters (Aristotle, 1958; Peters, 1983) handily sum up the equality-versus-fairness debate as follows: Fairness is about treating equals equally and unequals unequally. Of course, sorting out when people are equal or unequal is where the technical aspects of social policy debates focus, sometimes successfully and sometimes not. Those who focus on a one-size-fits-all concept of fairness or justice as simple equality miss the more subtle and contextually sensitive notion of social justice. Mere equal treatment ignores mitigating circumstances, circumstances such as poverty, discrimination, and mental and physical challenges, to name just a few. By contrast, social justice conscientiously tries to take into account individuating circumstances that are context variant and relevant to the equitable application of variant surface laws and other policies and rules. As noted earlier, the terms "same offense" and "same penalties" are deceivingly vague and imprecise. They do not capture either the heart of justice or the point of, say, punishment as opposed to penalties. Consequently, what appears clear on the surface of a law, policy, or other regulation may turn out to be a source of misunderstanding and turmoil in application.

Imagine the following display: the Ten Commandments, a statue of Socrates, and a statue of Justice. What could such a display mean?

The Ten Commandments represent one of the earliest times humans put prescriptions for action in writing as enforceable commands. They are meant to be an enduring and stable recognition that lines must be drawn. On the opposite end from the written law in our imagined display is Justice. Justice is blind. Blindness protects her from bias when rendering a decision in light of the law. But there is something more telling about Justice. She holds in her hand balance scales. The scales of Justice symbolize that she must know more than the law alone. She must have a *feel* for the law's administration. So justice requires that we move beyond law, policy, rules, and regulations. Justice, in contradistinction to sterile expression of law as portrayed in the Commandments, must have a feel for contextual variants and mitigating circumstances. But there is more to the display than law and justice. Specifically, what might we say about Socrates sitting in the middle between the law (Commandments) and the human need to sense circumstance (Justice)?

Socrates represents a school administrator (or, in the court, a judge). Socrates is pulled between two possible extremes. On one hand, there is the law. As written, the law appears cold, sterile, and yet certain and to the point. On the other hand, there is Justice. She is unbiased and tries to balance the facts of a situation to get a feel for what's at stake. Just what would put matters into balance? Socrates, the stand-in for every educational administrator, cannot allow himself to be pulled solely in the direction of how he feels about the matter or to ignore such compelling sensitivities and robotically force situations into a paradigm of sanctionable action. Instead, Socrates must pull everything together and through his experience of human affairs arrive at a decision reflective of legal intent and responsive to the actual facts at hand. This is no easy task, but it is one that every administrator must prepare herself to undertake from time to time.

Imagine two students late for gym class. The teacher has announced a zero tolerance policy for tardiness. The policy is well known to each student. The penalty for tardiness is four laps around a quarter-mile track. The first child is late because he was detained physically and bullied in the hallway by several older students. The second child, in a different class, saunters into gym late because he was flirting with admiring girls. Does it make sense to say the two students are guilty of the same offense? Zero tolerance policies focus on behavior alone and exclude consideration of intent and other mitigating circumstances. In the common law of democratic courts, intention and mitigating circumstances usually are considered relevant but, unfortunately, not in schools or select criminal cases for which zero tolerance policies are in place. If the teacher recognizes the two cases as categorically different in offensiveness, how can he justify assigning the same penalty to each student? And what should a principal do who knows that the teacher has such a rule? (See Case Study A.2 in Appendix A.)

In addition, what does it mean to say the teacher assigns the *same* penalty to each student? Can the penalty be deemed the same without consideration of the nature of the two students? Drunk drivers and assassins both kill people. But the law says that the condition of the drunk and his intent makes the case wholly different from the cold-blooded actions of an assassin. Therefore, the mitigating circumstances differentiating the two offenders will lead to two sharply different punishments. If this kind of reasoning makes sense in the law, then why not in the administration of order in the classroom, school, or district?

A REFLECTIVE BREAK

Imagine that two students are late in getting to football practice. The first student is 14 years old, in good health, but weighs 230 pounds and is only 5'4." The second student is the football quarterback, who stands 6'5" and weighs 190 pounds. Are the two students being assigned the same penalty when each is admonished to run four laps? How should the two students be penalized? Explain your reasoning.

Zero tolerance policies claim to assign the same penalty to each violator. Yet in the absence of any knowledge about the violators themselves, it is incautious to describe zero tolerance penalties and punishments in such cases as being the same for each malfeasant.

Legislators imposing zero tolerance on the courts and schools imposing such policies on themselves seem to have omitted the very practical need to do some meta-ethical analysis—clarify critical concepts—before rushing against the flow of the common law tradition and common-sense school management. Zero tolerance too often forces administrators laboring under such policies to limit or ignore the critical considerations represented by Socrates and especially Justice in our imaginary display described earlier. Such limits compromise the attempts of progressive schools and districts to sustain moral architectures conducive to student and staff development.

THE WISDOM OF THE LAW: ORDER AND SOCIAL JUSTICE

Is the law a source of wisdom? Should the law be a source of wisdom? Is the law always imposed on people from above, or is there an important sense in which people are said to *own* the law, especially in a democracy? Should the law serve human betterment, or is it free to ignore such considerations?

Consider again the questions pertaining to differences between equality on one hand and social justice and fairness on the other. We noted earlier that equality is a concept vastly different from concepts such as fairness and social justice. We also noted that administrators are well advised to do a little meta-ethical analysis to consider just how different these terms are from one another. But in practical administration, there is a need for more than meta-ethical analysis. As the symbolism of our imagined display suggests, between the feel of justice and balanced regard for the law as written there is a need for Socrates (our stand-in for administrators) to bring it all together with his practical understanding of human affairs and decide on a course of action. In short, the administrator must be a person of extraordinary common sense when administering law and policy in the school or district. Such common sense is presumably also what many people mean when they talk of wisdom and the law. So in completing our discussion of law as an element of public morality and featured component of moral architectures, we turn now to a discussion of the law's wisdom in balancing order and social justice.

Whenever one discusses wisdom, it is common for the mind to drift to the legendary wisdom of King Solomon as described in Jewish antiquity. Solomon knew the difference between equality and social justice. He also knew the importance of using his experience of practical affairs to get a grip on rightful administrative action.

Two women came to him claiming to be the mother of the same infant. In the absence of DNA, blood typing, and all the other resources of modern technology, Solomon had to make a right-minded decision in his administration of the law. Solomon's experience and understanding of human affairs led him to gamble that the real mother could not bear to see her child destroyed merely to ensure some legalistic notion of equality. So Solomon ordered that the child be severed in half and each alleging mother be given half, an equal amount of the disputed child. Solomon's gamble proved revealing. One woman was happy with the equal result. Equal result or not, the other woman willingly offered to give up her claim so the infant might live. Solomon knew then that this latter woman must be the mother, and so he awarded her the child. Solomon's handling of the case showed that equality is not the foundation of social justice;

rather, fairness is. It would have been horrendously unfair to destroy the infant to appease two disputing women. The true mother could not abide such merciless and unfair treatment of her infant.

Although Solomon is historically famous as an expert administrator of justice, we do not expect such heroic feats of understanding from contemporary school or district administrators, nor do we countenance Solomon's evident willingness to gamble on his understanding of human affairs. Still, we draw attention to this historically famous account of the administration of law to illustrate that the administrator can never fully abdicate the responsibility to judge or make decisions regarding each case with an eye to laws, policy, rules, and, most importantly, to individuating circumstances and social justice.

Zero tolerance policies may ease a teacher's or administrator's daily task of maintaining order or reduce the number of unjustified complaints about unfairness, but the price paid in terms of social justice is prohibitively high. Moreover, as mentioned often throughout this book, administrators are role models. The consistent and honorable attempt to treat everyone fairly goes far in role modeling a moral architecture of principle in the district and its schools. If systematically rigorous protocols—such as no tolerance policies—are substituted for doing everything possible to ensure social justice, then the moral architecture will flatten, leaving every person to seek his or her own well-being even at the expense of others (Milgram, 2004). Protecting oneself from harmful consequences becomes the driving force in such schools and districts. Schools and districts deserve more from employees.

SUMMARY

The school administrator who exhibits the wisdom to look beyond the law to see its intent will greatly increase the potential for building a rich, healthy, and strong moral architecture in schools or districts. This is true because no law or judicial decision can cover every ethical dilemma. So the administrator must also have an eye not just to surface-level law but to the moral architecture of her school and district. Successful education leadership subordinates the self-interested directives of outsiders interested only in schooling effects to the historic mission of education, which aims at bringing students together in a Great Conversation, respectful of fellow participants, humble of mind, and committed to seeking and sharing truth.

Wisdom is probably a good idea on which to close our exploration into the morality of ethical leaders. Not only is it a fitting close to this chapter on the nature of law, but it is a fitting close to the discursive part of the book and an apt segue to Appendix A. This appendix consists of a set of cases contributed by noted professors. It is wholly about giving you a chance to exercise what you have learned to apply from the eight chapters of instruction. Every case in Appendix A, like in every case previously and every case you are likely to confront in actual practice, will require you to rely on wisdom as well as knowledge of law, traditions, courtesies, grand theories of moral foundation, and virtue. Wisdom is what you will call on to identify the moral architecture that currently exists in your school or district, and wisdom will lead you to see what changes in that architecture will bring your school or district closer to fulfilling its educational and schooling responsibilities. Wisdom is an essential ingredient in an educational leader. The more you have, the better your influence on applicable moral architectures. The less you have, the more your school, your district, and perhaps your job may be in peril. Plato said leaders must have uncommon intelligence, a sophisticated educational preparation, and great practical experience. About that he is probably right because that is what it takes to acquire a robust and appropriate wisdom for educational leadership. Before you explore the questions, case studies, activity, and readings that follow, you may want to go to Appendix A to examine Case Study A.2 because it overlaps in important ways with the material in this chapter.

QUESTIONING THE AUTHORS **?**	Educators sometimes disagree on what is wise in cases revolving around gender, race, or ethnic tradition. How does one decide which proposed solution or option really is wise in such cases? How is a wise decision to be distinguished from a purely expedient, self-serving, or fearful one?

DISCUSSION QUESTIONS

1. Sometimes educational law seems too focused on specific cases, leaving little latitude for reflection. In contrast, professional ethics seems too focused on general principles. As an administrator, how would you make relevant law and professional ethics palpable to all faculty and staff in the moral architecture of your organization?

2. What are some key questions educational leaders should address with stakeholders when attempting to build a loftier moral architecture for the organization? How should they proceed with the development and implementation of plans and programs that lead to both educative and equitable opportunities for all?

CASE STUDIES

Case Study 8.1. The King of Snide at Westside Middle School

You are a school principal. You have a teacher that colleagues and students all refer to as the "king of snide" because of the many demeaning comments he makes to seemingly everyone around him except for his superiors. Eventually, you conclude that the teacher is destroying collegiality and preventing students from venturing forward with hypotheses and criticisms in their rightful attempt to participate in the Great Conversation. You have heard on more than one occasion that he ridicules students who disagree with him and that he tells students, "I don't suffer fools easily." Apparently he has even made this same comment to another colleague as well as a staff member. He is seriously disrupting the moral architecture of Westside Middle School. As principal, you thought of several options, such as talking with him about his comments and relevant portions of the code of ethics for teachers. You don't want to sound moralistic, so you consider documenting his prior and future caustic comments also. In addition, such documentation will be necessary for any personnel action you may take. But then you worry about setting up an unnecessarily confrontational environment too early on. Finally, you may simply take steps to ensure that his contract will not be renewed. But you recall how influential his family is in the community, and you recall that a month earlier the superintendent stressed that he didn't want any more lawsuits brought against the district. You are in the final year of a 5-year contract that may or may not be renewed.

As you considered your options, you attempted to divide your options into two somewhat overlapping categories: what you *could do* given the circumstances and what you *should do* given the circumstances. In the first case, you delineated what you thought would be effective, efficient, and expedient. In the second case, you considered what you thought were ethical ways of addressing the matter given the circumstances. What questions would you ask a trusted friend who is a principal in another school district? What details would you share with her? Would your conversation with her slant the discussion toward expedient or ethical outcomes?

Case Study 8.2. The Christian Biology Teacher

You have just hired a new biology teacher to teach honors biology. She has three master's degrees: one in biology, one in paleontology, and one in theology. Just before the academic year begins you learn that the new teacher occasionally speaks on the relationship of scripture and science in local churches. Being aware of church and state court rulings regarding the teaching of "scientific creationism" or "intelligent design theory," you worry about whether you should have a talk with her before the semester begins. You knew of her academic background when you hired her, but the recent flurry of talks in local churches has you a bit on edge. Will she spend a lot of class time discussing her personal views of origins or stick to the prescribed curriculum? Do you have any right to ask her about her intentions to teach science within the limits set by law? Are you intruding on her expertise unfairly and prejudicing your relationship by saying anything to her before there is even a single complaint? How might your decisions affect the school's moral architecture in the eyes of other faculty?

ACTIVITY

Activity 8.1

The law distinguishes between our sovereign sense of tolerance and intolerance. For example, the law allows kindergartens to remove copies of *Hustler* magazine and even the Bible from public school classrooms, albeit on different grounds. Censorship (often labeled "the problem of selection" by some ethicists) is an economic fact of school life. For instance, school libraries cannot purchase everything that is written; some books must be selected, others rejected, still others ignored. As Plato observed, the important question is not whether to have censorship or make selections but rather on what grounds the selections should be made. Who should decide the grounds and resulting criteria for selection or censorship, and who should implement them? Find a local district's policy specifying its selection or censorship policy. After reviewing relevant law and any interesting cases, amend the policy, making it both more comprehensive and consistent with the law and stakeholder intent.

FURTHER READING

Callan, E. (1997). *Educating citizens.* New York: Oxford University Press.

Fischer, L., Schimmel, D., & Kelly, C. (1999). *Teachers and the law.* New York: Longman.

Gutmann, A. (1999). *Democratic education* (Rev. ed.). Princeton, NJ: Princeton University Press.

Luban, D. (1988). *Lawyers and justice.* Princeton, NJ: Princeton University Press.

Stadler, D. (2007). *Law and ethics in educational leadership.* Upper Saddle River, NJ: Pearson Merrill/ Prentice Hall.

Tomasi, J. (2001). *Liberalism beyond justice.* Princeton, NJ: Princeton University Press.

APPENDIX A

Additional Case Studies in Educational Leadership

The importance of ethical action in contemporary multicultural schools and districts has been one of our underlying emphases in this book. This is evident in all that has been said about moral architecture and even more so in discussions of the Great Conversation. Finally, in Chapter 8 we noted that in addition to being familiar with foundational moral theory, being courageous and wise as an educational administrator is also critical.

More implicit throughout the book is another idea: that ignoring ethical considerations or discounting them as some sort of impractical luxury weakens institutional development and stakeholder respect for leadership. As Plato advised, leaders need to acquire practical experience of the world to serve skillfully. Therefore, we now share with you a set of original case studies developed by colleagues who are intimately familiar with both ethical and leadership challenges and issues. These are no substitute for being there, but the case studies are meant to bring you as vicariously close as one can come without being onsite and shouldering actual responsibility. You might want to visit Table A.1 before addressing these cases to remind yourself just how you might want to proceed when thinking through such matters. If you have not already done so, you may even want to revise the table, adding cells or thoughts that you think are helpful when analyzing case studies. Table A.1 is an abbreviated heuristic reminder of matters to be considered in light of all that you learned in Chapters 1–8. Again, you should revisit Table A.1 as you feel necessary as a poignant reminder of the concerns you think are most necessary to reflect on when encountering moral issues and dilemmas.

Administrators on the front line must make a large number of immediate decisions. Sometimes these decisions are made on an "instinctual or intuitive" level. In reality, these so-called intuitive decisions are probably nurtured a great deal by one's knowledge of ethical theory, personality, and character traits along with previous experience with students and similar situations. So, in part, the two-step approach is designed to convert this knowledge into practical wisdom by drawing focused attention to the steps involved and how judgments can be faulty at times.

The contributors of these case studies were selected in part for their representative and diverse backgrounds, their practical experience, and their stature as leaders in educational scholarship. Although each contributor raises a set of questions for her or his case study, the reader by now knows that there are nearly innumerable queries that can and should be posed.

Table A.1   A Two-Step Approach to Evaluating and Improving Moral Judgment

Step 1

Questions	Example	Rationale
What is my first impression of the situation?	She should be placed in an alternative school.	You are attempting to identify and test your current moral understanding and instincts.
What might have happened if I'd acted on my first impression?	She would have been unfairly disciplined.	You are attempting to determine whether your judgments and their consequences would be fair and wise.
What did I overlook in forming my first impression?	She had never done this before.	You are attempting to identify your blind spots and biases.
What did I assume that led to my first impression?	She is already a problem.	You are attempting to uncover your assumptions and presuppositions.
What do I need to do in the future to improve or refine my first impressions?	Ask more questions, listen more to staff and students.	You are attempting to identify steps you can take in the future that will improve your moral decision making.

Step 2

Questions	Example	Rationale
What is my second impression of the situation?	She is being bullied by classmates.	I learned from her classroom teacher and physical education instructor that classmates are provoking her at nearly every opportunity.
What might have happened if I had acted on my second impression?	Class bullies cease provoking her. She is counseled on how to respond to provocations.	I learned that the planned rewards for respecting others and the punishments for bullying them can alter classmates' behavior. The individual attention given to her in context will better prepare her for future bullying when it occurs.
What did I learn that changed or confirmed my initial impression?	Bullying is a problem that provokes and intimidates even our best students.	I learned that sometimes I am too involved in administrative trivia, and this compromises my ability to make quick, sound judgments, especially when I don't take the time to hear others' accounts.
How much confidence should I put in my immediate impressions?	As I learn more from my students and staff, I can become more confident about making quick decisions.	I learned that my most instant assumptions often do not serve the situation well. I should learn from students and staff as much as possible to become a better problem solver.

CASE A.1
Agonizing Over Ecstasy at Cedar Hill School

Daniel Vokey, *University of British Columbia*

Miss Chelsea is vice-principal of Cedar Hill Christian Secondary School, a small independent school in a prosperous suburban neighborhood. In the last term of her fourth year at the school, Miss Chelsea was approached by several teachers about a grade 12 student, Amie. Amie's erratic behavior had led them to suspect that she was under the influence of drugs while in their classes. All the teachers agreed that, since March, Amie seemed more uncoordinated, disoriented, and confused than she had been the previous term. Therefore, Miss Chelsea called Amie to her office and without revealing her sources explained her concerns. Amie reassured Miss Chelsea that she was fine and explicitly denied taking any illegal drugs. Miss Chelsea later contacted the school counselor and asked him to monitor the situation.

Later the same week, the coach for the school's senior hockey team noticed that his goaltender, Alain, was unusually agitated in class and in practice. When queried, Alain replied that he was nervous about an upcoming game. He also denied any involvement with drugs when asked. The coach informed Miss Chelsea about the matter, and she asked the coach to monitor Alain's behavior.

The next Monday, a father complained that two students, Sean and Brad, had taken his daughter off campus to smoke marijuana during the lunch period. According to the father, his daughter, Phyllis, and the boys had joined two others to share a joint. Miss Chelsea spoke with each student individually. Each acknowledged the lunchtime trip but denied smoking marijuana.

One week later, a mother turned in a daybook to Miss Chelsea that she had found under a bench at a bus stop a block from school grounds. The mother attached a note suggesting that the administration look through it before returning it to the student. When Miss Chelsea opened the daybook she discovered that it belonged to Amie. In the sleeve at the back she found a birthday card from Amie's boyfriend, Carl, promising her an ecstasy pill for her birthday party and mentioning the names of two other students who would be joining them in their special "celebration."

Miss Chelsea immediately initiated an investigation involving Amie, Carl, and the other students named in the binder: Alain and Brad. All were grade 12 students who had only a few weeks of classes left to complete high school. All had been students of Cedar Hill for 3 years or more. Interviews were conducted individually with the four students. All admitted that they smoked marijuana regularly; Amie, Carl, and Alain also confessed to recent experimentation with ecstasy. In accordance with school regulations, Miss Chelsea suspended all four students until a review panel composed of school administrators could be convened to consider their cases. Each student was reminded that, as stated in the "School Regulations" section of their *Student Handbook,* any staff member or student found to be under the influence of illegal drugs while at school was subject to dismissal or permanent expulsion.

At Cedar Hill, review panels are called on to make recommendations to the School Executive Board whenever the possibility of permanent expulsion is involved. The Executive Board retains final authority. The student and his or her guardians are provided with a copy of the review panel's recommendations

1 week before the Executive Board is convened. At the meeting, guardians are given an opportunity to address the recommendations of the review panel. The board meeting is attended by the local superintendent of independent schools, whose role is to ensure that all relevant information is considered and due process observed. At the end of the meeting, the board goes into executive session and makes a final determination of consequences based on the recommendation of the review panel, prior school and district precedent, and whatever additional evidence was presented at the meeting.

The review panel recommended that because all four students admitted to being regularly under the influence of marijuana during school hours, all four should be permanently expelled. Amie's mother argued that no consequences should be assigned because Miss Chelsea initiated her investigation only after illegally examining her daughter's daybook. The parents of the other students asked for leniency because expulsion would prevent the students from graduating that year, and the students had been cooperative with the investigation. In Alain's case, his father reminded the board of its ruling in a previous case of illegal drug use, in which the captain of the hockey team was suspended for only 4 weeks, dropped from the team, and put on probation for the rest of year.

The Executive Board suspended all four students from Cedar Hill for 5 weeks. This would allow the students to graduate pending adequate grades on their final examinations and no further violations. Any support the students needed to prepare for their examinations would have to be provided by tutors hired at the parents' expense.

Discussion Questions

1. Was Miss Chelsea justified, or even obligated, to examine the contents of Amie's daybook? (Relevant case law on this subject should be examined before rendering a decision.)

2. Did the punishment represent a defensible balance between justice and charity for each student involved, that is, was it fair?

CASE A.2
Justice and Zero Tolerance

Paul F. Bitting, *North Carolina State University*

As one of the few African Americans in my school and district, I am often expected to have a special influence over students of color. Ms. Scott and I had an agreement, and I promised that I would keep it. When she had a student, particularly a minority male student, who became so disruptive in her class that she felt compelled to send him out, she could send him to me and I would address the situation.

Recently, on a day when I was rushing to complete a major assignment for the district, Ms. Scott brought a young man to my room. He was a student of mixed race and very handsome. The two female students who were helping me noticed that right away. I told Ms. Scott, "I'm sorry, not today, I don't have time. I'm very busy." She asked again, and I said that this work had to be done.

She whispered, "He called me a m_____-f___ing b____, and you know what will happen to him if I send him to the office."

"Okay," I said, "Let him stay."

I turned to the student and said, "I really don't have time to talk with you today. Can you just find something to work on?"

He asked, "Can I help?"

Startled, I thought for a moment and then explained about some work I had to do on the computer. He said, "Okay, I can do that." And he did, and his work was as good as that of any of the students I had trained.

After he finished the work I gave him, I said, "Tell me your story." We had been discussing this management approach in a class I was taking for my specialist's degree in educational administration.

He told me that his younger brother had been a member of a gang and was involved in a drive-by shooting. Later, the brother had been assigned to the juvenile system and recently reassigned to an adult prison. His single mother, in despair and depression, was finding it difficult to go on.

"You love your mother and your brother, don't you?" I asked.

He nodded with tears in his eyes. "My mother loves us both, I know. It's just that she has so little time for me now with my brother's situation and all. She worries so about him."

He went on to explain that when he was little, his mother attended community college to get a degree in computers. She would take him with her whenever she went to the computer lab.

"That's where you learned about computers isn't it?" I asked. He nodded.

We talked about his anger and outburst and how we would work with that. Before he left for the rest of his classes, I promised him that we would talk more. I later wondered why we as a school didn't know about his situation. He was clearly a bright and capable student. I could see that anyone would want him as a student. He later told me that I was the first person he had ever talked to about his home situation.

I couldn't help but wonder about three things. What is there about school that makes it difficult for most teachers to talk about personal matters with students? What would it be like if we had a school full of adults who would ask, "Tell me your story," when something happened out of the ordinary and then listened? I wondered whether I would have time to have such interactions with students or to lend a hand to teachers like Ms. Scott when I became an administrator.

Discussion Questions

Consider the Rawlsian principle of justice as fairness. Consider how it applies to this case and answer the following questions:

1. Imagine that you are the building administrator. Ms. Scott has sent the student to you with a discipline referral explaining the profanity he used toward her. Your school has a zero tolerance policy regarding profanity. The policy is clear: The consequence for profanity is a 2-day suspension. What does justice require of you?

2. Does justice require that all be treated the same?

CASE A.3
A Matter of Integrity

William Hare, *Mount Saint Vincent University*

It had to come at some point, of course, and the day finally arrived at the end of March. The long-time head of science, Sarah Woodbury, was about to retire. It was hard to imagine the school without its distinguished head of science. Sarah had been an inspiration to her colleagues, setting an example of dedication, success, and enthusiasm that was unrivaled. It was not going to be easy to find someone to fill her shoes.

An appointment committee was created under the direction of Jack Blanchard, the principal. Two members were responsible for the initial review of credentials, and then the full committee of five would select one or two people to visit the school for onsite interviews. Three candidates looked very good. Each had several years of teaching and administrative experience and master's degrees. Each had also received glowing reports from their references. However, one candidate emerged as the front-runner: Mitchell Clarke, head of science at Springfield Academy. He had been at Springfield for 10 years, 5 as head of department, and had a long list of professional development workshops and seminars, indicating his ongoing commitment to teaching. He had even contributed a chapter to a textbook on science for high school students. He had bachelor's and master's degrees from major universities. In addition, Clarke had obtained a master's degree in educational leadership from another small university that was wholly unfamiliar to the committee. The committee invited Mr. Clarke to interview.

However, something was nagging at Jim Sears, one of the teachers on the appointment committee, although he had hesitated to raise it at the meeting once the momentum in favor of inviting Clarke for an interview began to develop. Truth to tell, he was reluctant to raise a doubt about the qualifications of someone who might well be his head of department next term. In his experience, these things rarely remained confidential, and whistleblowers often paid a heavy price. He was vaguely worried about the possibility of legal troubles and seemed to remember that defamation cases had been initiated in some instances where credentials had been challenged. He had been troubled all along by the fact that he could not find on Clarke's résumé a period of leave that coincided with his studies for the master's degree in educational leadership. He told himself that it was probably a program taken through distance education and not requiring any residence. Was it really his business to look into the matter any further?

Jim couldn't leave the matter alone. He looked up the university in question on the Internet, and his worst fears were soon confirmed. The "university" was a diploma mill run from a post office box. Its name was a close variant of the name of a reputable university and would be mistaken for the same at a casual glance. It was "accredited," of course, but a little research soon revealed that the accreditation agency was also spurious, probably set up by the bogus university itself. A master's degree ("indicate your preferred major field") cost just under $2,000 and was available in 14 days. No one could plausibly claim that they had been deceived into thinking the program was genuine, although a desperate appeal for "credit for life experience" could probably be anticipated.

What could possibly have induced the candidate to list something so absurd? Did it mean that Clarke would be any less effective if he were appointed? How could it detract from his knowledge and skills, which were apparently beyond dispute? His impeccable references indicated that his colleagues held him in high regard. If Jim were to remain silent, perhaps the matter would never become an issue. The interview was scheduled for the next day. Jim stared at the e-mail to his colleagues long and hard before finally clicking "Send."

Discussion Questions

1. What are the main ethical issues in this case? Which ethical theory in particular is most appropriate for addressing these issues?

2. Should the assessment of teachers and department heads be confined to questions of skill and competence, or is it important to consider matters relating to the teacher's character? If the appointment committee had been looking for a new principal and discovered an applicant who met all relevant qualifications but had a doctoral degree from a diploma mill, how, if at all, would it change your answers to the prior question?

3. Was the principal or the committee at fault for not spotting the flaw that so agitated Jim Sears?

CASE A.4

Possibilities at Lone Mountain

Ernestine K. Enomoto, *University of Hawaii*
Bruce H. Kramer, *St. Thomas University*

Joshua Levin is the principal at a middle school in a sprawling suburban district. Last spring, the school district reluctantly joined a voluntary desegregation consortium of 12 other districts, and consequently the school has begun receiving students from the city. Transported by bus from their homes, the new students, many of whom are minorities, are picked up as early as 5:30 AM in order to be at school by 7:30 AM. After school, they leave at 3:30 PM but sometimes reach home as late at 6:00 PM. Although there was some tension at the school initially, there have only been a few disturbances among the students. Nonetheless, the newcomers generally keep their distance from the other students. They cluster together during recess and sit apart during lunch hour. Outside class, they hardly speak to other students.

The one bright spot is that one of the region's best ice rinks is located next to the school. Its athletic director, Tom Apollo, provides after-school programs and coordinates winter sports for the district. For the newcomers to the school, this could be their first opportunity to learn to skate and possibly compete in skating sports. Tom said that he was committed to helping the students develop integrated teams for skating sports and even said he would solicit corporate and community support for uniforms and equipment.

But here is Joshua's dilemma. Athletic activities are expensive to support, and the community would like to see a well-rounded program of sports offered. To enable the newcomers to participate,

Joshua would need to consider how he might fund their participation. Besides even the basics of equipment and supplies, bus transportation would be a major problem, especially given the rising cost of gas and personnel needed for extra runs. The urban students in particular would need transportation if they were to participate. The school would need to pay those costs. Joshua would also need to secure approval from his school board along with additional funding from it and would have to make cuts in smaller ongoing programs such as girls' soccer and boys' tennis. And he reminds himself he must consider whether the expenditure of all this time, effort, and money would be fair to students who cared little for sports and athletics.

Dr. Brennon, the district superintendent, is not sympathetic with Joshua's proposal. "If these new kids are not causing trouble, all the better. Let's worry about test scores and academics, not athletics." Even some veteran teachers at the school are similarly unsympathetic. Joshua knows personally the fun of skating sports, and he has made it a point to get to know many of the newcomers. He thinks his plan will help students integrate and succeed at school. Yet even the newcomers' own parents have expressed little interest in his plan. The one mom he did hear from said adamantly that she wanted her son to concentrate on school, *not* sports. It's hard to argue about the importance of a solid academic foundation.

Throughout his career in education, Joshua Levin has been deeply committed to educational equity. He took leadership courses to become more effective at ensuring equity regardless of student background or racial mix. He worked hard to build community coalitions and did volunteer work in the inner city. But is this program within the scope of what he should be addressing at his school here and now? Do such athletic activities really matter, or are they strictly extracurricular? Should he focus on a more general plan to integrate minorities with the majority of the student body? And what about the girls who make up that majority?

Joshua feels somewhat constrained by the rules and even by his understanding of his own professional responsibilities. He truly believes in the promise of this new opportunity, so should he push ahead with his plans? He dreams of other opportunities for the newcomers that he believes will occur if he can succeed in this mission.

Discussion Questions

1. Is there a right course of action based on Joshua Levin's duties and responsibilities as principal? How might this action clash with what he desires for the new students? What constitutes good leadership in this case?

2. Has the principal attempted to integrate all points of view in this situation? What other viewpoints have not yet been considered? How might Joshua give fair consideration to all viewpoints in resolving his dilemma?

3. What might be some likely consequences of Joshua's proposal? What short-term and long-term consequences should be considered in making ethical decisions in this case?

4. What issues relate to providing equity and equal educational opportunity? How might Joshua take these considerations into account when trying to make the best decisions for all students at the school?

CASE A.5

Principal as Buffer at Man Dorr Primary

Kamla Mungal, *University of West Indies*

Principal Karen Kochar shook her head in dismay, as she could not believe what the school supervisor was asking her to do. She knew that this one act might erase the gains she had made over the past 2 years. The school was finally improving, and she had made significant progress in her attempts to motivate teachers and students. As a young principal who was well qualified for the position, she knew that she was constantly under scrutiny and made every attempt to convince the school supervisors that she had taken charge and was in control of the school.

Man Dorr Primary is located in the main city of the area, the most southerly island in the school district. Despite having many fine educators, the school district is known for its highly authoritarian leadership culture in many institutions.

The school had experienced declining levels of performance in the past 10 years, and students' academic underperformance was a cause for concern by the school district. In addition, the community was experiencing increased poverty, crime, violence, and drug trafficking. Staff morale had fallen, and the parents were often heard reminiscing about the past high performance of the school in all areas of the curriculum.

When Principal Kochar was appointed to the school 2 years ago she recognized that it would take time to gain teachers' confidence and to engender a culture of high expectations for both teachers and students. The staff was quite talented and eager to demonstrate their skills. Improving performance involved instituting structures for school-based management and team decision making, trying innovative teaching strategies, tracking individual students' performance on tests, establishing policies for inclusion, and improving parental involvement in the teaching and learning process.

The staff eagerly jumped on the bandwagon of each new initiative. They were quite pleased every time their small successes attracted recognition from the principal. They shared their stories and highlighted individual students who had made notable improvements in either academics or other pursuits.

The school supervisor, Mrs. Thomas, issued a directive to Ms. Kochar to classify teachers' performance according to their students' performance on the national assessment. Mrs. Thomas was a much-respected senior supervisor who was promoted through the system and had participated in all of the major programs of the school district and region. She knew the regulations and was renowned for her unwavering demand for compliance with rules and regulations.

The new performance management appraisal (PMA) system explicitly linked teachers' ratings to their students' performance on standardized tests. Teachers had become accustomed to celebrating and to being rewarded for their students' incremental successes in the value-added system that was the operational policy of the school. They had worked hard to improve their students' basic skills as identified in the curriculum framework. Yet there was no way to immediately capture such gains in the PMA.

Ms. Kochar looked at 8-year old Darren Ali across the school yard. He was obviously engrossed in his social studies textbook. She recalled when she first met Darren and how he would not sit still in his classroom, looking for every opportunity to disrupt other students and classes. Her thoughts were also distracted by the suggestion of a literacy fair, put forward by a group of teachers just that morning, to highlight the achievements of the students in language arts.

It was clear that the PMA would place teachers at the school in the category of low performers based on the proposed classification system. Ms. Kochar thought of how best to address the demands of the system while maintaining the strategies and techniques that had worked for her to improve the school. Despite the promotion to school supervisor that she was expecting, she could not sacrifice the improvements the school had realized over the last 2 years. She looked at Mrs. Thomas squarely and started to outline an approach that she thought would work in the interest of all.

Discussion Questions

1. What ethical theories appear to guide the actions of the principal and the school supervisor?

2. Would you consider the position of the school supervisor to be an ethical one?

3. Discuss the principal's conflict of responsibilities as highlighted in this case.

4. How would you advise Ms. Kochar to accommodate the PMA system? What risks are there for the various stakeholders?

CASE A.6

Professional Ethics and the Micropolitics of Decentralization: The Dilemma of District Office Middle Managers

Lars G. Björk, *University of Kentucky*

The Clark County Public School District is located in a midsized community. The most recent census reports that roughly 64% of the 35,000 children served by the district are African American, and most are also from low-income families. A broad-based school improvement effort was launched by the newly elected school board to get decision making down to a level where problems can be identified and resolved quickly. The new board hired a superintendent, Bob Villareal, who realizes that restructuring a highly centralized district with 4,500 employees will be a challenge.

One of his first initiatives was to establish a comprehensive plan for decentralization. As the number of district-level administrators was reduced, the deputy superintendent for instruction, Mr. Bagley, became increasingly resistant to decentralization. Before Mr. Villareal's appointment, Mr. Bagley, an African American, had been the only minority with a senior administrative position.

One of the central features of the restructuring was to shift financial responsibility directly to the schools. Jack Wharton, the district's chief financial officer, handed out the *Preliminary Budget Preparation Booklet* at a district budget meeting and explained that site-based managers would be responsible for budget decisions. Mr. Bagley, a sincere social reformer and advocate for minorities, complained, "I am increasingly being held accountable for delivering state and federally funded programs, and now I no longer control how funds earmarked for such purposes are to be spent!"

Mr. Bagley sent a memorandum to his program staff and principals and directed them to submit all program changes and budget requests to him at least a week before their submission to the central budget office.

Although the principals and other staff were well aware that Mr. Bagley's memorandum contradicted the district's new policy, they admired his courage and also prudently avoided confrontation with him. They did as he asked. It was business as usual.

In short, Mr. Bagley had become insubordinate and was undermining Mr. Villareal. Mr. Bagley has long been a highly visible and greatly admired administrator in the local community. The superintendent sent out a general memo to all administrative staff again reiterating how the new decentralization policy would be implemented. He sent an e-mail to Mr. Bagley asking for a meeting at Mr. Bagley's earliest convenience. Mr. Bagley responded in an e-mail that he was tied up all week working on the curriculum for Black History Month. He asked the superintendent whether financial management was something that should be put on the back burner or just left to the preferences of individual schools. The e-mail was sent a week ago, and neither administrator has contacted the other since.

Discussion Questions

1. Is there evidence of any lack of respect between these two as individuals? Should that matter to the superintendent when considering what to do about Mr. Bagley's evident insubordination?

2. Are the participants' race and ethnicity matters to be addressed in the search for the morally right thing to do in this case?

3. What loyalties should Mr. Bagley's most immediate subordinates exhibit in the emerging confrontation? How should such loyalties be decided?

CASE A.7
A Professional's Personal Challenge

JoAnn Franklin Klinker, *Texas Tech University*

Principal Gray felt sorry for the distraught woman in front of him. She had dark circles under her eyes, and her voice cracked with exhaustion. Although unaware of it, she was wringing her hands. He noticed they were rough and red. That meant she'd been doing the laundry by hand again for her family of four because she couldn't afford to get the washing machine repaired. Ever since her husband began his fight against cancer 2 years ago, Sandra and her family had fallen further into poverty. And he also knew what she wanted and why he had to say no.

Sandra Smith teaches Spanish to the 9- to 12th-grade students at Salem High School. She frequently leaves during the school day for family reasons. Everyone was sympathetic at first, but colleagues eventually tired of filling in for her, and substitutes are unavailable.

Colleagues are willing to be inconvenienced for a short time period, but they let it go on too long, and, quite reasonably, they want their own lives back. "Her students need her here too," they rightly observe.

"My husband had a rough night last night, Joe. He's in a lot of pain, and I'm worried about him." She drew a deep breath. "I really need to leave after lunch today."

"We've talked about this, Sandra. I've told you, this has to stop," Principal Gray said.

"I know I promised it wouldn't happen again, but he's worse than I've ever seen him," Sandra replied.

"The students need you too. We should have docked your pay before, Sandra. We are doing all we can. You need to meet us part way." She'd already used up all of her sick days, personal leave days, and even the days that others had volunteered to give her. They'd talked about her taking family medical leave, but even if she had it wouldn't have solved his problem. Spanish teachers were scarce, and substitutes were even harder to find.

"I know. That's why I made the effort, and I stayed the morning, but I really need to go now, Joe. We have professional development this afternoon. I don't need to be here for that. I'll only miss two shortened periods with the kids. They won't mind. I'll give them a worksheet. I promise they'll behave. I scolded them good after the last time."

"What did the doctor say when you left school early last week?" Principal Gray asked.

"I'm so glad you let me go with him." Sandra smiled at him. "There's a new treatment they want to try, but he has to get a little better before they do it. He's trying, Joe. You're his friend, you know he's a fighter. But if I'm not there, he doesn't eat, and he doesn't take his meds. He fights so hard, but the depression is. . . ." Her voice faltered, and she looked away.

Principal Gray sighed. He thought back to the job he'd had before this one. It wasn't a memory he was proud of. He'd refused to let the art teacher at his previous school leave during his planning period to check on his sick wife. That night, the art teacher found her dead on the kitchen floor. The coroner's office said she'd choked to death. He knew it hadn't been his fault, but he'd left that job soon afterward.

"Have Joy cover for me," Sandra said, interrupting his thoughts. "She won't mind. I covered for her when her kids were sick."

"Joy has been in your classroom five times in the last 8 weeks. Ted has been there six times, and Clay as well. I've covered for you four times in the last month. The teachers are complaining, the parents too, and the kids are out of control whether you're here or gone. It has to stop, Sandra."

"I know they're upset with me. I guess I can't blame them. No one wants to be inconvenienced." She looked at him. "Can you cover for me? Please, Joe."

"I can't. I have a meeting with the superintendent, that baseball discipline issue—the parents are coming in to talk about it—and we're dismissing at 2:00 PM for professional development. I need you here."

"Please reconsider," Sandra asked.

He looked at her. Tears again. He hated it when teachers cried. He looked at his watch. "It's 12:00 now. By the time you drive home, it will be 12:30. I'll excuse you from the faculty meeting. You can leave at 2:00." And he knew as soon as he said the words that tomorrow morning he'd have two or three teachers in his office, maybe a parent or two, complaining that Sandra had again been given special treatment. Even the superintendent had already told him that he was too lenient with her and that there were even concerns circulating among members of the school board.

"You're just afraid for your job. You don't care about me," she said.

"The kids need you, Sandra. We pay you to do the job you were hired to do. I expect you to do it."

"And if I go home and find him dead, how are you going to feel then?" Sandra said and then ran out of the room.

Discussion Questions

1. On the surface, what is the moral dilemma that Principal Gray confronts?

2. This case study is based on the foundational moral theory of utilitarianism. Examine your school policy and you will find that most policies are written from this philosophical viewpoint. How does utilitarianism serve, or undermine, what is best for the school, individual students, and individual teachers?

3. Principals acting friendly toward teachers is generally a good thing. But what are the ethical risks of principal–teacher friendships? What are the implications for optimally effective leadership?

CASE A.8
Rights of Students Versus Rights of Teachers

John Keedy, *University of Louisville*

On one occasion when I was a principal, I served in a school in a small town (population 1,000), Hebron, located between two old industrial mill cities. There was little employment in Hebron. Unemployment might have reached as high as 30%. Staff at Hebron Elementary School always braced themselves for the first of the month, when families evicted from apartments in larger towns would suddenly appear to enroll their children. Most of the citizens either worked in a largely blue-collar town nearby or commuted to a somewhat larger town for higher-paid white-collar jobs. The general economic description of Hebron would be lower middle class (e.g., truck drivers, grocery clerks, farm hands) with some middle-class professionals (e.g., realtors, retirement village staffers, teachers).

Hebron Elementary had 260 students in Grades K–6, with two teachers per grade. Staff consisted of one administrative position with a part-time secretary; 17 full-time certified teachers, including a special education teacher, a Title One teacher, a teacher of behavior-disordered students serving the entire district, and her assistant; and part-time itinerant physical education, art, and music teachers. The school was governed by its own three-member school committee (the counterpart to a school board), with a regional junior high and high school serving Hebron and four nearby towns. The district had six local school committees: a committee serving each of the five towns and a coterminous committee of 23 members with oversight of the two regional junior high and high schools.

In my second year as principal, a teacher was accused of physically intimidating a student and was facing a possible lawsuit. The teacher simply quit, giving 2 weeks' notice, and returned to a carpentry job. Given that teachers in most nearby towns made much more than Hebron Elementary teachers and given that time was short, we were forced to depend for the most part on word of mouth for selecting candidates to serve the remainder of the school year. Two candidates surfaced: Mrs. Green, a 40-year-old mother of two and graduate of a regional teachers' college, and Ms. James, a mid-30s graduate of a liberal arts college holding an emergency teacher certification.

Our school lacked a personnel committee, as is often found in larger schools. Instead, the principal simply made a recommendation to the school committee, who then had to act on the nomination. The predicament arose from two circumstances. First, Mrs. Green's husband, a state trooper, had recently been laid off because of state budget cuts. She shared with me during her job interview that "I would much prefer to be a stay-home mom and be home when my two children return from school, but I now feel forced to work due to a hefty home mortgage payment and other pressing financial obligations with my husband out of work." Mrs. Green was supported informally by three of my teachers because of her financial hardship and her past work as a loyal member of the local teachers' association. One of the teachers pressing especially hard was Tom, a mid-40s "senior teacher" who acted as principal in my absence.

Despite the pressure from Tom and the other two teachers, I chose to go with Ms. James. During her interview she had shared with me her central teaching principles. These included encouraging students to become actively engaged in their work through classroom discussion, continually assessing student reading and writing in social studies, grouping and regrouping when necessary, and working with individual students as needed. My formal teacher observations and informal walk-throughs had convinced me that some Hebron teachers often did not have the students' academic benefit at heart; instead, they just covered the textbooks and hung onto their jobs. All too often students were completing worksheets at their desks and then correcting their own work by checking the answer grids at the teachers' desks for multiple-choice questions on assigned readings. I also checked with one of my best teachers about hiring Ms. James. She observed, "She would be far better for the kids" but requested that her preference be kept strictly confidential because she feared retribution from colleagues.

I had less than 2 weeks to make the decision and to recommend to the school committee my choice for teacher. Despite the predicament, my choice was to do what I thought would benefit the children. My choice was less than democratic, but I think it was right nonetheless.

Discussion Questions

1. What contextual variables should have affected my decision the most?

2. In the real world of school administration, there are always mixes of motives that bear on any decision to be made. What was the mix of motives in this case?

3. Would it have been ethically wrong for me to recommend the other applicant on the grounds of her family and financial situation, her teaching certification, her service to the local professional organization, and the support of other teachers?

CASE A.9
When a Picket Fence Becomes an Offense in Standardized Testing

Elizabeth Campbell, *University of Toronto*

It was that time of year again: time to administer the series of tests in what had become a high-stakes exercise in public accountability. Some teachers agreed with the principal that the tests generally served a beneficial purpose by providing valuable information on student academic progress. Other teachers vigorously objected to the tests on what they claimed were grounds of professional ethics. They claimed that the tests created so much stress for students and teachers alike that they compromised the learning process. They believed that because most of their students were from immigrant families, language difficulties unfairly disadvantaged their students. Even for those fluent in English, cultural assumptions embedded in the test questions confused students but had very little to do with the students' actual proficiency. In addition, they claimed that prohibiting teachers from offering assistance to their elementary students during the tests was unnatural for the students and oppressive. Teachers were permitted only to read out loud the questions verbatim. They were not allowed to make clarifications or offer definitions. Finally, the offended teachers thought it an insult to their professionalism that at the end of each test, they were required to submit a letter testifying that they followed proper procedures in administering the test.

In part because overall test results are reported publicly school by school, the principal felt pressure from the school district to improve test scores. And as the principal, she was expected to oversee the testing process and ensure that test validity had not been compromised.

On the first day of the testing week, the principal strolled the hallways where the Grade 3 classrooms were located. As she passed by Jasmine Grey's class, she noticed that on the blackboard, there was an outline of what looked like a picket fence. She recalled that one of the Grade 3 test questions asks students to calculate an addition and subtraction problem by counting slats on a picket fence. She surmised that Jasmine must have drawn the fence for the students, and this was in violation of the testing procedure. She anticipated that Jasmine, a long-time vocal critic of the cultural biases in some standardized tests, would defend her action on grounds of giving her students a fair shot at answering a question when none of them had probably ever seen a picket fence.

Feeling shaken, the principal hurried away before Jasmine could see her. She needed to think. As she returned to her office she noticed another Grade 3 teacher, Justine Earl, following the required testing procedure. Clearly, Justine's students would not have the advantage of Jasmine's. Unlike Jasmine, Justine had always been supportive of the tests and believed in their academic purpose and authority. She would never have drawn a picket fence on the board. Besides, such an act could be seen as professional misconduct; Justine would never consider such risks.

Thirty minutes later, the teachers were coming by the office to drop off tests and their letters certifying proper administration of the test. Jasmine handed in the package of tests but no letter of certification. The principal was compelled to ask her why the letter was not included. Jasmine replied, "I don't want to lie to you. I didn't follow the so-called proper procedures." She explained about the drawing on the board and continued, "If it'll make it easier for you, I'll sign the certification letter. I did what I thought was right. I'm sorry, but I guess now you'll have to do what you think is right."

Discussion Questions

1. What should the principal do about Jasmine's behavior? What options are open to her?

2. On what ethical principles is each option based, and what are the likely consequences or implications of each option in both the short term and the long term?

3. What should the principal do with the completed tests?

4. To what extent and in what ways should any of the following influence the principal's decision?

   - If Jasmine had not confessed and instead submitted her signed form as if nothing had happened
   - If Justine and some of the other Grade 3 teachers had heard about Jasmine's action and complained that by advantaging her own students, she created a situation in which their own students would not be compared fairly
   - If there were still 4 more days left in the testing period, and Jasmine could be prohibited from administering any further tests

CASE A.10
When the Saints Come Marching In

Sylvia Méndez-Morris, *Texas Tech University*

Principal Ralph Hester is a 63-year-old white man with 38 years' experience as an educator, 15 of which have been as a school administrator. He has been the principal at East Wayside Elementary School for the last 6 years, establishing a reputation as firm and fair leader. He is an elder at First Wayside Church, grew up in the community, attended Wayside Independent School District schools, and is known as a solid individual. One of his teachers is Yolanda Smith. She is a 47-year-old white woman and a member of Unity Baptist Temple. She has 22 years' elementary teaching experience and has been a fifth-grade teacher at East Wayside Elementary School for almost 8 years. She moved to Wayside with her family from a tiny farming community close to the Ohio River.

Mr. Hester has met the entire Dominguez family, including Xoilo's father, Mr. Carlos Dominguez, and mother, Dr. Sara Chopra. Mr. Dominguez is a 36-year-old Chicano doctoral student at the local branch of Courtland State University (CSU) and, like the rest of his family, a practicing Hindu. Dr. Sara Chopra is a 34-year-old professor at CSU. They have one child, Xoilo.

The Dominguez family has lived in Wayside City for 4 years and seems to have adjusted to living in a predominantly white, Bible-belt community. Xoilo is a shy, computer-savvy fifth-grade student who earns good grades and enjoys skateboarding. Twice he has made the honor roll. From the very beginning, he made friends with two other boys, Jason and Jorge. They often spend time in each other's homes; in fact, they seem inseparable at times.

All seemed to be going well for Xoilo as far as Mr. Hester could see until recently. According to the Mr. Dominguez, Xoilo came home for a third time complaining about the Christian music Mrs. Smith played in the classroom during their silent reading time. She sometimes even went so far as to discuss the lyrics with students afterwards. Xoilo complained that because he was Hindu the Christian music distracted him, and discussion of its lyrics offended him.

When Xoilo first talked to his parents about Mrs. Smith playing Christian music, they advised him to talk to her and resolve it that way. The second time Xoilo complained to his parents, Mr. Dominguez e-mailed Mrs. Smith and says he politely reminded her that playing Christian music at school was probably a violation of the principle of separation of church and state. Mrs. Smith reportedly responded that she would not accept "mandates from liberal heathens who are trying to destroy American values."

And yet there's more, Mr. Hester thought. Two days earlier, Xoilo cried because of the things that Mrs. Smith had reportedly yelled at him in front of the class when he once again asked her not to play Christian music. He reminded her that he was a Hindu and did not want to listen to religious praise he "did not believe in." Her response, according to Xoilo, was to call him a "devil worshipper" and a heathen.

The next day Mr. Dominguez and Dr. Chopra called Mrs. Smith in person for an appointment. They claim that Mrs. Smith raised her voice while speaking with Dr. Chopra and even slammed the phone down after stating that she would not meet with "heathens." Dr. Chopra then called Mr. Hester and reported to him their side of the story. Mr. Hester subsequently called Mrs. Smith into his office to hear her side of the story and to find out what caused such reported actions in a teacher that he knew well and respected. He had on one occasion heard her call Xoilo a heathen as he was passing by her room but assumed that had been intended as a humorous aside. Was there something more? Was she having severe emotional problems?

After hearing her describe how she has always played music from her Sunday school classes and never had a complaint before, he called Dr. Chopra's office and arranged for an appointment with everyone involved. He then asked Mrs. Smith to bring the CDs that she played in her classroom and any documentation that she might have regarding Xoilo "ordering" her not to play that music.

Whom should Mr. Hester believe? He remembered another case a few years before. Mr. Lopez, a member of Mr. Hester's church, told him that Mrs. Smith had one day after school told his daughter that only certain Baptists would be part of the rapture and be saved. He had told Mr. Lopez that he knew that Yolanda sometimes gets overzealous but that she was "really harmless." He conveyed the complaint to Mrs. Smith and told her that he had "taken care of it" but that she needed to exercise some restraint because she was a public school teacher.

Principal Hester was conservative in his own religious beliefs, and in many ways his beliefs were similar to Mrs. Smith's. In fact, he had dropped out of CSU's master's program because he was not allowed to write his thesis on the leadership style of Jesus Christ. He was offended by what he perceived as CSU's bigotry precluding him from writing a leadership (not a religious) thesis featuring Christ. His Internet searches had showed similar articles on Mohammed, the Dalai Lama, Gandhi, and so many others. But that didn't cause his supervisor to change his mind. Grounds for tolerance and intolerance are sometimes hard to demarcate. He wanted to get things right this time for all involved.

He had planned for a short meeting, but when Mrs. Smith arrived with her church pastor and both were carrying Bibles, he worried that things were much worse than he may have suspected. Was the preacher accompanying Mrs. Smith to advise about her mental state, comfort her, or defend the reckless actions that had been reported about her classroom behavior? Mr. Dominguez then arrived with Mr. Lopez. Things were not going to be easy. But it is Mr. Hester's job to get it right and not let any biases from the past or present contaminate his thinking.

Discussion Questions

1. What, if anything, should Mr. Hester say to the pastor and Mr. Lopez about their presence at this meeting?

2. As Mr. Hester, what moral perspective would help guide you in your interactions with Mrs. Smith and the Dominguez family? What legal considerations ought to be considered as well?

3. What should Mr. Hester do to respect both Xoilo's and Mrs. Smith's religious beliefs?

4. How should Mr. Hester's own previous experiences and knowledge of this student and this teacher help him understand the situation?

5. How would you summarize what Mr. Hester needs to do in this situation, and what are the moral grounds for such action?

CASE A.11
Defending the Unempowered

Paul A. Wagner, *University of Houston–Clear Lake*
Douglas J. Simpson, *Texas Tech University*

Imagine you are a principal in a large high school in one of the following districts: Providence, Rhode Island; Madison, Wisconsin; Austin, Texas; or San Francisco, California. A library paraprofessional is accused of sexual harassment by a senior cheerleader named Margie. The paraprofessional has a 2-year degree but very limited skills in English. He likes to write poetry. Margie claims that he has e-mailed her six poems. None is sexually explicit, but each is romantic in character. After receiving the first three poems Margie asked him to stop. The paraprofessional sent her three additional poems, all of the same type. Margie confronts you in your office and charges him with sexual harassment. She says this 31-year-old man also seems to make it a point to brush up against her from time to time, and so now she won't go to the library. She has told several of her friends on the cheerleading squad about her plans to make an accusation of sexual harassment. Two try to dissuade her. The two eventually approach you after learning of Margie's charges. Windswept is the captain of the cheerleaders, and she claims there is nothing untoward about the employee's behavior. Summersun, the other girl, backs Windswept up. Both claim they each received one poem from the employee in question but not by e-mail. Their impression was that he truly wanted their feedback on style and content. They suggest that Margie is arrogant, snobbish, and somewhat prejudiced toward minorities and that that may be underlying her hostility toward this employee.

Margie's father owns the largest car dealership in town, and he is also owner of a large real estate concern. He is active in local and state politics but in the state's minority, conservative party. You have met him before and know that he believes his daughter can do no wrong. After alerting the superintendent to the problem, what should you do? You are not hesitant to admit that you fear the local press. How are they likely to spin the story?

Sexual harassment laws are very important, and they are there to protect the unempowered, namely youth subject to predatory behavior by staff and fellow students. On the other hand, the employee is an immigrant to this country who seems earnest and is working hard to improve his lot in life. He clearly enjoys being friends with the students and has even mentioned to you once that they like him because of his poetry. He is single, and there has never been another charge like this against him.

Discussion Questions

1. What should you do?

2. How much should you try to anticipate the local press when figuring out the right course of action?

3. District and school moral architecture aim at genuine inclusion, and this demands that you act to protect the unempowered. But who exactly is unempowered: the 17-year-old girl, who admittedly seems to you very nice and exceedingly proper in all that she does, or your employee, who is a bit rough around the edges, unfamiliar with local taboos, and yet seemingly very earnest about doing a good job?

4. Local union officials have already begun telling the employee that if he is reprimanded in any way he should go to the press and maybe sue. Margie's father is sure to sue if something isn't done. So what will you do?

American Association of School Administrators Statement of Ethics for Educational Leaders

An educational leader's professional conduct must conform to an ethical code of behavior, and the code must set high standards for all educational leaders. The educational leader provides professional leadership across the district and also across the community. This responsibility requires the leader to maintain standards of exemplary professional conduct while recognizing that his or her actions will be viewed and appraised by the community, professional associates and students.

The educational leader acknowledges that he or she serves the schools and community by providing equal educational opportunities to each and every child. The work of the leader must emphasize accountability and results, increased student achievement, and high expectations for each and every student.

To these ends, the educational leader subscribes to the following statements of standards. The educational leader:

1. Makes the education and well-being of students the fundamental value of all decision making.

2. Fulfills all professional duties with honesty and integrity and always acts in a trustworthy and responsible manner.

3. Supports the principle of due process and protects the civil and human rights of all individuals.

4. Implements local, state and national laws.

5. Advises the school board and implements the board's policies and administrative rules and regulations.

6. Pursues appropriate measures to correct those laws, policies, and regulations that are not consistent with sound educational goals or that are not in the best interest of children.

7. Avoids using his/her position for personal gain through political, social, religious, economic or other influences.

8. Accepts academic degrees or professional certification only from accredited institutions.

9. Maintains the standards and seeks to improve the effectiveness of the profession through research and continuing professional development.

10. Honors all contracts until fulfillment, release or dissolution mutually agreed upon by all parties.

11. Accepts responsibility and accountability for one's own actions and behaviors.

12. Commits to serving others above self.

Source: Adopted by the AASA Governing Board, March 1, 2007. Reprinted with permission from AASA.

National Education Association Code of Ethics of the Education Profession

The educator, believing in the worth and dignity of each human being, recognizes the supreme importance of the pursuit of truth, devotion to excellence, and the nurture of the democratic principles. Essential to these goals is the protection of freedom to learn and to teach and the guarantee of equal educational opportunity for all. The educator accepts the responsibility to adhere to the highest ethical standards.

The educator recognizes the magnitude of the responsibility inherent in the teaching process. The desire for the respect and confidence of one's colleagues, of students, of parents, and of the members of the community provides the incentive to attain and maintain the highest possible degree of ethical conduct. The Code of Ethics of the Education Profession indicates the aspiration of all educators and provides standards by which to judge conduct.

The remedies specified by the NEA and/or its affiliates for the violation of any provision of this Code shall be exclusive and no such provision shall be enforceable in any form other than the one specifically designated by the NEA or its affiliates.

PRINCIPLE I: COMMITMENT TO THE STUDENT

The educator strives to help each student realize his or her potential as a worthy and effective member of society. The educator therefore works to stimulate the spirit of inquiry, the acquisition of knowledge and understanding, and the thoughtful formulation of worthy goals. In fulfillment of the obligation to the student, the educator:

1. Shall not unreasonably restrain the student from independent action in the pursuit of learning.

2. Shall not unreasonably deny the student access to varying points of view.

3. Shall not deliberately suppress or distort subject matter relevant to the student's progress.

4. Shall make reasonable effort to protect the student from conditions harmful to learning or to health and safety.

5. Shall not intentionally expose the student to embarrassment or disparagement.

6. Shall not on the basis of race, color, creed, sex, national origin, marital status, political or religious beliefs, family, social or cultural background, or sexual orientation, unfairly:

   • Exclude any student from participation in any program.
   • Deny benefits to any student.
   • Grant any advantage to any student.

7. Shall not use professional relationships with students for private advantage.

8. Shall not disclose information about students obtained in the course of professional service unless disclosure serves a compelling professional purpose or is required by law.

PRINCIPLE II: COMMITMENT TO THE PROFESSION

The education profession is vested by the public with a trust and responsibility requiring the highest ideals of professional service. In the belief that the quality of the services of the education profession directly influences the nation and its citizens, the educator shall exert every effort to raise professional standards, to promote a climate that encourages the exercise of professional judgment, to achieve conditions that attract persons worthy of the trust to careers in education, and to assist in preventing the practice of the profession by unqualified persons. In fulfillment of the obligation to the profession, the educator:

1. Shall not in an application for a professional position deliberately make a false statement or fail to disclose a material fact related to competency and qualification.

2. Shall not misrepresent his/her professional qualifications.

3. Shall not assist any entry into the profession of a person known to be unqualified in respect to character, education, or other relevant attribute.

4. Shall not knowingly make a false statement concerning the qualifications of a candidate for a professional position.

5. Shall not assist a noneducator in the unauthorized practice of teaching.

6. Shall not disclose information about colleagues obtained in the course of professional service unless disclosure serves a compelling professional purpose or is required by law.

7. Shall not knowingly make false or malicious statements about a colleague.

8. Shall not accept any gratuity, gift, or favor that might impair or appear to influence professional decisions or action.

Source: Adopted by the NEA 1975 Representative Assembly. Reprinted with permission.

National School Boards Association Code of Ethics for School Board Members

The NSBA Board endorses the following code for local school board members.

As a member of my local Board of Education I will strive to improve public education, and to that end I will:

- attend all regularly scheduled board meetings insofar as possible, and become informed concerning the issues to be considered at those meetings;

- recognize that I should endeavor to make policy decisions only after full discussion at publicly held board meetings;

- render all decisions based on the available facts and my independent judgment, and refuse to surrender that judgment to individuals or special interest groups;

- encourage the free expression of opinion by all board members, and seek systematic communications between the board and students, staff, and all elements of the community;

- work with other board members to establish effective board policies and to delegate authority for the administration of the schools to the superintendent;

- communicate to other board members and the superintendent expression of public reaction to board policies and school programs;

- inform myself about current educational issues by individual study and through participation in programs providing needed information, such as those sponsored by my state and national school boards association;

- support the employment of those persons best qualified to serve as school staff, and insist on a regular and impartial evaluation of all staff;

- avoid being placed in a position of conflict of interest;

- take no private action that will compromise the board or administration, and respect the confidentiality of information that is privileged under applicable law; and

- remember always that my first and greatest concern must be the educational welfare of the students attending the public schools

Source: Reviewed and approved by the Board November 10, 1999.

Glossary

Accountability: Initially the term was derived from the worlds of business and commerce. All activity undertaken in the name of business can be assigned some cost or benefit. (This is no longer true. Even in the business world there is now much talk of value-added activity: activity for which there may be no discrete economic indicators.)

Today the term *accountability* is used in organizational contexts of all sorts. A person or organization is said to be accountable when discrete, observable standards are set and subsequent performance is measured against the performance standards.

There is a danger that the terms *accountable* and *accountability* will be misused in a moral context. Such terms stand in sharp contrast to morally descriptive ones such as *responsible* and *responsibility*. One cannot meaningfully be held accountable for something for which one senses no responsibility. Acknowledgment of responsibility opens the door to successful implementation of accountability systems.

Action: Action has replaced behavior as the focal point of cutting-edge research in areas such as cognitive psychology, cognitive anthropology, and economics. Roughly speaking, the word *action* refers to an event that consists of a behavior (or set of behaviors)

in addition to some information processing and often some intention or purpose.

Administrative law: Rules and regulations made by a government agency. The agency itself must be created through legislative action, with its authority and limits generally spelled out. Subsequent court decisions may limit or expand the authority of a government agency to create or withdraw from imposing further regulation. Both the U.S. Department of Education and the state boards of education are examples of such agencies with the power to create rules and regulations exhibiting the force of public law.

Altruism: *Altruism* means focusing on the needs of others without calculating self-benefit. Scientists such as Lee Alan Dugatkin, David Sloan Wilson, and Elliot Sober and psychologists and economists such as Dawn Schroeder, Lawrence Kohlberg, Anatol Rapaport, Robert Frank, and many others have shown that the disposition to act altruistically is widely distributed. Biological scientists such as Dugatkin have shown altruism exhibited in most higher species from guppies onward. The most likely hypothesis about human beings is that they sometimes act selfishly (psychological egoism) and sometimes unselfishly (altruism). Of course, how one acts in any given case never determines how one *ought* to act.

Authority: Because of institutional position, experience, or expertise one person is charged with directing or limiting the actions of others.

Autonomy: Autonomy is the exercise of one's wits to make decisions on the basis of good reason. It is not simply a right to do what one wants. A bear eliminates as it will in the forest, but no one describes such action as anything other than the bear doing what it wants. Infants cry when they want, but more mature humans have the ability to act contrary to how they want on the basis of good reason. It is this capacity that is identified by the term *autonomy,* and it is the development of this capacity that is said to be an educational objective. The exercise of autonomy is generally considered a right of adults to be protected by a democratic republic.

Boss: A person in a position to control others through institutionally formalized variance in social roles.

Bullying: When a person possessing power disproportionate to that of others uses that power to intimidate and manipulate.

Character: Character is an aspect of personal identity that merits praise or rebuke. For example, one is praiseworthy for consistently honest action and blameworthy for consistently dishonest action. In ordinary language, a person is held responsible for his or her manifest character. In contrast, people do not ordinarily hold others responsible for their personalities. Rightly or wrongly, folk psychology has it that a person is responsible for the character he or she develops but not for his or her personality. Persons are not held responsible for traits wholly genetic in origin or otherwise outside the person's control.

Character trait: A character trait is an element of character. Normally, character traits are thought of as virtues and vices. A person is

said to be capable of developing or eliminating his or her virtues and vices, respectively.

Chauvinism: Favoring one's own without due regard to empirical data or circumstances.

Community: Any group of people sharing some common vision. An individual may be a member of more than one community.

Compassion: A desire to empathize with others suffering some disadvantage and a desire to assist them in some appropriate way.

Consequence: Anything that causally follows from an action is a consequence. For example, teachers may give students rewards for good behavior and punishments or penalties for bad or inappropriate behavior. Properly speaking, all are consequences.

Courtesies: Practices fostered to promote mutual respect between members of a community.

Discipline: Following a rule one believes is based on good reason. For example, people speak of a well-disciplined army, a well-disciplined student, a well-disciplined investor, and so on. Armies, students, or investors hypnotized or otherwise blind to what they are doing are not, properly speaking, well disciplined. Discipline, properly speaking, is not about punishing, penalizing, or any other use of power to force one's will on others.

Disparate impact: One of two basic types of discrimination defined by Title VII. Disparate impact occurs when school district policy or practice has a disproportionate impact on members of a protected class. Disparate treatment, as defined by Title VII, occurs when a school intentionally treats people differently because of their race, sex, national origin, age, or disability.

Duty: The consequence of the creation and assignment of rights. In the domain of morality, a duty exists when a moral agent recognizes a compelling obligation to act or forgo acting on behalf of another.

Education: From the ancient Greek word *educare,* meaning "to lead out." Education has been written about from the earliest times and from all cultures. In summary, it is most effectively thought of as participation in the Great Conversation of Humankind. In collective fashion, humans and humans alone seek to articulate and record both the small and great truths of the world, the transitory and the enduring.

Epistemology: The study of justifications to know. If asked to respond to the question "How do you know X is true?" the *criteria* for determining whether an answer is accurate and sufficient are the proper subject matter of epistemology.

Equal Access Act: Federal law requiring secondary schools that allow noncurriculum clubs to meet during or after the school day (creating a limited open forum) to allow other legal organizations to use school facilities as well. These include prayer groups, the Gay and Straight Alliance, and other alternative lifestyle groups.

Equality: Treating everyone the same. When this is done without regard to relevant differences, unfairness can result.

Equity: This term denotes the spirit and habit of right dealing with others. It is usually defined in terms of principles of fairness and justice (*Miller v. Kenniston,* 86 Me. 550, 30 A. 114). In a more restricted jurisprudential sense, it is a branch of remedial justice based on well-settled and well-understood principles and precedents beyond the strict lines of positive law (*Isabelle Properties v. Edelman,* 297 N.Y.S., 572 574, 164 Misc. 192). In the courts, equity is relied on to secure relief where the administration of law is necessarily incomplete (*Laird v. Union Traction Co.,* 208 Pa. 574 57 A. 987).

Ethical dilemmas: When there is no evidential or referential pattern favoring one position over another at the outset, and the tension of "getting it right" seems in serious doubt.

Ethical issues: When principles, traditions (including codes, policies, and laws), or virtues seem to favor a certain orientation to problem solving, yet mitigating circumstances make follow-through a challenge, the pragmatic effect is to compromise implementation of policy and action and makes the challenge an issue.

Excuses: Statements made to show why an evident violation of an ideal should be ignored. Excuses attempt to identify extenuating circumstances beyond one's control. (See *Ought implies can.*)

Existentialists: Ranging from atheists Jean-Paul Sartre (1993) and Franz Fanon to agnostic Albert Camus and Christian Søren Kierkegaard, existentialists deny the existence of any formal grounds for moral choice. For Sartre that leaves only the option of authentic choice, of choosing what one truly wants and not in consequence of outside forces and other directives. For Kierkegaard, morals are mere sociological conventions that more often than not approach God's will but are not isomorphic with it. God speaks to individuals alone, and when the voice of providence is present the individual can't help but know it is God's will for him or her alone.

Fair: Assigning to no one a disadvantage before an activity commences. This does not prohibit differential treatment of persons, only the assignment of disadvantages (events inhibitory of self-fulfilling actions). In more rough-and-ready fashion we might say that as a rule, fairness is a matter of treating equals equally and unequals unequally.

Favoritism: Preferring one person, subject, talent, behavior, or event to the detriment of others.

Focus: Directed attention to some matter, free from distracting influences.

Freedom: Absence of restraint.

Grading: Discriminating between levels of achievement.

Hamilton equation: $r \times b > c$. This means the closer the relative (r), genetically speaking, and the more benefit (b) to that relative, the more the actor is likely to take risks to secure the relative's benefit. The closeness of the genetic overlap must be greater than or equal to the cost (c) to the actor. The bottom-line implication here is that an identical twin is likely to sacrifice even her life for her twin but not for her second cousin twice removed. According to Hamilton, this is a natural consequence of evolutionary history and doesn't require further investigation into the special nature of humans or of providence. More than even Rapaport's Tit for Tat, which is heuristically useful for modeling complex social behavior with simple rules that could have been evolutionarily derived, Hamilton proposed his rule as a biological law establishing the foundation of morality.

Harassment: With deliberate and malicious intent, a person attempts to limit another's exercise of autonomy. (This definition should not be confused with statutory definitions of sexual harassment.)

IDEIA 04 (Individuals with Disabilities Education Improvement Act of 2004): Federal law defining the legal rights held by children with disabilities. This act is a refinement of the "least restrictive environment" legislation initiated by PL 94-142 in 1975 and extended by the Individuals with Disabilities Act of 1997. This legislation and accompanying court law are the source of requirements for free appropriate education to the handicapped and individual education plans for the handicapped as prescribed by admission, dismissal, and review committees. Administrators should be aware that if they make an inopportune call and litigation results, parents win in more than 50% of all cases, and these are the issues for which schools are most often brought to court (Zirkel, 2002).

Immorality: In *Youngman v. Doerhoff,* 890 S.W. 2d 330 (Mo. Court of Appeals, 1994) the court defined *immorality* as "contemplated behavior sufficiently contrary to justice, honesty, modesty, or good moral conscience, or behavior involving baseness, vileness or depravity so as to support the inference that the teacher understands the conduct to be wrong." This suggests a strong court sympathy with G. E. Moore's intuitionism.

Indoctrination: Causing someone to accept a belief, practice, or attitude for which he or she is unable to provide justification. A person may indoctrinate another with no intention of doing so. Indoctrination is identified by what happens to the person indoctrinated, not by the intent, or lack thereof, by a causative agent. Furthermore, *indoctrination* does not denote mischief on the part of the causative agent.

The word *indoctrination* acquired an unattractive connotation in the latter half of the 20th century, but this connotation has not yet become part of the denotation of the term. Military and religious orders may be said to indoctrinate people. Sometimes this is a good thing and sometimes not. Indoctrination always involves risk inasmuch as it delimits the autonomy of the person indoctrinated. Strictly speaking, kindergarten teachers may be said to indoctrinate students in counting and "The Alphabet Song."

Information: Information is a set of rule-governed symbols. By itself information has no meaning.

Intersubjective agreement: Abundant evidence from neuroscience shows that the perceptions of one person do not map onto the perceptions of another in any wholly precise and exacting fashion. Nevertheless, when one English speaker says to another English speaker, "Hand me that piece of chalk," the subsequent action of the listener usually leads to the satisfaction of the speaker. Objectively speaking, the two could not have the same perception of the piece of chalk. Nevertheless, it is evident from the listener's response to the request that there is sufficient agreement between the two on the appropriateness of subsequent action. This agreement is said to be intersubjective. Although each person has his or her own sense of the perceived, there is sufficient overlap to allow successful and shared communal action. Such intersubjective agreement provides a basis for all sorts of social commerce, including such things as the moral and the pedagogical.

Intuitionism: This is a philosophical position that says the intuitions one has about matters of ultimate right or wrong are profoundly reliable when issuing forth from the right source and evident in the most visceral of one's sensibilities.

Intuitions: Beliefs people hold as if they were true despite the fact that the believer cannot articulate any reasoned grounds for such belief. These are deeply held beliefs, to be distinguished from mere hunches or transient guesses, as one might rely on when answering a multiple-choice test item about which one has little or no clue.

Is–ought gap: List all the sentences describing how the world *is*. The list does not describe how the world *ought* to be. There is a logical gap between factual statements about how the world *is* and prescriptive recommendations about how it *ought* to be. For example, at one time the average cholesterol level in the United States was 225. Doctors did not accept how the world was and instead encouraged people to get their cholesterol below 200. Doctors knew how the world was but thought they *ought* to make it better by telling people to reduce their cholesterol. Philosopher David Hume was the first to notice the logical consequences of the "is–ought gap" more than 300 years ago.

Jurisprudence: This is the meta-theory of law. Jurisprudence is the study of court-rendered justice, the theoretical foundations of judicial practice, the proper role of an officer of the court, the nature of evidence, admissible rules of inference, venue, jurisdiction, and the purpose of law generally. In its most general form jurisprudence constitutes the philosophy of law.

Knowledge: Information that maps onto reality in a reliable and uncontroversial fashion is knowledge. The mapping-on effect of knowledge reflects meaning. This includes differences between "knowing how" and "knowing that."

Law: The law is a subset of moral discourse. More specifically, the law is the set of morals that those who hold the sovereignty of state endorse and enforce. For example, when the law offends people's moral sense, they may set out to change it. Consider debates about such things as abortion, capital punishment, tax evasion, product liability, and corporal punishment in the schools. Each of these debates reflects basic moral commitments. Contract law is essentially the law of promise keeping. (Promise keeping is a moral issue. The consequences of breaking promises can be addressed in communal fashion through the law.) Even procedural issues of venue and jurisdiction in the courts reflect something of the adjudicating community's moral sense of fair play.

Learning: Learning is a matter of acquiring new attitudes, skills, beliefs, behaviors, habits, and feelings. It is also a shift in conceptual horizon. In the words of philosopher Gilbert Ryle, learning is a "success verb." To say that "Smith is learning mathematics" means that Smith *is acquiring* relevant attitudes, skills, beliefs, and so on. Success verbs stand in sharp contrast to "task verbs," such as "teaching" and "aiming." Task verbs depict an intentional effort but are not suggestive of success. A marksman may aim at the target, but this says little about the likelihood of his hitting it. Similarly, instructors may teach mathematics, but observers may still ask, properly speaking, "Did the students learn anything?"

License: The absence of community social norms prohibiting or inhibiting a range of behavior.

Metaphysics: This is a traditional branch of philosophy. It theorizes about what is said to be beyond the bounds of physical description. For example, some say that the best metaphysicians today are physicists theorizing about events before the big bang, quantum entanglement, the possibility of multiple universes, and the end of the universe. None of these speculations can be addressed within the confines of physical law or experiment. Theology, new age advice, and so-called folk psychology are also beyond the reach of physical law and so are subject to metaphysical analysis.

Morality: Doing right by self and others. It involves addressing questions such as "Whom do I owe?" "What do I owe?" "How do I know when I have at least minimally fulfilled my duties?" and "What counts as heroic in seeking the well-being of self and others?"

Morals: Statements that prescribe or prohibit action. The key moral term (implicit or explicit) in such sentences is the self-revealing *should* or *ought*. For example, the moral "Murder is wrong" implies "A person *ought not* murder another." Similarly, ethics, strictly speaking, are statements prescribing or prohibiting behavior.

Motivating: This is the act of creating an allure while removing distractors.

Multiculturalism: As with all "isms," there is variation concerning what should be included in the ideology. Whatever else might be said about this particular ideology, there are two concepts (sometimes at tension with one another) that characterize it. One is the idea that respect for the personhood of an individual must always be preserved. The second is that in order to respect the individual, disparaging evaluations of incidentals of the individual's social inheritance should be avoided.

Obligation: An intellectual awakening to the fact that if people do not act as they ought, they will suffer guilt. Failure to suffer guilt when knowingly engaged in wrongdoing is central to the psychiatric diagnosis of a sociopath. For all others, guilt is educative. It informs people of their obligations.

Organization: A community exhibiting operational structure.

Ought* implies *can: As early as 1954, philosopher R. M. Hare, in his book *The Language of Morals,* made an issue of reminding readers that no one can be held responsible for doing that which he or she could never possibly do. To say that someone *ought* to do some act is to presume that the person is in fact empowered to do it. A common mistake people often make when first working with the Wagner–Kierstead Moral Self-Assessment Protocol is to create an objective that is impossible to fulfill. A lot of heartache can be avoided if the user of the protocol will just remember when framing his or her objectives, "*Ought* implies *can*."

Paternalism: This is the realm of discourse pertaining to the circumstances that justify one person acting or making decisions for another. For example, although smoking may be generally unwise, in the United States it is left up to the adult whether he or she should undertake such behavior. In contrast, society limits the right of children to purchase cigarettes, and parents may prohibit children from using cigarettes. Indeed, in the latter case, parents may be criticized for failing in their moral obligation to their children if they allow their children to smoke. It is generally recognized that those in position of authority or society at large may act to protect the infirm, mentally incapacitated, or innocent. All others are allowed to exercise their own autonomy even if their choices seem to others to be generally unwise. The schools have a special obligation to act paternalistically toward students in the legal doctrine of in loco parentis. This means the schools are expected to act paternalistically in the role of parents in a varying range of matters. The courts have in recent years limited the role of in loco parentis, particularly in the case of adolescents, but the schools still shoulder a responsibility for protecting students from unwise choices such as the use of drugs on school grounds.

Penalties: Penalties are negative consequences assigned to an action. In sharp contrast to punishments, no moral condemnation is necessarily involved in the use of penalties. In contrast to punishments, penalties are merely a matter of negative reinforcement aimed at extinguishing behavior.

For example, parking tickets and most traffic tickets assign penalties. If a person parks next to an expired parking meter, he or she may be assigned a penalty (fined). In general, this involves no moral condemnation. Perhaps the person is late for a test. She parks in a 30-minute parking space knowing full well she will be in the test for at least 2 hours. She is fined and pays for the convenience of parking close by.

In contrast, violations of the law such as failing to stop at a stop sign or exceeding the speed limit by 30 mph or more are ticketed for "reckless and imprudent driving" and are said to be a "punishable offense." When arrested for punishable offenses, violators may not just mail in a fine but must appear in court. In criminal proceedings, the judge expresses the community's moral disapproval.

A teacher may be penalized for coming late to an in-service workshop. In contrast, a teacher is generally punished for selling grades to students. To confuse the concepts of punishment and penalty trivializes the offensiveness of punishable offenses.

Personality: Personality is a facet of personal identity. Personality traits include such things as being extroverted or introverted, happy or sad, and morose or optimistic. It is often said, though not perhaps in any fully accurate sense, that people are not responsible for their personality traits. People are said to inherit the traits that make up personality from their parents (genetic contribution) and from family, friends, and society (environmental contribution).

Personality trait: An element of one's personality, as opposed to one's character. People are generally held blameless for personality defects. Such defects may be treated therapeutically. Similarly, personality assets may be acknowledged as talents or a form of giftedness.

Plan: Based on a continuous inventory of resources, a plan prescribes the resources to be used, who will use them, and who will benefit from their use.

Professionalism: Pertains to the shared moral vision of a community of trained specialists.

Protocol: A protocol is a stepwise procedure for ensuring the completion of some task.

Psychological egoism: A theoretical descendant of empiricism and later (and more specifically) behaviorism. Today the term *psychological egoism* encompasses any theory of motivation limiting itself to the self-interest of the acting agent. Roughly put, this includes all approaches giving rise to folkisms such as "Motivation is a matter of the carrot or the stick," "What's in it for me?," or, in more summary fashion, "Everyone acts out of self-interest." As Elliot Sober and David Sloan Wilson (1998) show in *Unto Others,* their exhaustive review of the literature, there has never been any experimental evidence or even a compelling argument mustered to support a defense of self-interest as the sole source of motivation.

Punishment: Punishment occurs when a person in proper authority over another deliberately and intentionally assigns to the other a negative consequence for violating the moral order and makes the other mindful of the nature and extent of the violation. There is no "nonmoral" punishment. For example, the law prohibiting murder exists to secure the community's sense of moral order. In addition, philosopher of education Robin Barrow points out, if the reason for the negative consequence is not made clear to the offender, then properly speaking no punishment occurs. In such cases, the negative consequences may often be rightly felt by the punished as nothing more than an act of bullying on the part of the authority, the person exhibiting superior power.

It is impossible to give a full account of the concept of punishment in a glossary. The reader may run a library search of the concept and discover that thousands of articles and treatises have been written on the subject over the years. The concept of punishment is so richly textured that it requires extensive knowledge of many complex ideas for full understanding. Other ideas involved in understanding punishment include authority, moral order, educative, deliberate, and violation, to name but a few. The reader should avoid trivializing the concept of punishment, either as a result of careless use or exposure to curricular materials that focus solely on extinguishing behaviors.

Racism: Disfavoring others because of their race.

Responsibility: Responsibility is a moral commitment to manage some range of potentialities. For example, an administrator may ask another administrator to be responsible for oversight of a school sporting event while she runs an errand. The other administrator agrees to be responsible for the first administrator's assigned task, but there is no list of behaviors either has agreed to ensure. Rather, the person accepting responsibility has undertaken the task of managing an indefinable and potentially unlimited number of possibilities.

One can compile a list of responsibilities, but responsibilities are not the same as what it means to *be responsible.* Some responsibilities can be operationally defined and people subsequently held accountable for shortcomings. However, in other cases, there is no meaningful way to operationally define a responsibility. For example, in at least one traditional marriage vow, the partners agree "to have and to hold, in sickness and health, in good times and bad." This moral commitment for which each assumes responsibility is not reducible, in any satisfying way, to a list of measurable objectives. Nevertheless, generations of married couples have successfully lived up to one another's expectations of their partner's responsibilities without the benefit (and restricting confinement) of such a list.

Educators are responsible for the educational well-being of their students. Being responsible in this sense cannot be restricted to a list of measurable behaviors for which the educator can be held accountable. The moral commitment of seeking the educational well-being of students looms much larger than can be captured on any list.

Right: A human artifact. Rights are prescribed, specific protections for the purpose of managing social relations. Rights create license for one or more persons simultaneous with the creation of duties on the part of others. In this sense, rights and duties are properly understood as two sides of a single concept. Whenever a right is created, a duty is created that thereafter obligates one or more other people.

Rudeness: Action that diminishes the show of respect due others.

Sexism: Disfavoring others because of their gender.

Strong character: A person of strong character is said to willfully pursue his or her favored virtues and avoid offending vices. A person of strong character is ordinarily thought to have integrity, holding herself personally accountable for any lapse of commitment.

Surface-level morals: As psychologist Marc Hauser (2006) explains, these are the prescriptions and prohibitions evident in a community or culture consequent to deep-level moral universals interacting with contingencies of the local environment. The rules and conventions that exist in different cultures to keep people from hurting themselves are the surface-level rules. These may vary depending on surrounding contingencies. The driving

deep-level concern that makes such rules a focus of attention may be that people not render themselves unnecessarily vulnerable to commonly avoidable environmental threats.

Teach: *Teach* is a task verb. It identifies the task one undertakes when deliberately trying to bring specific attitudes, skills, beliefs, feelings, behaviors, and habits into the life of another.

Training: Teaching skills and facts for the purpose of carrying out explicitly defined tasks.

Understanding: This and the concept of consciousness are probably the two most difficult concepts to define in all of the cognitive sciences, neuropsychology, and artificial intelligence. At the very least, understanding involves a feel for the application of knowledge, flexibility, heuristic tools, and speed in the application of knowledge to address a presenting need. Vaguely put, one can say that understanding is *meaningful*.

Universality, principle of: The principle of universality says that every moral decision must be such that anyone in the same circumstance would find compelling reason for agreement on the right-mindedness of the act, rule, or policy under consideration.

Vice: A disposition to act in a way contrary to the actor's sense of right is a vice. The actor has privileged access to his or her vices. Depending on how he or she *behaves,* others may never learn of the actor's vices. The reason vices are ordinarily thought to be a part of one's character rather than one's personality is that it is believed one is responsible for the strength of a vice in his or her life. If one repeatedly gives in to a disposition, it becomes more strongly entrenched in one's character. The more one overrides the disposition, the weaker it becomes. Consequently, a person is held responsible for evident vices as much as for evident virtues.

In cases of psychopathology such as kleptomania, a person is not held responsible for his actions. The disposition to steal is thought to be so strong that the person cannot control it. The disposition to steal is said to be a defect of *personality* necessitating therapeutic intervention. People are not held responsible for their psychopathologies. In contrast, however, they are held responsible for giving in to their own acknowledged vices. The distinction between vices and psychopathologies is not always clear. In practice, there is much disagreement over whether a given action is a result of psychopathology or willful vice.

Violence: A deliberate effort to do harm to another. The harm desired reflects malicious intent. Malicious intent is key to the difference between innocent or accident injury on one hand and violence on the other.

Virtues: Like vices, virtues are thought to be traits of character. Possession of a virtue is praiseworthy, and its absence can be grounds for disapproval. Scholars such as Martin Seligman have concluded that there is much more agreement than disagreement on what counts as virtuous. They claim that this is true across cultural, geographic, and historic borders. For example, people everywhere seem to agree that

courage is a virtue. However, they often disagree on what counts as an appropriate example of such a virtue. Although people disagree on specific instances of virtue, in principle they agree on the praiseworthiness of traits such as courage, honesty, integrity, respectfulness, charitableness, loyalty, compassion, dedication, justice, and fair-mindedness.

The reason virtues are thought to be praiseworthy is that there is a commonly accepted sense that one builds one's own complement of virtues. People are not born virtuous. For example, an infant is not said to exhibit any virtue. Infants are regarded as simply innocent. Infants make no deliberate moral decisions. In contrast, the adult who acts virtuously is praised if he or she seems to be acting in the face of counterbalancing influences. For example, many people admire Jamie Escalante's and Marva Collins's courage for teaching inner-city children calculus and the liberal arts, respectively, despite experts' insistence that this could not be done.

Weak character: When, despite the absence of any overwhelming psychopathology, a person continues to violate his or her own moral ideals, the person is said to exhibit weakness of character.

References

Applbaum, A. (1999). *Ethics for adversaries.* Princeton, NJ: Princeton University Press.

Adams, R. M. (2002). *Finite and the infinite goods.* New York: Oxford University Press.

Adams, R. M. (2005). *A theory of virtue: Excellence in being for the good.* New York: Oxford University.

Adler, M. (1998). *Paidea proposal.* New York: Touchstone.

Alexander, H. (2007). *The structural evolution of morality.* Cambridge: Cambridge University Press.

Alexander, L., & Sherwin, E. (2008). *De-mystifying legal reasoning.* New York: Cambridge University Press.

Al-Ghazali. (1963). *Incoherence of the philosophers* (S. A. Kamali, Trans.). Lahore: Pakistan Philosophical Congress.

American Association of School Administrators. (1981). *Code of ethics.* Adopted by the AASA Governing Board, March 1, 1981.

Amrein, A., & Berliner, D. (2003). The effects of high-stakes testing on student motivation and learning. *Educational Leadership, 60*(5), 32–36.

Anderson, J., Rungtussanatham, M., & Schroder, R. (1994). A theory of quality management underlying the Deming management method. *Academy of Management Review, 19*(3), 472–509.

Aquinas, Saint Thomas. (2001). *Aquinas's shorter Summa: Saint Thomas' own concise version of his* Summa Theologica. Manchester, NH: Sophia Institute Press.

Ariely, D. (2008). *Predictably irrational.* New York: Harper.

Aristotle. (1958). *The politics* (E. Barker, Trans. & Ed.). New York: Oxford University Press.

Audi, R. (2002). *The architecture of reason.* New York: Oxford University Press.

Audi, R. (2005). *The good in the right: A theory of intuition and intrinsic value.* Princeton, NJ: Princeton University Press.

Augustine. (1998). *Saint Augustine's confessions* (H. Chadwick, Trans.). New York: Oxford University Press.

Austin, J. L. (1962). *How to do things with words* (J. O. Urmson & M. Sbisà, Eds.). Cambridge, MA: Harvard University Press.

Axelrod, R. (1984). *The evolution of cooperation.* New York: Basic Books.

Axelrod, R. (1997). *The complexity of cooperation.* Princeton, NJ: Princeton University Press.

Bakunin, M. (1970). *God and the state.* New York: Dover.

Barash, D. P. (2003). *The survival game.* New York: Times Books.

Baron, J. (2000). *Thinking and deciding.* Cambridge, MA: Harvard University Press.

Baron, J. (2005). *Rationality and intelligence.* Cambridge: Cambridge University Press.

Barry, B. (2001). *Culture and equality: An egalitarian critique of multiculturalism.* Cambridge, MA: Harvard University Press.

Beck, L. G. (1994). *Reclaiming educational administration as a caring profession.* New York: Teachers College Press.

Beckner, W. (2004). *Ethics for educational leaders.* Boston: Pearson Education.

Benhabib, S. (2004). *The rights of others: Aliens, residents, and citizens.* Cambridge: Cambridge University Press.

Berliner, C., & Biddle, B. (1995). *The manufactured crisis.* Upper Saddle River, NJ: Addison-Wesley.

Berliner, D. (2005). The near impossibility for testing for teacher quality. *Journal of Teacher Education, 55*(3), 205–213.

Black, H. C. (Ed.). (1951). *Black's law dictionary* (4th ed.). St. Paul, MN: West Publishing.

Blackburn, S. (1984). *Spreading the word: Groundings in the philosophy of language.* New York: Oxford University Press.

Blackburn, S. (2001). *Ruling passions: A theory of practical reasoning.* New York: Oxford University Press.

Blackburn, S. (2003). *Being good.* New York: Oxford University Press.

Blasé, J., & Anderson, G. (1995). *The micropolitics of leadership.* New York: Teachers' College Press.

Born, D., & Whitfield, D. (Eds.). (2004). *Great conversations.* Chicago: Great Books Foundation.

Boyes-Stones, G., & Brittain, C. (2008). *The Platonist revival.* New York: Cambridge University Press.

Braithwaite, J. (2002). *Restorative justice and response regulation.* New York: Oxford University.

Brighouse, H. (2006). *On education.* New York: Routledge.

Buzzelli, C., & Johnston, B. (2002). *The moral dimensions of teaching: Language, power, and culture in classroom interaction.* New York: Routledge Farmer.

Byrne-Jiminez, M., & Orr, M. (2007). *Developing effective principals through collaborative inquiry.* New York: Teachers College Press.

Callan, E. (1977). *Educating citizens.* New York: Oxford University Press.

Campbell, D. T., & Overman, E. S. (1991). *Methodology and epistemology for the social sciences.* Chicago: University of Chicago Press.

Campbell, D. T., & Russo, J. (2001). *Social measurement.* San Francisco: Sage.

Campbell, E. (2004). *The ethical teacher.* Maidenhead, UK: Open University Press.

Canfield, J., & Hansen, M. (2001). *Chicken soup for the soul.* Deerfield Beach, FL: Health Communications.

Carter, S. (1997). *Integrity.* New York: Harper.

Chen, C., & Lee, Y. (2008). *Leadership management in China.* Cambridge, MA: Harvard University Press.

Chomsky, N. (1988). *Language and problems of knowledge.* Cambridge, MA: MIT Press.

Chomsky, N., & Pateman, B. (2005). *Chomsky on anarchism.* Boston: AK Press.

Churchland, P. (1995). *The engines of reason.* Cambridge, MA: MIT Press.

Clark, F., Higgens, A., & Kohlberg, L. (1991). *Lawrence Kohlberg's approach to moral education.* New York: Teachers College Press.

Clark, M. (1984). Record keeping in two types of relationships. *Journal of Personality and Social Psychology, 47*(4), 549–557.

Clark, M., & Mills, J. (1979). Interpersonal attraction in exchange and community relations. *Journal of Personality and Social Psychology, 37*(1), 12–24.

Coles, R. (2000). *Moral life of children.* New York: Atlantic Monthly Press.

Coulter, A. (2006). *Godless: The church of liberalism.* New York: Crown.

Crick, F. (1995). *An astonishing hypothesis.* New York: Scribner.

Crisp, R. (2006). *Reasons and the good.* New York: Oxford University Press.

Crosby, P. B. (1985). *Quality improvement through defect prevention: The individual's role.* Winter Park, FL: Philip Crosby Associates.

Cua, A. (1979). *Dimensions of moral creativity: Paradigms, principles and ideals.* Philadelphia: Pennsylvania State University Press.

Darling-Hammond, L. (1998). Teachers and teaching. *Educational Researcher, 27*(1), 5–15.

Darling-Hammond, L. (2004). Standards, accountability, and school reform. *The Teachers' College Record, 106*(6), 1047–1085.

Darling-Hammond, L. (2006). *Powerful teacher education.* San Francisco: Jossey-Bass.

Darling-Hammond, L., French, J., & Garcia-Lopez, S. P. (2002). *Learning to teach for social justice.* New York: Teacher's College.

Darling-Hammond, L., La Fors, J., & Snyder, J. (2001). Educating teachers for California's future. *Teacher Education Quarterly, 28*(1), 9–55.

Darling-Hammond, L., & Snyder, J. (2000). Authentic assessment of teaching in context. *Teaching and Teacher Education, 16*(5–6), 523–545.

Darwall, S. (2006). *The second-person standpoint: Morality, respect, and accountability.* Cambridge, MA: Harvard University Press.

Dawson, R. (2001). *Confucius: The analects.* New York: Oxford University Press.

Deal, T. E., & Peterson, K. D. (1999). *Shaping school culture.* San Francisco: Jossey-Bass.

Deming, W. E. (1982). *Quality, productivity and competitive position.* Cambridge, MA: MIT Press.

Deming, W. E. (2000). *The new economics for industry, government, education* (2nd ed.). Cambridge, MA: MIT Press.

Denyer, N. (2008). *Plato.* Cambridge, MA: Harvard University Press.

De Waal, F. (2006). *Our inner ape: A leading primatologist explains why we are who we are.* New York: Riverhead Trade.

Dewey, J. (1908). *Moral principles in education.* Carbondale: Southern Illinois University Press.

Dewey, J. (1960). *The quest for certainty.* New York: Putnam. (Original work published 1929)

Dewey, J. (1938). *Experience and education.* New York: Free Press.

Dokic, J., & Engel, P. (2006). *Frank Ramsey.* New York: Routledge.

Drucker, P. (1967). *The effective executive.* New York: Collins.

Dryfoos, J. (1996). Full service schools: A revolution in health and social services for children and families. *Educational Leadership, 53*(7), 18–23.

Dugatkin, L. (1999). *Cheating monkeys and citizen bees.* New York: Free Press.

Dugatkin, L. (2006). *The altruism equation.* Princeton, NJ: Princeton University Press.

Dupre, A. (2009). *Speaking up: The unintended costs of free speech in public schools.* Cambridge, MA: Harvard University Press.

Dworkin, R. (1988). *Law's empire.* Cambridge, MA: Belknap.

Eldridge, N. (1985). *Timeframes: Re-thinking the Darwinian revolution.* New York: Simon & Schuster.

Englehardt, T. (1986). *The foundations of bioethics.* New York: Oxford.

Fasching, D. J. (1997). Beyond values: Story, character, and public policy in American schools. In J. L. Paul, N. H. Berger, P. G. Osnes, Y. G. Martinez, & W. C. Morse (Eds.), *Ethics and decision making in local schools: Inclusion, policy, and reform* (pp. 99–122). Baltimore: Paul H. Brookes.

Fehr, E., & Fischbacher, U. (2003). The nature of human altruism: Proximate and evolutionary origins. *Nature, 425,* 785–791.

Fischel, W. (1967). *Ibn Khaldun in Egypt.* Berkeley: University of California Press.

Fischer, L., Schimmel, D., & Kelly. C. (1999). *Teachers and the law.* New York: Longman.

Fiske, A. (1992). The four elementary forms of sociability: Framework for a unified theory of social relations. *Psychological Review, 99*(4), 689–723.

Fletcher, G. P. (1993). *Loyalty.* New York: Oxford University Press.

Foot, P. (2002). *Moral dilemmas and other topics in moral philosophy.* Oxford: Clarendon.

Frank, A. (2009). *The constant fire: Beyond the science and religion debate.* Cambridge, MA: Harvard University Press.

Frank, R. H. (1988). *Passion within reason: The strategic role of the emotions.* New York: Norton.

Frankl, V. (1959). *Man's search for meaning.* Boston: Beacon.

Freire, P. (1998). *Pedagogy of freedom: Ethics, democracy, and courage.* Lanham, MD: Roman & Littlefield.

Freire, P. (2000). *Pedagogy of the oppressed.* New York: Continuum.

Fulghum, R. (2004). *All I really need to know I learned in kindergarten.* New York: Random House.

Fullan, M. (2003). *The moral imperative of school leadership.* Thousand Oaks, CA: Corwin.

Fullan, M. J. (2004). *Leadership and sustainability.* Thousand Oaks, CA: Corwin.

Gabor, A. (1986). *The man who discussed quality.* New York: Penguin.

Gardara, P., & Contreras, F. (2009). *The Latino crisis: The consequences of failed school policies.* Cambridge, MA: Harvard University Press.

Gardner, H. (1991). *The unschooled mind: How children think and how schools should teach.* New York: Basic Books.

Gardner, H. (1993). *Frames of mind: The theory of multiple intelligences.* New York: Basic Books.

Garner, B. (Ed.). (2004). *Black's law dictionary* (8th ed.). St. Paul, MN: West Group.

Gaylin, W. (1979). *Caring.* New York: Avon.

Gaziel, H. (1997). Impact of school culture on effectiveness of secondary schools with disadvantaged students. *The Journal of Educational Research, 90*(5), 310–318.

Gaziel, H. (2003). Images of leadership and their effect upon school principals' performance. *International Review of Education, 49*(5), 475–486.

Gazzaniga, M. (2006). *The ethical brain.* New York: Dana.

Gellman, R. A., & Delucia-Waak, J. (2006). Predicting school violence: A comparison of violent and non-violent students on attitudes toward violence, exposure to violence, and post traumatic stress disorder symptomology. *Psychology in the Schools, 43*(5), 591–598.

Gert, B. (1996). *The moral rules.* New York: Harper Torchbooks.

Gert, B. (2004). *Common morality.* New York: Oxford University Press.

Gibbard, A. (1990). *Wise choices, apt feelings.* Cambridge, MA: Harvard University Press.

Gibbard, A. (2003). *Thinking how to live.* Cambridge, MA: Harvard University Press.

Gibbard, A. (2008). *Reconciling our aims: In search of a basis for ethics.* New York: Oxford University Press.

Gilligan, C. (1982). *In a different voice: Psychological theory and women's development.* Cambridge, MA: Harvard University Press.

Glickman, C. D. (2004). *Leadership for learning: How to help teachers succeed.* Alexandria, VA: Association for Supervision Development.

Glimcher, P. W. (2004). *Decisions, uncertainty, and the brain: The science of neuroeconomics.* Cambridge, MA: MIT Press.

Gneezy, U., & Rustichini, A. (2000). A fine place. *Journal of Legal Studies, 29*(1), 1–17.

Goldratt, E. (2004). *The goal.* Great Barrington, MA: North River Press.

Goldstein, R. (2006). *Incompleteness: The proof and paradox of Kurt Godel.* New York: W.W. Norton.

Goodlad, J. (2004). *Romances with schools: A life of education.* New York: McGraw-Hill.

Goodlad, J., & Lesnick, H. (2004). *Moral education.* Boston: Allyn & Bacon.

Gordon, L. (2008). *An introduction to African philosophy.* New York: Cambridge University Press.

Gould, S. (2002). *The structure of evolutionary theory.* Cambridge, MA: Belknap.

Griffin, J. (1986). *Well-being: Its meaning, measurement and moral importance.* New York: Oxford University Press.

Gross, M. (2000). *The conspiracy of ignorance.* New York: Harper.

Gross, M. L. (1997). *The end of sanity: Social and cultural madness in America.* New York: Avon.

Gunter, H. (2001a). Critical approaches to leadership in education. *Journal of Educational Inquiry, 2*(2), 94–107.

Gunter, H. (2001b). *Leaders and leadership in education.* London: Routledge and Kegan Paul.

Gutmann. A. (1999). *Democratic education* (Rev. ed.). Princeton, NJ: Princeton University Press.

Habermas, J. (1979). *Communication and the evolution of society.* Boston: Beacon.

Hacking, I. (1975). *Why does language matter to philosophy?* Cambridge: Cambridge University Press.

Haidt, J. (2003). The moral emotions. In R. J. Davidson, K. R. Scherer, & H. H. Goldsmith (Eds.), *Handbook of affective sciences* (pp. 852–870). Oxford: Oxford University Press.

Haidt, J., & Joseph, C. (2004). Intuitive ethics: How innately prepared intuitions generate culturally variable virtues. *Daedalus,* pp. 55–66.

Haladayna, T. M., Nolen, S. B., & Haas, N. S. (1991). Raising standardized achievement test scores and the origins of test score pollution. *Educational Researcher, 20*(5), 2–7.

Hamilton, W. D. (1964). The genetical evolution of social behavior. *Journal of Theoretical Biology, 7,* 1–52.

Hamilton, W. D. (1975). Innate social attitudes in man. In R. Fox (Ed.), *Biosocial anthropology* (pp. 133–153). New York: Wiley.

Hare, R. M. (1954). *The language of morals.* New York: Oxford University Press.

Hare, R. M. (1992). *Essays on religion and education.* Oxford: Clarendon.

Hare, R. M. (2000). *Sorting out ethics.* Oxford: Oxford University Press.

Hare, W. (1993). *What makes a good teacher?* London, ON: Althouse.

Hart, H. L. A. (1963). *Law, liberty and morality.* Palo Alto, CA: Stanford University Press.

Hart, H. L. A. (1997). *The concept of law* (2nd ed.). New York: Oxford University Press.

Hauser, M. (2006). *Moral minds: How nature designed our universal sense of right and wrong.* New York: Ecco.

Haybron, D. (in press). *The pursuit of unhappiness: Well-being and the limits of personal authority.* New York: Oxford University Press.

Haydon, G. (2000). *Values, virtues and violence: Education and the public understanding of morality.* Oxford: Blackwell.

Haynes, F. (1998). *The ethical school.* London: Routledge.

Hekman, S. J. (1995). *Moral voices, moral selves: Carol Gilligan and feminist moral theory.* University Park, PA: Penn State Press.

Hellman, D. (2008). *When is discrimination wrong?* Cambridge, MA: Harvard University Press.

Hirsch, E. D. (2006). *The knowledge deficit.* New York: Houghton Mifflin.

Hirst, P. H. (1990). *Logic of education.* New York: Routledge.

Hobbes, T. (1996). *Leviathan* (R. Tuck, Ed.). Cambridge: Cambridge University Press. (Original work published 1651)

Hofstader, D. (1979). *Godel, Escher and Bach.* New York: Basic Books.

Howard, R., & Korrer, C. (2008). *Ethics for the real world.* Cambridge, MA: Harvard University Press.

Howard, V., & Scheffler, I. (1995). *Work, education and leadership.* Bern: Peter Lang.

Howe, K., & Miramontes, O. (1992). *The ethics of special education.* New York: Teachers College Press.

Hoyle, J. R., English, F. W., & Steffy, B. E. (1998). *Skills for successful 21st century school leaders: Standards for peak performers.* Arlington, VA: American Association of School Administrators.

Hume, D. (1966). *Enquiry concerning the principles of morals.* Oxford: Oxford University Press. (Original work published 1748)

Hume, D. (2000). *A treatise of human nature.* Oxford: Oxford University Press. (Original work published 1739)

Hursthouse, R. (1999). *On virtue ethics.* New York: Oxford University Press.

Hutchins, R. (Ed.). (1952). *Great books of the Western world.* Chicago: Great Books Foundation.

Ionesco, E. (1962). *Exit the king* (D. Watson, Trans.). New York: Grove.

Isaacson, W. (2007). *Einstein: His life and universe.* New York: Simon & Schuster.

Jackson, F. (2000). *From metaphysics to ethics: A defense of conceptual analysis.* New York: Oxford University Press.

Jagger, A. (2006). *Just methodologies: An interdisciplinary feminist reader.* Boulder, CO: Paradigm.

Jazzar, M., & Algozzine, B. (2006). *Critical issues in educational leadership.* Boston: Pearson.

Johnson, B. (2008). *Radical hope: Ethics in the face of cultural devastation.* Cambridge, MA: Harvard University Press.

Johnson, S. M. (1966). *Leading to change: The challenge of the new superintendency.* San Francisco: Jossey-Bass.

Joyce, R. (2006). *The evolution of morality.* Cambridge, MA: MIT Press.

Juran, J. M., & Blanton, A. B. (1998). *Juran's quality handbook* (5th ed.). New York: McGraw-Hill.

Kaiser, J. S. (1996). *The 21st century principal.* Mequon, WI: Stylex.

Kant, I. (1998). *Groundwork to the metaphysic of morals* (M. Gregor, Trans.). Cambridge: Cambridge University Press.

Katz, M. S., Noddings, N., & Strike, K. A. (Eds.). (1999). *Justice and caring: The search for common ground in education.* New York: Teachers College Press.

Kierkegaard, S. (2000). *The essential Kierkegaard* (E. Hong, Ed.). Princeton, NJ: Princeton University Press.

Kierstead, F. D., & Wagner, P. A. (1993). *The ethical, legal, and multicultural foundations of teaching.* Madison, WI: Brown & Benchmark.

Knapp, M. C., & Talbert, J. (2003). *Leading for learning: Reflective tools for school and district leaders.* Seattle: Center for the Study of Teaching a Policy, University of Washington.

Koble, M., & Garcia-Carpintero, M. (2008). *Relative truth.* New York: Oxford University Press.

Koerner, J. D. (1963). *The miseducation of the American teacher.* Boston: Houghton Mifflin.

Kohlberg, L. (1981). *The philosophy of moral development: Moral stages and the idea of justice.* New York: HarperCollins.

Kohn, A. (2004). *What does it mean to be well-educated?* Boston: Beacon.

Kohn, M. (2008). *Trust: Creating the common good.* New York: Oxford University Press.

Korsgaard, C. M. (1996). *Sources of normativity.* Cambridge: Cambridge University Press.

Kouzes, J., & Posner, B. (1993). *Credibility.* San Francisco: Jossey-Bass.

Kouzes, K., & Posner, B. (2006). *A leader's legacy.* San Francisco: Jossey-Bass.

Kowalski, L. T. J. (Ed.). (2004). *School district superintendents: Role expectations, professional preparation, development and licensing.* Thousand Oaks, CA: Corwin.

Kropotkin, P. (2002). *Peter Kropotkin: A collection of revolutionary writings.* New York: Dover.

Kultgen, J. (1988). *Ethics and professionalism.* Philadelphia: University of Pennsylvania.

Lai, K. (2008). *An introduction to Chinese philosophy.* Cambridge, MA: Harvard University Press.

Lao Tzu. (1979). *The complete works of Lao Tzu* (H. C. Ni, Ed. and Trans.). San Francisco: Seven Stars Communication.

Laozi. (2001). *Dao de jing: The book of the way.* (M. Roberts, Trans.). Berkeley: University of California Press.

Levine, A. (2008). *The general will.* New York: Cambridge University Press.

Lipman, M. (2003). *Thinking in education.* Cambridge: Cambridge University Press.

Long, A. A. (2002). *Epictetus: A stoic and Socratic guide to life.* New York: Oxford University Press.

Luban, D. (1988). *Lawyers and justice.* Princeton, NJ: Princeton University Press.

Lynch, M. (2004). *True to life.* Cambridge, MA: MIT Press.

Lyubomirsky, S., et al. (2005). Pursuing happiness: The architecture of sustainable change. *Review Journal of General Psychology, 9*(2), 111–132.

MacIntyre, A. (1981). *After virtue.* Notre Dame, IN: University of Notre Dame Press.

MacKinnon, C. (2006). *Are women human? And other international dialogues.* Cambridge, MA: Belknap.

Mangin, M. (Ed.). (2007). *Effective teacher leadership.* New York: Teachers College Press.

Martinich, A. P. (1999). *Hobbes: A biography.* New York: Cambridge University Press.

Maxey, S. J. (2002). *Ethical school leadership.* Lanham, MD: Scarecrow.

McLaughlin, B., et al. (2009). *The Oxford handbook of philosophy of mind.* New York: Oxford University Press.

McNeil, L. (2000). *Contradictions of school reform.* New York: Routledge.

Meeker, M. (2002). *Epidemic.* Washington, DC: Lifeline.

Melchert, N. (2006). *The Great Conversation: A historical introduction to philosophy.* Oxford: Oxford University Press.

Milgram, S. (2004). *Obedience to authority.* New York: Gardners Books/HarperCollins.

Mill, J. S. (1989). On Liberty *and other writings* (S. Collini, Ed.). Cambridge: Cambridge University Press. (Original work published 1851)

Mill, J. S. (2007). *Utilitarianism.* New York: Dover.

Millgram, E. (2005). *Practical reasoning and morality.* Cambridge: Cambridge University Press.

Moore, G. E. (1936). *Ethics.* London: Thorton Butterworth.

Moore, G. E. (1993). *Principia ethica* (T. Baldwin, Ed.). Cambridge: Cambridge University Press. (Original work published 1903)

Mullen, J. D. (1981). *Kierkegaard's philosophy.* New York: New American Library.

Murphy, J. (Ed.). (2002). *The educational leadership challenge: Reforming leadership for the 21st century.* 101st Yearbook of the National Society for the Study of Education. Chicago: National Society for the Study of Education.

Murphy, L., & Nagel, T. (2003). *Myth of ownership: Taxes and justice.* Oxford: Oxford University Press.

Myers, D. (1999). Close relationships and the quality of life. In D. Kahneman, E. Diener, & N. Schwarz (Eds.), *Well-being and the foundations of hedonic psychology* (pp. 374–391). New York: Russell Sage.

Myers, D. (2005). Teaching tips from experienced teachers. *Observer, 18,* 3.

Neill, A. (1995). *Summerhill School.* New York: St. Martin's.

Nichols, S., & Berliner, D. (2005). *The inevitable corruption of indicators and educators through high-stakes testing* (pp. 1–180). Retrieved December 15, 2006, from http://GreatlakesCenter.org

Nichols, S., & Berliner, D. (2007). *Collateral damage: How high-stakes testing corrupts America's schools.* Cambridge, MA: Harvard University Press.

Nichols, S., Glass, G., & Berliner, D. (2006). High-stakes testing and student achievement: Does accountability pressure increase student learning? *Educational Policy Analysis Archives, 14*(1).

Nida-Rumelin, J. (1997). *Economic rationality and practical reason.* New York: Springer.

Nighardt, J. G. (1961). *Black Elk speaks: Being the life story of a holy man of the Oglala Sioux.* Lincoln: University of Nebraska Press.

Noddings, N. (1988). An ethic of caring and its implications for instructional arrangement. *American Journal of Education, 96*(2), 215–229.

Noddings, N. (1992). *The challenge to care in schools.* New York: Teachers College Press.

Noddings, N. (2003). *Caring: A feminine approach to ethics and moral education.* Berkeley: University of California Press.

Noddings, N. (2007). *When school reform goes wrong.* New York: Teachers College Press.

Nowack, M. W. (2006). *Evolutionary dynamics.* Cambridge, MA: Belknap.

Nussbaum, M. (2008). *Liberty of conscience.* New York: Basic Books.

Nussbaum, M. C. (2006). *Frontiers of justice.* Cambridge, MA: Belknap.

Ortega y Gasset, J. (1931). *Revolt of the masses.* New York: W. W. Norton.

Peirce, C. S. (1992). *The essential Peirce, selected philosophical writings, Vol. 1 (1867–1893)* (N. Houser & C. Kloesel, Eds.). Bloomington: Indiana University Press.

Pellicer, L. O. (2007). *Caring enough to lead: How reflective practice leads to moral leadership* (3rd ed.). Thousand Oaks, CA: Corwin.

Peters, R. S. (1981). *Moral development & moral education.* New York: HarperCollins.

Peters, R. S. (1983). *Concept of education.* New York: Routledge and Kegan Paul.

Peterson, C., & Seligman, M. (2004). *Character strengths and virtues.* Washington, DC: Oxford University Press.

Phillips, R., & Freeman, R. E. (2003). *Stakeholder theory and organizational ethics.* San Francisco: Berrett Koehler.

Piaget, J. (1995). *The essential Piaget* (100th Anniversary Ed.; H. Gruber & J. J. Voneche, Eds.). New York: Jason Aronson.

Plato. (1992). *The republic* (D. Lee, Trans.). New York: Penguin.

Popham, J. (2001). *The truth about testing.* Washington, DC: ASCD.

Posner, R. A. (1998). The problematics of moral and legal theory. *Harvard Law Review, 111,* 1637–1717.

Poundstone, W. (2008). *Gaming the vote.* New York: Hill & Wang.

Power, C. F., Higgins, A., & Kohlberg, L. (1991). *Lawrence Kohlberg's approach to moral education.* New York: Columbia University Press.

Prawat, R. (1992). Teachers' beliefs about teaching and learning: A constructivist perspective. *American Journal of Education, 100*(3), 354–395.

Price, T. (2008). *Leadership ethics.* Cambridge, MA: Harvard University Press.

Putnam, H. (2002). *The collapse of the fact value dichotomy and other essays.* Cambridge, MA: Harvard University Press.

Putnam, H. (2004). *Ethics without ontology.* Cambridge, MA: Harvard University Press.

Quine, W. V. O. (2004). *The pursuit of truth.* Cambridge, MA: Harvard University Press.

Rapaport, A. (1991). Ideological commitments and evolutionary theory. *Journal of Social Issues, 47,* 83–89.

Rawls, J. (1969). A sense of justice. In J. Feinberg (Ed.), *Moral concepts* (pp. 120–140). London: Oxford University Press.

Rawls, J. (1971). *A theory of justice.* Cambridge, MA: Belknap.

Rawls, J. (2001). *Justice as fairness.* Cambridge, MA: Harvard University Press.

Rawls, J., & Hermann, B. (2002). *Lectures on the history of moral philosophy.* Cambridge, MA: Harvard University Press.

Rebore, R. (2001). *The ethics of educational leadership.* Upper Saddle River, NJ: Merrill Prentice Hall.

Rest, J. R. (1979). *Development in judging moral issues.* Minneapolis: University of Minnesota Press.

Rice, D. (1997). *A guide to Plato's* Republic. New York: Oxford University Press.

Rich, J. M. (1984). *Professional ethics in education.* Springfield, IL: Charles C. Thomas.

Ridley, M. (2003). *Nature via nurture: Genes, experience and what makes us human.* New York: HarperCollins.

Rothschaeffer, W. A. (2008). *The biology and psychology of moral agency.* New York: Cambridge University Press.

Ryle, G. (1949). *The concept of the mind.* Chicago: University of Chicago Press.

Salomone, R. (2000). *Visions of schooling: Conscience, community, and common education.* New Haven, CT: Yale University Press.

Sapir, E. (1921). *Language: An introduction to the study of speech.* New York: Classic Books.

Sartre, J. P. (1993). *Being and nothingness* (H. Barnes, Trans.). New York: Simon & Schuster.

Saussure, F. (2002). *Writings in general linguistics.* Paris: Editions Gallimard.

Scanlon, T. (1998). *What we owe others.* Cambridge, MA: Harvard University Press.

Scheffler, I. (1973). *Reason and teachers.* Indianapolis: Bobbs-Merrill.

Scheffler, I. (1974). *Four pragmatists: A critical introduction to Peirce, James, Mead, and Dewey.* London: Routledge and Kegan Paul.

Scheffler, I. (1985). *Of human potential: An essay in the philosophy of education.* Boston: Routledge and Kegan Paul.

Schmidtz, D. (1996). *Rational choice and human agency.* Princeton, NJ: Princeton University Press.

Schmoker, M., & Wilson, R. (1993). *Total quality education.* Bloomington, IN: Phi Delta Kappa Foundation.

Schwartz, B. (2002). *Psychology of learning and behavior* (5th ed.). New York: Norton.

Scriven, M. (1976). *Evaluation thesaurus.* Boston: McGraw-Hill.

Searle, J. (1995). *The construction of social reality.* New York: Free Press.

Seligman, M. (1996). *The optimistic child.* New York: Harper Perennial.

Sergiovanni, T. J. (1984). Leadership and excellence in schooling. *Educational Leadership, 41*(5), 4–13.

Sergiovanni, T. J. (1990). Adding value to leadership gets extraordinary results. *Educational Leadership, 47*(8), 23–27.

Sergiovanni, T. (1992). *Moral leadership: Getting to the heart of school improvement.* San Francisco: Jossey-Bass.

Sergiovanni, T. J. (1996). *Moral leadership: Getting to the heart of school improvement.* San Francisco: Jossey-Bass.

Sergiovanni, T. J. (2005). *Strengthening the heartbeat: Leading and learning in schools.* San Francisco: Jossey-Bass.

Shealy, M. W. (2006). The promises and perils of "scientifically based" research for urban schools. *Urban Education, 41*(1), 5–19.

Shriberg, A., Shriberg, D., & Kumari, R. (2005). *Practicing leadership: Principles and applications* (3rd ed.). Hoboken, NJ: Wiley.

Sigmund, P. (1987). *St. Thomas Aquinas on politics and ethics.* New York: W.W. Norton.

Simmonds, N. (2007). *Law as a moral idea.* New York: Oxford University Press.

Simmons, R. G., & Black, A. (1991). African American versus white children and the transition into junior high school. *American Journal of Education, 99*(4), 481–520.

Sizer, T. R., & Sizer, N. F. (1999). *The students are watching: Schools and the moral contract.* Boston: Beacon.

Skyrms, B. (2004). *The stag hunt and the evolution of social structure.* Cambridge: Cambridge University Press.

Smith, L. (2009). *Aristotle and the philosophy of friendship.* Cambridge, MA: Harvard University Press.

Snyder, J. (1994). Change forces: Probing the depths of educational reform. *American Journal of Education, 102*(3), 378–382.

Snyder, K. J., Acker-Hocevar, M., & Snyder, K. S. (2004). *Leadership on the edge of chaos: Leading schools into the global age.* Milwaukee: ASQ Quality Press.

Sober, E. (1975). *Simplicity.* New York: Oxford University Press.

Sober, E., & Wilson, D. S. (1998). *Unto others: The evolution and psychology of unselfish behavior.* Cambridge, MA: Harvard University Press.

Sommers, C. H. (1994). *Who stole feminism?: How women have betrayed women.* New York: Simon & Schuster.

Sommers, C. H. (2000). *The war against boys.* New York: Simon & Schuster.

Sowell, T. (1995). *Race and culture: A world view.* New York: Basic Books.

Sowell, T. (2005). *Black redneck and white liberals.* New York: Encounter Books.

Spring, J. (2004). *Conflict of interests: The politics of American education* (5th ed.). Highstown, NJ: McGraw-Hill.

Stadler, D. (2007). *Law and ethics in educational leadership.* Upper Saddle River, NJ: Pearson Merrill/Prentice Hall.

Starratt, R. J. (1994). *Building an ethical school: A practical response to the moral crises in schools.* London: Falmer.

Starratt, R. J. (2004). *Ethical leadership.* San Francisco: Jossey-Bass.

Stein, A. (2005). *Foundations of evidence law.* New York: Oxford University Press.

Sternberg, R. (1997). *Thinking styles.* Cambridge: Cambridge University Press.

Sternberg, R. J. (2003). *Wisdom, intelligence, and creativity synthesized.* New York: Cambridge University Press.

Stevenson, C. L. (1944). *Ethics and language.* New Haven, CT: Yale University Press.

Strike, K. (1991). The moral role of schooling in a liberal democratic society. *Review of Research in Education, 17,* 413–483.

Strike, K. (1999). Can schools be communities? *Administration Quarterly, 35*(1), 46–70.

Strike, K. (2006). *Ethical leadership in schools.* San Francisco: Sage.

Strike, K., Haller, E., & Soltis, J. (1998). *The ethics of education administration.* New York: Columbia University Teachers College Press.

Strike, K., Haller, E., & Soltis, J. (2005). *The ethics of school administration* (3rd ed.). New York: Teachers College Press.

Strike, K., & Soltis, J. (2004). *The ethics of teaching.* New York: Columbia University Teachers College Press.

Tarski, A. (1981). *Logic, semantics and mathematics.* Indianapolis: Hackett.

Taylor, C. (2005). *The ethics of authenticity.* Cambridge, MA: Harvard University Press.

Taylor, C. (2007). *A secular age.* Cambridge, MA: Harvard University Press.

Thompson, M. (2008). *Life and action.* Cambridge, MA: Harvard University Press.

Thorndike, E. L. (1940). *Human nature and the social order.* New York: Macmillan.

Tiberius, V. (2008). *The reflective life.* New York: Oxford University Press.

Tomasi, J. (2001). *Liberalism beyond justice.* Princeton, NJ: Princeton University Press.

Tooby, J., & Cosmides, L. (1998). Friendship and the banker's paradox: Other pathways to the evolution of adaptions for altruism. In W. G. Runciman, J. M. Smith, & R. I. M. Dunbar (Eds.), *Evolution of social behavior patterns in primates and man* (pp. 299–323). Oxford: Oxford University Press.

Townsend, M. (1995). Effects of accuracy and plausibility in predicting results of research findings on teaching. *British Journal of Educational Studies, 65*(3), 359–365.

Turiel, E. (2005). Thought, emotions, and social interactional processes in moral development. In M. Killen & J. G. Smetana (Eds.), *Handbook of moral development* (pp. 7–37). Mahwah, NJ: Erlbaum.

Valliant, G. (1998). *Adaptation to life.* Cambridge, MA: Harvard University Press.

Vogel, L. R., Rau, W. C., Baker, P. J., & Ashby, D. F. (2006). Bringing assessment literacy to the local school: A decade of reform initiatives in Illinois. *Journal of Education for Students Placed at Risk, 11*(1), 39–55.

Vohs, K., Mead, N., & Goode, M. (2006). The psychological consequences of money. *Science, 314,* 1154–1156.

Vygotsky, L. (1962). *Thought and language.* Cambridge, MA: MIT Press.

Wagner, P. (1981). Simon, indoctrination and ethical relativism. *Journal of Educational Thought, 15*(3), 187–194.

Wagner, P. (1992). *Understanding professional ethics.* Indianapolis: Phi Delta Kappan Fastback.

Wagner, P. (1997). Total quality management: A plan for optimizing human potential? In H. Siegel (Ed.), *Reason and education: Essays in honor of Israel Scheffler* (pp. 241–258). Dordrecht, The Netherlands: Springer.

Wagner, P. A. (1982). Moral education indoctrination and the principle of minimizing substantive error. In *Proceedings of the 31st annual meeting of the Philosophy of Education Society. April 26–29, 1981* (pp. 191–198). Normal: Illinois State University.

Wagner, P. A. (1997). The teacher and the propagandist: In dilemma. *Project in Professional Ethics Newsletter,* pp. 1–3.

Wagner, P. A., & Benavente, L. (2006). Misunderstood purpose and failed solutions. *Current Issues in Education, 9*(2).

Wagner, P. A., & Benavente, L. (2008). Genuine religious tolerance: Is it a thing of the past in public schools? *Interchange, 39*(3), 327–350.

Wagner, P., & Benavente, L. (in press). The autistic society and its classrooms. *The Educational Forum.*

Walker, M. (2006). *Moral repair.* Cambridge: Cambridge University Press.

Walton, M. (1986). *The Deming management method.* New York: Perigree.

Warneke, G. (2008). *After identity: Re-thinking race, sex and gender.* New York: Cambridge University Press.

Wedekind, C., & Milinski, M. (2000). Cooperation through image scoring in humans. *Science, 288,* 850–852.

Whitney, J. (1994). *The trust factor.* Highland, NJ: McGraw-Hill.

Whorf, B. (1964). *Language, thought and reality.* Boston: MIT Press.

Wilder, R. (2007). *Talks from the teacher's lounge.* New York: Delacorte.

Wilson, D. S. (2002). *Darwin's cathedral.* Chicago: University of Chicago Press.

Wilson, J. Q. (1997). *The moral sense.* New York: Free Press.

Wittgenstein, L. (1967). *Lectures and conversations on aesthetics, psychology, and religious belief.* Berkeley: University of California Press.

Wright, R. (1995). *The moral animal.* New York: Vintage.

Yell, M. (2005). *Law and special education* (2nd ed.). New York: Prentice Hall.

Zagzebski, L. T. (1996). *Virtues of the mind.* Cambridge, UK: Cambridge University Press.

Zagzebski, L. T. (2001). The uniqueness of persons. *The Journal of Religious Ethics, 29*(34), 12.

Zagzebski, L. T. (2004). *Divine motivation theory.* Oxford: Oxford University Press.

Zakhem, A. J. (Ed.). (2007). *Stakeholder theory.* New York: Prometheus.

Zimmerman, M. J. (1996). *The concept of moral obligation.* Cambridge: Cambridge University Press.

Zirkel, P. (2002). Courtside: An unmitigated disaster. *Phi Delta Kappan, 83,* 5.

Zirkel, P. (2006). The remedial authority of hearing and review officers under the Individuals With Disabilities Education Act. *Administrative Law Review, 56,* 401.

Zirkel, S. (2004). Fifty years after *Brown v. Board of Education:* The promise and challenge of multicultural education. *Journal of Social Issues, 60,* 1.

Index

Abduction, 41–42
Absolutist policy (case), 154
Academic freedom (case), 149
Accommodating faulty policies (case), 81
Accommodation, principles vs., 56–57
Accountability, 13, 177
Accounting, moral issues of, 83–86
Accounting ledgers, 94
Action, 1, 177
Action theory, 2
Administration, school and district. *See* School and district administration
Administrative courage (case), 101
Administrative law, 137, 177
Administrators:
  commitment to Great Conversation, 70
  creating policy, 70
  ethical perspective, 68
  fear of litigation, 113
  ongoing review of moral architecture, 124
  See also Leader; Leadership; School and district administration
Advocating for children (case), 165
All I Really Need to Know I Learned in Kindergarten (Fulghum), 24
Altruism, 10, 36, 177
Ambitions, professional (case), 64
American Association of School Administrators, Statement of Ethics for Educational Leaders, 170–171
American Law School Association Committee on Ethics, 2
American Psychological Association, universal virtues study, 9

Aristotle:
  advice for educators, 23
  "government by law and not by men," 143
  leadership virtue of justice, 63
  moral truth, 21
  Politics, The, 13, 127, 143
  "ruled by principle," 123
  self-actualization, 127
  social contract and, 27–30
  theory without practice, xiii
  treatment of equals, 111
  virtue theory and, 22–24
Assessment:
  of education, 96–99
  values and, 95
Attitudes:
  appropriate for Great Conversation, 53–54
  schooling dispositions and, 57–60
Authoritarian leaders (case), 159
Authority, 3, 178
Autonomy, 91–92, 178
Axelrod, R., 34–35, 38

Barriers, eliminating, 73
Behavior:
  acceptable vs. unacceptable, 25
  effect of zero tolerance policies on, 106
Behavioral approaches to learning, 98–99
Bentham, Jeremy, 31
Betterment, human:
  theory of, 7
  within education, 13, 60
Biological universalism, 35–37
Bitting, Paul F., 154

Björk, Lars G., 160
Black Elk, 39
Bolling v. Sharpe, 140
Bootstrapping process in education, 54
  intrusions as constraint on, 125
  virtues, Great Conversation and, 121–22
Boss, 41
  defined, 178
  ethical perspective, 68
  role of, 69
Briggs v. Elliot, 140
Brown v. Topeka Board of Education,
  86, 140–141
Budgets, district and school, 99
Bullying, 90–91
  defined, 178
  professional (case), 101

*California's Consolidated State Performance
  Report: Amended Part II,* 126
Campbell, Elizabeth, 165
Career and Technology Education (CTE)
    legislation:
  as intrusion, 125
  ultimate cost of, 127–128
Caring, ethic of, 16
Case matrix, xviii–xxi
Categorical imperative (CI), 30
Character, 5–6, 178
Character trait, 178
Chauvinism, 110, 178
Chicken Soup for the Soul (Canfield &
  Hansen), 24
Child abuse, reporting, 141–143
Child protective services, calling, 141–143
Children, advocating for (case), 165
Civil disobedience, 137
Civil Rights Act of 1964, 86
Code of ethics:
  American Association of School
    Administrators, 170–171
  moral vision and, 14
  National Education Association, 172–174
  National School Boards Association, 175
  physicians', 13–14
  See also Statement of ethics
Collateral Damage (Nichols and Berliner), 127
Collegial advice (case), 148

Common law, 108
Communication problems (case), 160
Community, 1
  defined, 178
  moral architectures of school and
    districts and, 124–125
Compassion:
  cases about, 133, 153, 161
  defined, 178
  Great Conversation and, 58
Competence:
  cases about, 149, 156
  increased confidence and increased, 127
Competing duties (case), 19
Conflicts of duty, 92–94
Confucius:
  advice for educators, 27
  emphases and questions, 28
  rational thinking and, 26
Conscience, personal (case), 117
Conscience and public law (case), 165
Consequences, 32, 178
Consistency (case), 153
Costs and benefits, meta-language
  of, 83–86
Costs and benefits of inclusion:
  accounting and, 83–86
  assault on inclusion, 89–92
  assessing education, 96–99
  conflicts of duty and, 92–94
  education, evaluation and funding, 94
  education for inclusion, 86–89
  stakeholder groups and, 99–100
Courage, 23
  administrative (case), 101
  law and, 136
Courtesies, 5, 178
Covering aesthetic, 103–104
Cowardly strategies (case), 133
Crosby, Phillip, 71–72
Cultural differences (case), 168

Darrow, Clarence, xvi
Data collection and review, 73–74
*Davis v. County School Board of Prince
  Edward County,* 140
Decision making:
  democratic (case), 163

hasty (case), 148
instinctual or intuitive, 151
Deming, W. E., 71
  data collection challenges, 73–74
  moralism, 72–73
  social and managerial idealism, 72–73
Democratic decision making (case), 163
Democratic leadership, 8
Democratic openness, 70
Desires and duties (case), 157
Dewey, John, xiii, 42, 77, 132
Differential treatment of students, 111, 120
Discipline, defined, 178
Disloyalty, professional (case), 160
Disparate impact, 111, 178
Disparate power holders (case), 168
Dispositions:
  educational, 55
  schooling, attitudes and, 57–60
Distribution of wealth, 99
District administration. *See* School and district
  administration
Diverse moral opinions (case), 133
Doing good, political and economic
  challenges to, 60–62
Doing the right thing (case), 133
"Do no harm," 13–15, 92
Double helix metaphor, 121
Dugatkin, L., 36–37
Duties, competing (case), 19
Duty, 2
  conflicts of, 92–94
  defined, 178–179
  empathy and (case), 163
Duty and honesty vs. compassion and
  paternalism (case), 133

Eagle Scout, expulsion for pocket knife,
  106–109
*East Hartford Education Association v. Board of
  Education of East Hartford,* 92
Education, 3, 179
  as ideal, 96, 121
  assessing, 96–99
  bootstrapping process in, 54
  comprehensive instructional purposes of, 59
  evaluation, funding and, 94
  human betterment evolving within, 60
  ideal of, 121–122
  morally prescriptive shared vision in, 49–51
  reasons for, 50
  schooling vs., 61–62, 114–115
  self-actualization and, 127
  social engineering, schooling and focus of,
    129–130
  true value of, 76
Educational goals, test scores and (case), 81
Educational leaders:
  accommodation vs. principles, 56–57
  as change agents, 57
  roles of, 57
  See also Leaders; Leadership
Educational purpose, four corners of. *See* Four
  corners of educational purpose
Eisenhower, Dwight, 47
Electronic dangers (case), 116
Empathy and duty (case), 163
Empowerment, law and, 136
Enomoto, Ernestine K., 157
Epistemology, 55, 179
Epperson v. Arkansas, 92
Equal Access Act, 111, 179
Equality, 111
  defined, 179
  equity and (case), 157
  use of term, 144
Equality of punishment (case), 154
Equality-versus-fairness debate, 144
Equality of wrongdoing (case), 154
Equal rights amendments, 140
Equity, 85, 179
Equity and equality (case), 157
Escalante, Jamie, 126
Ethical dilemmas, 1, 179
Ethical issues, 1, 179
Ethical priorities (case), 133
Ethic of caring, 16
Ethics:
  morals vs., 1
  professional, 13–14, 15–18
  school law and, 136
  See also Code of ethics
Ethnocentric curricula (case), 81
Evaluation:
  education, funding and, 94
  values and, 95

Evolutionary account of moral origins, 120
Evolutionary psychology, 36
Evolution of Morality, The (Joyce), 120
Exclusions from Great Conversation, 87
Excuses, 179
Existentialists, 39, 179

Fair, 179
Fairness, 88–89
  case about, 153
  equality vs., 144
  procedural (case), 19
Faulty policies, accommodating (case), 81
Favoritism, 89, 180
Fear, eliminating, 73
Fearing the influential (case), 65
Feminism, sympathy theory and, 40
Fighting a losing battle (case), 65
Financial rewards, rejecting (case), 81
First Amendment rights, 15
Flaws and faultfinding (case), 156
Focus, 55, 180
"Follow along with" vs. "follow," 48
Following rules (case), 45
Foundational moral theory, 49
Four corners of educational purpose:
  acquiring information, 54–55
  attitudes appropriate for Great
    Conversation, 53–54
  challenge of accommodating, 56
  dispositions, 55
  illustration, 52
  learning, 51–53
Frankl, Victor, xii
Fraternité, 77
Freedom, 42, 180
Freire, Paulo, 31, 115
Friendship and leadership (case), 161
Funding, evaluation, education and, 94
Funds, expenditure of, 99

Gardner, Howard, 78, 99
Gebhardt v. Belton, 140
Gender exclusion, 87
"Getting one's ducks in a row," 73–74
Good intentions (case), 19
"Government by law and not
    by men," 143

Grading:
  case about, 81
  defined, 180
Great Conversation of Humankind:
  administrators commitment to, 70
  attitudes appropriate for, 53–54
  bootstrapping principles, virtues and, 121–122
  commitment to inclusion, 15
  compassion and, 58
  concept of, xii
  elements of justice and, 119
  exclusions from, 87
  fostering, moral architecture and, 125
  goals of inclusion and, 89
  knowledge and, 97
  leading the, 12–13
  as moral compass, 14
  participation in, 114–115
  truth, moral commitment and, 10–12
  use of term, 4, 11

Hamilton equation, 36, 180
Harassment, 91, 180
Hare, William, 156
Hasty decisions (case), 148
Hate speech, 111–113
Hennessy v. Webb, 141
Higher-order virtues, 103–104
High-stakes testing, 74–76, 98
Hippocrates, 13–14
Hobbes, Thomas, 27–30
Human betterment:
  evolving within education, 60
  realization in education, 13
  theory of, 7
Humans, animating moral faculty of, 21
Hume, David, 37–39, 41
Hurt feelings and underserved
    students (case), 64

Ideal of education, 96, 121
Idealism:
  in moral vision, 123
  pragmatic, 76–78
  social and managerial, 72–73
Identifying the unempowered (case), 168
Immigrants, new (case), 168
Immorality, 103, 180

Imposing values (case), 101
Inclusion:
    assault on, 89–92
    costs and benefits of. *See* Costs and
        benefits of inclusion
    education for, 86–89
    general challenge of, 86
    general concerns, 88
    goals of, 89
    Great Conversation and, 15
    significant benefits for few, 31
Individuals with Disabilities Education Act
    of 1990 (IDEA), 86
Individuals with Disabilities Education
    Improvement Act of 2004 (IDEIA),
    86, 89, 180
Indoctrination, 54, 180
Inferential ability, 41–42
Influential, fearing the (case), 64
Information, defined, 181
In loco parentis, 92
Innocent, protecting the (case), 65
Institutional integrity (case), 116
Insubordination (case), 116
Integrity:
    institutional (case), 116
    leadership and, 62
    personal (case), 64
Intentions, good (case), 19
Intersubjective agreement, 104, 181
Intuition, 16
    providential, 39
Intuition, defined, 181
Intuitionism, 181
*Isaacs ex. rel. Isaacs v. Board of Education of
    Howard County*, 92
Isabelle Properties v. Edelman, 179
Is-ought gap, 39, 181

Joyce, Richard, 120
Juran, Joseph, 71–72
Jurisprudence, 135–138, 181
Justice:
    as blind, 144
    bootstrapping principles and, 121
    law, order and feel of, 143–146
    law and, 136
    leadership virtue of, 63

    as linchpin concept, 119–120
    pragmatics of, 119
    pragmatic value of, 130–132
    promising and, 120–121
    properly working moral architectures,
        122–123
    scales of, 144
    social, order and, 146–147
    use of term, 119

Kant, Immanuel, 30, 38
Keedy, John, 163
Kennedy, John F., 5
Kierkegaard, Sören, 39, 41
King, Martin Luther, Jr., 24, 115
King Solomon, 146–147
Klinker, JoAnn Franklin, 161
"Knowing how" vs. "knowing that," 78
Knowledge:
    defined, 181
    Great Conversation and, 97
    Greek search for, 8
Kohlberg, Lawrence, 33, 120
Kramer, Bruce H., 157

Laird v. Union Traction Co., 179
*Landstrom v. Illinois Department of Children
    and Family Services*, 142
Language differences, 88
Lao Tzu, 26, 28, 94
Law, 2
    common, 108
    conscience and (case), 165
    defined, 181
    as moral asset, 138
    moral courage, prudence and, 141–143
    nature of, 138–141
    order, and the feel of justice, 143–146
    as public morality, 135
    role in moral evaluation, 135–150
    as surface to moral architecture, 135
    wisdom of, 146–147
    See also School law
Leaders:
    educational. *See* Educational leaders
    practical experience of, 151
Leadership:
    based on surface rules, 107

democratic, 8
Eisenhower on, 47
ethical perspective, 68
friendship and (case), 161
law and, 136
maximizing, 3
as moral architecture, 47–66
moral architecture and, 3–6
moral nature of, 1–3
moving beyond management, 69–71
responsible, 123
in school and district administration, 67–69
shared vision and, 48–49
strength of, 110
sustainable, 47–49, 62–63
See also Administrators
Learning:
behavioral approaches to, 98–99
as corner of educational purpose, 51–53
defined, 182
educationally valuable, 93
Learning tasks, prioritizing, 93–94
Legal intent, 136
License, 120, 182
Litigation, administrative fear of, 113
Long v. Board of Education of Jefferson County, 92
Low-performing students and low-performing teachers (case), 159

Machiavelli, 41
McLaughlin v. Tilendis, 141
Management:
leadership moving beyond, 69–71
in school and district administration, 67–69
Manager:
ethical perspective, 68
role of, 68–69
Managerial idealism, 72–73
Mann, Horace, 129
Méndez-Morris, Sylvia, 166
Metaphysics, 105, 182
"Might makes right," 103, 109, 129
Mill, John Stuart, 31–32, 38
Miller v. Kenniston, 179
Minimizing substantive moral error, principle of, 43
Model Child Protection Act with Commentary, 141

Moore, G. E., 37–39, 41
Moral architecture:
building a rich, 130–131
covering aesthetic of, 104
elements of, 6–7
elevating school and district, 128–129
flat vs. elevated, 6, 122–123
hiddenness of, 124
key questions in building, 105
law as surface to, 135
leadership and, 3–6, 47–66. *See also* Leadership
model for analyzing, 17–18, 104
moral foundation of, 104
properly working, 122–123
scaffolding of, 104
sustaining, 125–128
use of term, xiii
Moral artists, 105
Moral commitment, 10–12
Moral courage, prudence, law and, 141–143
Moral disrupters (case), 148
Moral ecology, 47
Moral error, principle of minimizing substantive, 43
Moralism, 72–73
Morality, 2
defined, 182
meta-ethical vs. prescriptive, 8
prescriptive, 8–10
Moral judgment, evaluating and improving, 152
Moral life, communal, do's and don'ts of, 8–9
Moral nihilist, 94
Moral opinions, diverse (case), 133
Moral origins, evolutionary account of, 120
Moral principles, highest-order, 122
Moral realism:
emphases and questions, 28
rationality and, 24–27
Moral rules, surface-level. *See* Surface-level moral rules
Morals, 1
defined, 182
ethics vs., 1
Moral scaffolding, 104, 106, 122
Moral theory:
foundational, 49
intuitionism, 37–39
pragmatic assessment of, 43–44

pragmatism, 41–44
rationality and moral realists, 24–27
scientific theory vs., 21–22
social contract, 27–30
social sympathy, 37, 39–41
universalism, 30–31
virtue theory, 22–24
Moral truth, Aristotle on, 21
Moral vision:
  code of ethics and, 14
  idealism in, 123
Mother Teresa, 40
Motivating, defined, 18
Motives and consequences (case), 163
Multiculturalism, 11, 182
Multiple intelligences, theory of, 78
Mungal, Kamla, 159
Murphy, Liam, 83–84
Myers, David, 99
Myth of Ownership, The (Murphy and Nagel),
  83–84

Nagel, Thomas, 83–84
National Education Association, Code of
  Ethics of the Education Profession, 172–174
National School Boards Association, Code of
  Ethics, 175
New immigrants (case), 168
Nietzsche, Friedrich, 94
Nihilist, moral, 94
No Child Left Behind (NCLB):
  change in shared vision and, 49
  as intrusion, 125–126
  school administration and, 75–76
  state immunity statutes under, 141
Noddings, Nel, 40, 41

Obligation, 2, 182
Open inquiry, premature, 70
Openness with staff (case), 64
Openness to suggestions, 70
Organization, 4, 182
Ortega y Gasset, José, xv, 25, 28
Ought implies *can,* 81, 106, 182–183

Paradigmatic individual, 9
Pascal, Blaise, 94
Paternalism, 57, 133 (case), 183
Peirce, C. S., 41

Penalties, 32, 183
Personal conscience (case), 117
Personal disregard (case), 160
Personal integrity and professional ambitions
  (case), 64
Personality, 5, 182
Personality trait, 183
Personal risk and staff needs (case), 64
Pesce v. J. Sterling Morton High School, 142
Philosophy, jurisprudence and, 135–138
Piaget, Jean, 33
Picarella v. Terrizzi, 142
Plans, 71, 183–184
Plato:
  advice for educators, 25–26
  covering aesthetic, 113
  emphases and questions, 28
  moral realist, 26
  practical experience of leaders, 151
  truth and justice, 104–105
Plessy v. Ferguson, 140
Pocket knife, Eagle Scout expulsion
  for, 106–109
Policy:
  accommodating faulty (case), 81
  administrator and creation of, 70
  point of, 74–75
  reviewing, 71–72
  in school and district administration, 67–69
Policy and supervisors (case), 160
Politics, The (Aristotle), 13, 127, 143
Practice, theory responsive to, 79–80
Practice without theory, xiii
Pragmatic idealism, 76–78
Pragmatics of justice, 119
Pragmatism, 41–44, 72–73
  emphases and questions, 44
  moral theory and, 43–44
  today's pragmatists, 42
Premature open inquiry, 70
Prescriptive morality, 8–10, 103
Pride, developing, 73
Principal seminars, 79
Principles, accommodation vs., 56–57
Principles and directives (case), 159
Principle of universality, 32, 32–33
Private lives (case), 117
Procedural fairness (case), 19
Procedural problems (case), 166

Professional ambitions (case), 64
Professional bullying (case), 101
Professional commitment (case), 117
Professional competence (case), 149
Professional disloyalty (case), 160
Professional ethics, 13–18
Professionalism, 16
  case about, 45
  compassion and (case), 161
  defined, 184
  moral obligation and, 50
  teacher (case), 148
Professional judgment (case), 156, 166
Professions, four historic, 50–51
Promising, 29, 120–121
Proportionality (case), 153
Protecting the innocent (case), 65
Protocol, 29, 184
Providential intuition, 39
Prudence, moral courage, law and, 141–143
Psychological egoism, 104, 184
Psychology:
  evolutionary, 36
  universalist, 33–34
Public law, conscience and (case), 165
Public morality, law as, 135
Public pressure (case), 117
Public values, prioritized importance of, 83
Punishment, 31
  defined, 184
  equality of (case), 154
Putnam, Hilary, 42, 77

Quotas, eliminating, 73

Racial exclusion, 87
Racism, 10, 111–113, 184
Rapaport, A., 34–35, 38
Rationality:
  emphases and questions, 28
  moral realists and, 24–27
Rawls, John, 33–34, 38, 119–120
Realism, 26
  See also Moral realists
Redistribution of wealth, 84, 99
Reflective equilibrium, 32
Reflective thinking (case), 154
Rejecting financial rewards (case), 81

Religion, promoting (case), 101
Religious tolerance, 15–16, 149, 166
Responsibility, 3, 184–185
Revolt of the Masses, The (Ortega y Gasset), xv
Rightness and prudence (case), 157
Rights, 15, 185
Risk, personal, staff needs and (case), 64
Rival goods (case), 161
Rudeness, 110, 185
Rules, following (case), 45
Ryle, Gilbert, 78

Safe environment, providing, 113–114
Santa Fe v. Doe, 92
Satisficing, 100–101
Scaffolding, moral, 104, 122
Scheffler, Israel, 42
  fraternité, 77
  pragmatism, 72–73
School and district administration:
  "getting one's ducks in a row," 73–74
  leadership, 69–71
  leadership, management and policy, 67–69
  making theory responsive to
    practice, 79–80
  No Child Left Behind and, 75–76
  point of policy, 74–75
  policy vs. people review, 71–72
  pragmatic idealism, 76–78
  See also Administrators
Schooling:
  comprehensive instructional
    purposes of, 59
  education vs., 61–62, 114–115
  focuses of, 60
  social engineering and, 129–130
  use of term, 60
School law:
  ethics and, 136
  See also Law
School segregation cases, 140–141
Schwartz, Barry, 98–99
Secular Age, A (Taylor), 49
Self-actualization, 127
Seligman, Martin P., 99
Sergiovanni, Thomas, 1, 71–72, 74
Sexism, 10, 185
Shared vision, morally prescriptive, 49–51

Simpson, Douglas J., 168
Sixth sense, 38
    See also Intuition
Sober, E., 36–38
Social contract, 27–30, 34
Social engineering, 129–130
Social idealism, 72–73
Social justice, order and, 146–147
Social sympathy, 37, 39–41
    emphases and questions
        need for, 39
    sense of bondedness and, 40
Socrates, educational administrators as,
        145–146
Solomon (King), 146–147
Staff, openness with (case), 64
Staff needs, personal risk and (case), 64
Staff timidity (case), 101
Standardized tests, 98
Starratt, Robert, 1
Statement of ethics:
    American Association of School
        Administrators, 170–171
    See also Code of ethics
Stereotypes (case), 133
Stossel, John, 106–108
Strike, Kenneth, 32–33
Strong character, 6, 185
Students:
    differential treatment of, 111
    low-performing (case), 159
    underserved (cases), 64, 161
Sufficient elevation, 85
Summative test data, 126–127
Surface-level moral disagreements, 59
Surface-level moral rules, 26
    admissibility under the categorical
        imperative, 30
    covering aesthetics as, 103
    defined, 185
    governing solely by, 109
    leadership based on, 107
    operational efficiency and, 122
    providing safe environment and,
        113–114
    transient, 108
    zero tolerance policies and, 106
Sustainable leadership, 62–63

Taylor, Charles, 49
Teach, 76, 185
Teacher circles, 79
Teacher professionalism (case), 148
Teachers, low-performing (case), 159
Ten Commandments, 144
Test data, summative, 126–127
Testing, high-stakes, 74–76
Testing procedures, violating (case), 165
Test scores, NCLB and, 75
Test scores and educational goals (case), 81
*Texas State Plan for Career and Technology
    Education, 2005–2007,* 128
Theory, responsive to practice, 79–80
Theory of multiple intelligences, 78
Theory without practice, xiii
Threats (case), 45
Timidity, staff (case), 101
Tinker v. Des Moines, 92
Title VII, 178
Tit for Tat computer program, 35
Training, 50, 185
Transculturalism, 122
Truelove v. Wilson, 141
Truth, Great Conversation and, 10–12

Understanding, 2, 185
Unempowered, identifying the (case), 168
Universalism:
    biological grounds of, 35–37
    emphasis and questions, 38
    Kantian, 30–31
    principle of universality, 32–33
    universal gaming, 34–35
    universalist psychology, 33–34
    utilitarian, 31
Universality, principle of, 185
Universal virtues, APA study of, 9
U.S. Constitution, First Amendment of, 92
U.S. Supreme Court:
    school segregation cases, 140–141
    See also entries for specific cases
Utilitarians, 31

Value-added activities, 95
Values:
    evaluation and, 95
    imposing (case), 101

Vice, 9, 185–186
Violating testing procedures (case), 165
Violence, 1, 186
Virtues, 41
  defined, 186
  higher-order, 103–104
Virtue theory, 22–24
Vision, shared, 48–49
Vokey, Daniel, 153

Wagner, Paul A., 168
Weak character, 6, 186
Wealth redistribution, 84, 99

Wilson, D. S., 36–38
Wisdom, law and, 136
Wright, Shannon, 36
Wrongdoing, equality of (case), 154

Youngman v. Doerhoff, 180

Zagzebski, Linda, 23–24
Zero tolerance policies, 103–110
  hidden bigotry and, 109
  penalties and punishments and, 145–146
  predictable consequences of, 143
  surface-level rules and, 106

About the Authors

Paul A. Wagner, PhD, is director of the Project in Professional Ethics, University of Houston–Clear Lake and a professor in the educational leadership program. He has also taught economics for undergraduates and business management theory and organizational behavior to business graduate students at the University of Houston–Victoria. He is a former executive secretary of the Philosophy of Education Society and vice-president of the Association of Philosophers in Education, and he has served on the national ethics committee of the 40,000-member Association of Public Administrators. He was a founding member of the State of Texas annual ethics workshop for senior-level officials. He has served as a consultant to a number of major corporations, universities, medical schools, and technical schools in the area of strategic planning. He is the author of *Understanding Professional Ethics,* a Phi Delta Kappan fastback, and the author of more than 120 publications. He has served as an ethics consultant to both Leadership Houston and the American Leadership Forum.

Douglas J. Simpson, PhD, is professor and Helen DeVitt Jones Chair in Teacher Education at Texas Tech University. He is the author or coauthor of numerous publications, including *John Dewey and the Art of Teaching, The Pedagodfathers: The Lords of Education, Recreating Schools: Places Where Everyone Learns and Likes It, The Teacher as Philosopher,* and *Educational Reform: A Deweyan Perspective.* He has held tenured positions at the University of Louisville, Memorial University of Newfoundland, Tennessee State University, and Texas Christian University and taught in the fields of ethics and teaching, curriculum and instruction, school psychology, and educational theory. He spends time each week at Phyllis Wheatley Elementary School, where he interacts with students pursuing ethical, historical, and geographic interests. He is a former president of the American Educational Studies Association and the Society of Professors of Education.

About the Case Study Authors

Paul F. Bitting is an associate professor, Department of Educational Leadership and Policy Studies, North Carolina State University. Paul is a former teacher, counselor, and administrator at Stephen Decatur Junior High School, Brooklyn, New York, and Jackie Robinson Junior High School, Manhattan, New York. The focus of his research and scholarly activity has been on the social and cultural factors that affect underserved populations.

Lars G. Björk is professor and acting chair, Department of Educational Leadership Studies, University of Kentucky. His works include *Higher Education Research and Public Policy, Minorities in Higher Education, The Study of the American Superintendency, The New Superintendency, The Superintendent as CEO,* and *The Contemporary Superintendent.*

Elizabeth Campbell is a professor, Department of Curriculum, Teaching and Learning, Ontario Institute for Studies in Education, University of Toronto. She is a member of the cross-disciplinary Centre for Ethics at the university and the author of *The Ethical Teacher.* Her scholarship is in professional ethics and moral agency in teaching, the moral and ethical dimensions of teaching and schooling, and teacher education.

Ernestine K. Enomoto is an associate professor at the University of Hawaii–Manoa, where she teaches in educational administration. Her scholarship has focused on leadership and organizations serving multiethnic student populations. She coauthored with Bruce H. Kramer *Leading Through the Quagmire,* proposing an inquiry method to harness democratic ethics for fair deliberation and conflict resolution.

William Hare is professor of education, Mount Saint Vincent University, Halifax, Nova Scotia, where he teaches philosophy of education. His books include *Open-Mindedness and Education, In Defence of Open-Mindedness,* and *What Makes a Good Teacher.* His most recent book is *Key Questions for Educators,* coedited with John Portelli.

John Keedy is a professor, Department of Leadership, Foundations, and Human Resource Education, University of Louisville. He has served as a principal in both Massachusetts and Virginia. He is widely published in leadership journals and serves on the editorial boards of the *Journal of School Leadership* and *Education and Urban Society.*

JoAnn Franklin Klinker is an assistant professor in the educational leadership program at Texas Tech University. Her research interests are ethical decision making, emotion and decision making, and democratic leadership. A former high school principal, JoAnn is particularly interested in bridging the gap between theory and practice in educational leadership programs.

Bruce H. Kramer is associate dean of the School of Education at the University of St. Thomas (Minnesota) and was formerly chair of the Department of Leadership, Policy and Administration. His research interests focus on the application of critical pragmatism to the ethical judgments of leadership. With Ernestine K. Enomoto, he is the coauthor of *Leading Through the Quagmire*.

Sylvia Méndez-Morris is an associate professor in educational leadership at Texas Tech University. Her research and teaching interests include Chicanas and Latinas in educational leadership, leadership for social justice, equity issues in leadership, and instructional improvement for English language learners.

Kamla Mungal is a part-time lecturer, School of Education, University of the West Indies. Until recently, she was principal of the Mt. D'Or Government Primary School in Trinidad and Tobago and has worked with principals of primary schools across Trinidad and Tobago. She is currently manager of academic administration at Arthur Lok Jack Graduate School of Business, University of the West Indies.

Daniel Vokey is an associate professor at the University of British Columbia. His research seeks to integrate Eastern and Western perspectives on how professionals can cultivate practical wisdom for leadership and teaching. In addressing this topic Daniel draws from his background in moral philosophy, career in adventure-based experiential education, and study and practice of Mahayana Buddhism.